The Path through Grief

The Path through Grief

A Practical Guide

Marguerite Bouvard
in collaboration with Evelyn Gladu

Brewer Press
P.O Box 812446
Wellesley, MA 02181

First Edition 2 3 4 5 6 7 8 9

Breitenbush Books, Inc.,
P.O. Box 02137, Portland, Oregon 97202
James Anderson, Publisher
Patrick Ames, Editor-in-Chief
Designed by Ky Krauthamer and Ben Waggoner
Set in New Baskerville

Breitenbush Books are distributed by Taylor Publishing Co.,
1550 West Mockingbird Lane, Dallas, Texas 75235

Library of Congress Cataloging-in-Publication Data
Bouvard, Marguerite Guzman.
The path through grief: a practical guide /
Marguerite Bouvard in collaboration with Evelyn Gladu —1st ed.
Bibliography: p.   ISBN 0-932576-66-4 (pbk.)
1. Grief. 2. Bereavement—psychological aspects.
3. Death—psychological aspects. I. Gladu, Evelyn.   II. Title.
BF575.G7B675 1988
155.9'37—dc19   88-12135

Manufactured in the United States of America.

With thanks to Jacques for the countless hours of editing, printing, formatting, shipping, and for his constant support in this project; and to Bette for her encouragement.

Acknowledgements

Thanks to Ed Meyers, Dr. Theresa Amabile, to Omega, and to all those who have shared their stories with us and whose lives have touched us.

The lines from "Of Grief" are reprinted from *Collected Poems, 1930-1973* by May Sarton, by permission of the author and W. W. Norton & Co., Inc., New York. Copyright 1974 by May Sarton. "Visits" and "Flood" by Ruth Feldman, from *The Ambition of Ghosts*, Green River Press, University Center, Michigan, 1979. "The Tender Plant" courtesy of Eugene T. Maleska. "When the waters of loss rose" by Ruth Feldman, from *To Whom It May Concern*, William L. Bauhan, New Hampshire, 1986. "Grief" by Beatrice Hawley, from *Nothing Is Lost*, Apple-wood Press, Cambridge, Massachusetts, 1979, courtesy of John Jagel. "The Funeral" by David Citino, from *The Gift of Fire*, The University of Arkansas Press, Fayetteville, Arkansas, 1986.

Contents

How Friends & Co-Workers Can Help

Reaching the Other Side of Grief: The Final Phase

The Path through Grief

Introduction

Why this book

I have always considered that the most important aspect of my job as
college professor was to help each student acknowledge and value his
or her own experience and feelings. Therefore, I typically spend many
hours talking to students in my office. It's in conjunction with these
conversations with my students that I found them coming to me to discuss loss: the loss of parents, of siblings, and of friends. They came to
my office to talk because the suffering they were experiencing seemed
invisible to their friends and sometimes even to their families. Their
feelings of anger, guilt and despair seemed somehow unnatural to
them. They had difficulty even admitting to themselves the intensity
of their emotions. But I also discovered that this was not only a
problem facing young adults. Many of my friends had experienced
loss, and yet no one wanted to talk to them about their losses.

I decided to make a documentary film about grief based on the
experience of a student of mine who had lost both parents and who
was able to talk openly about her loss. I felt that seeing this young
woman relate her experience would free others to express themselves
and also reduce their sense of isolation. This film was the first step in
a research project on grieving which I conducted over the past several
years and which resulted in this book.

Part of my research was devoted to interviewing people who had
experienced different kinds of loss. Some of these interviews are
recorded as narratives within each chapter of this book. Like the film,
they are intended as mirrors in which we can see our own stories and
which can diminish the feeling of loneliness so many of us face when
we have lost someone. I wanted to be able to write a book that would
not only help people who were experiencing grief, but would also
place mourning in perspective, not as an aberration, but as part of our
lives. I wanted to help not only those who were dealing with loss, but

friends and acquaintances of the bereaved.

During my investigations of grief, I met Evelyn Gladu, director of the Omega Program in Somerville, Massachusetts, which provides emotional support services for the ill and bereaved. We found that we had similar outlooks and similar purposes and decided to collaborate on this book. I felt that her quiet understanding, compassion, and years of experience as counselor to the bereaved would bring a unique perspective to the project.

Why we grieve alone

While we have begun to admit the reality of death and dying in our culture, we have yet to acknowledge publicly the problems of the survivors and the importance of mourning in our lives. After a death, we are left with disrupted lives and with months and often years of pain and suffering. Yet in our contemporary society, we consider mourning as morbid, something to be avoided at all costs. However it is the denial of mourning which is unnatural and unprecedented in history.

The emotions associated with grief are very powerful, and include anger, guilt, despair, and sadness. Imagine how they are heightened when society denies their very existence. Not only do we experience intense emotions when we grieve, but in addition we are made to feel that somehow these emotions are inappropriate. Just at the time when we are in need of social support, we find ourselves isolated, without a common ritual or even a language with which we can communicate our feelings to others.

When asked to list the major emotions we experience in our daily lives, very few people would include sadness, or even consider it a powerful and enduring emotion. On the contrary, sadness is often regarded as an unacceptable sign of fragility or vulnerability. Therefore the experience of sorrow may come as a great shock to us. We have not been prepared for its intensities by our education, by social ritual, or by the stream of publications and visual media that provide us with common experiences and fill so much of our lives.

Years ago, when it was normal to die at home, the close involvement of family members with the care and then the funeral and burial of the dead person helped family members to view the death as a natural part of the life cycle, not as something horrible to be avoided. The transformation of our view of death was part of the technological revolution which ended a rural way of life and which brought changes not only in life style but also in ways of viewing illness. With the advances in modern medicine, death has come to be avoided at all costs, as the enemy, the ultimate failure.

Not only death, but mourning also was considered the province of the family and the community. In the past, a period of time was set aside for the purpose of mourning and it was understood that during this period, the grieving person would be the object of special care and concern. The bereaved wore black to show that he or she was in mourning. A period of seclusion of the grieving was customary to allow the survivor to shelter his or her grief from the world and to wait until the pain diminished before returning to society. While we might not wish to return to wearing black, we still need to have others acknowledge our pain and to accompany us during the difficult period of transition to a new life.

We still need to be able to communicate both the event of death and our own distress. It was common practice in the past to send announcements of the death of a loved one to those who lived far away, and possibly to hang out a bouquet of flowers on the front door to let neighbors know that a death had occurred within the family. These served as social cues. Friends and neighbors would respond with various expressions of sympathy, letters or visits. Today, the fact of death is communicated in the obituary columns of newspapers, an impersonal though necessary gesture, and one which may not elicit much response beyond attending the funeral. Although our social practices have changed, we still need a social acknowledgement of our sorrow, and social rituals to accompany us as we traverse the phases of mourning.

It's as if our very consciousness of mourning had disappeared along with the rituals. In our contemporary society, we don't think about loss or grief. We prepare for happiness and success, not for personal catastrophe. The freedom and optimism which pervade our culture and which are so liberating are reinforced in our school curriculum. However, rarely is the other side of reality acknowledged and it is only recently that colleges have begun to offer courses on death and dying. Usually these are included in psychology or sociology curricula and are intended for future health care providers. However, since everyone will experience the death of loved ones during their lives, all students could benefit from learning about mourning. Even primary school children could be introduced to loss and death in a way that corresponds to their special developmental needs. The fact is that the future we all dream of may hold loss and illness as well as joy and achievement. If we are introduced to these aspects of our lives, not as aberrations but as part and parcel of the normal human journey, we will not be bewildered and caught off guard when we experience sorrow. Nor will we feel as if we have somehow failed when we are visited by loss.

In today's society, we all seem to believe that cheerfulness, a friendly face, a smile, is a socially necessary form of behavior. Perhaps it's part of the Anglo-Saxon ethos to maintain a calm demeanor in all circumstances. While this style of behavior is certainly grounded in a deep courtesy for others, it can also be traced to an uneasiness with deep-seated emotions. These deeper emotions can be less easily controlled, and therefore are alarming. A doctor who just emigrated from the Soviet Union once remarked that he found Americans phenomenally cheerful people. He was used to hearing melancholy complaints from his patients back home. However, in America when he would ask even his gravely ill patients how they were doing, they always responded, "Just fine." So we often believe that we must answer, "I'm doing fine," when people query us after a loss or during an illness. However, we also need to learn how to acknowledge the profound pain that we all experience at certain times in our lives.

The range of emotions which are allowed social expression varies from culture to culture. In Latin societies, both sexes are allowed the release of tears in public. Greeks and Italians expect a very open show of emotions at funerals and are encouraged to express their grief during mourning. However, we tend to praise the person who shows control of his or her emotions. Perhaps anger or outrage are tolerable, but sadness embarrasses us. It reveals our fragility in a world in which we are always supposed to be in control.

All of us try to draw a line between our private and public lives. Certainly this is very necessary to protect the intimate details of our existence. However, this rule is difficult to apply to the intense and disruptive emotions of grief, because these feelings may affect our working patterns and our sense of competence.

Another obstacle to learning about the emotions that will accompany us in our passage through the stages of life is the fact that death and illness occur in hospitals, out of sight. Science has not only reduced the mortality rate and alleviated the pain associated with illness, it has also brought us modern institutions of health care. We rarely learn about death and illness as part of family or community life because they occur away from our daily lives and within institutions. Moreover, the influence of the family is minimal within these institutions.

Hospitals where so many people die today are places of cure, and hospital staff have great difficulty communicating with dying patients and their families. Typically they may be afraid of being caught up in emotional, dramatic situations with the patient or with his family, and prefer to carry on without acknowledging the fact of death. When my aunt was dying of cancer, my cousin, who is a doctor, and who was treating her, made me promise not to tell her that she was dying. As she became permanently bedridden, she and I corresponded a few times a week, and her letters testify to the loneliness she felt during this period. She knew she was dying, yet because of the silence surrounding her she felt compelled to keep silent herself, and thus was unable to share her feelings and anxieties.

The culture of individualism and the weakening of social and extended family ties resulting from social mobility may have freed us to live, study and work wherever we please without constraints. However, this freedom is not without costs. Religious ties and many social rituals for bereavement have fallen in disuse. These rituals serve many purposes. They are part of the process by which we learn about the roles we will assume in society. Without them, we must learn without guidance how to experience and incorporate sadness in our lives. It is an experience that may continually surprise us, and that may add to the outrage we already feel in the face of death and its apparent injustice.

Given the great variety of religious practices in our society, not only mourning rituals but the whole question of the funeral service must frequently be decided upon without the benefit of precedent. When my mother died, she was living in another city. This situation is not uncommon. The question arose of where to have the funeral, what type of service to have, and even what type of burial. I decided to have the funeral services in my home town rather than in my mother's, so that I could house family members who were coming from abroad. Many families are separated by long distances or practice different religions, so that the location and type of service can be a difficult decision to make, and might even become a source of conflict.

The ceremony of the funeral makes the reality of death a little more acceptable. It provides a safe and sheltering environment for those who were the closest to the deceased. It is a time to express our feelings and to receive support from others. Therefore the type of service can have an important impact on the grieving family. The selection of eulogies and readings, the decisions on whether to have an open or closed casket, or whether to select cremation, give a very important sense of participation if all the family members are included. Depending on the way it is handled, the funeral can either be an empty ceremony or a significant way of saying good-bye to the deceased. In the narratives, we will find different types of funeral arrangements, and varying levels of comfort with them.

Today, it is becoming more common for the dying to express their wishes and actively participate in the preparation for the funeral service. In Chapter 5, Eric discusses the funeral arrangements for his wife and how he honored her wishes. This is not only helpful to the dying, like Eric's wife, who receive acknowledgment from those who are close, but also to the family member, who is given an opportunity to help carry out the dying person's wishes. Last spring I attended the funeral services for a friend of mine who was a poet. She had arranged the services with her pastor, and he read several of her poems during the eulogy and shared significant moments of her life. Afterwards, there was a receiving line of relatives which allowed all those who attended to express their condolences in person.

While new rites for funerals are a way of reawakening community participation in the rituals surrounding death, we are still faced with major questions after the funeral of a loved one. The real process of separation begins after the funeral, yet there are no common practices to help us through the long period of adjustment and the reforging of new roles.

While bereavement rituals vary among societies, there are certain common threads in all societies. Most importantly, these rituals permit the public expression of private distress. Because there are no longer any commonly accepted rites for mourning, the anguish of someone who has suffered loss today is frequently endured in private. The suffering of the mourner may be increased by being ignored. When one of my colleagues lost her son, a few close friends sent her affectionate notes, but when she returned to work after the funeral, she was greeted by silence. No one mentioned the death of her son. She felt as if her pain was invisible, and didn't matter to others at all. After the death of a loved one, we need more than ever to be accepted, to have our pain acknowledged.

But it wasn't necessarily a deliberate omission on the part of her co-workers as much as an absence of guidelines for facing the situation, and perhaps an uneasiness at the reminder of their own mortality. Such an event generates conflicting feelings. At the same time we may be relieved that our own families were spared, may feel a deep sympathy, and also a frightening sense of our own vulnerability. Perhaps we think we are protecting our friends by not mentioning the deceased, but in reality, it is ourselves that we are protecting. Or perhaps we want to do too much, feel that we must make it all right. It may be difficult for us to acknowledge that in a world where there seems to be a solution to every problem, a cure for so many illnesses, there are things we cannot fix.

The very powerful emotions we experience during grief are

demanding of us and take a long time to abate. Yet many people expect those who are mourning the loss of a loved one to return to normal activities and behavior soon after the funeral. Leaves of absence are normally granted for attending funerals, usually a day or two, but a leave of absence for mourning would be considered strange and unnecessary. Yet the emotions we experience while grieving cause us great fatigue. It may feel as if we are recovering from a long and difficult illness. While in the long run work can be both absorbing and healing, it can be extremely burdensome immediately after a death, and we are generally less than effective in our jobs. If at all possible, taking time for the express purpose of mourning is extremely helpful to the grief-stricken person.

As we experience grief, we are truly on uncharted territory. We don't know just how long or how intensely we should feel the anger, pain and guilt resulting from loss. Nor do we know how to behave towards others. Often we feel guilty because our emotions continue unabated, and because we are fearful of imposing our sadness on others.

The father of one of my students was killed in an explosion while working inside a manhole. Because her mother "fell apart" during the year after the death, Joan took up the burden of household management. She told me that she felt nothing at the time. I asked her if she had discussed her feelings with anyone, and she replied that she didn't want to burden others. One of the outcomes of this postponement of her own grief was the development of an ulcer. It may be actually harmful to our health to deny our most powerful emotions. It is a paradox that by facing them we eventually pass through them, and reach the other side of grief where loss is no longer the center of our lives. My student is now talking about the anger and sadness she feels about the death, and feels that it is all right to grieve. Just as the dying are made to feel that they have an obligation to keep silent and thus spare those around them, the grieving who are in need of comfort and support feel that they have to keep a "stiff upper lip," so as not to disturb family and friends. However, maintaining a stoic silence may have serious consequences for our well-being.

Mourning is not an illness or an aberration. The pain of grief is an important part of our journey through life. Trying to control our feelings will not make them disappear. On the contrary, if we try to block them or to bury them, they will surface later on in our lives, and may cause us serious physical and emotional problems. It is perhaps a paradox that if we acknowledge our grief and make room for the sorrow of loss in our lives, we can then put these emotions behind us. These extreme feelings of anguish are normal and they also serve a very important purpose in our lives. Through the hard work of grieving, we are actually healing ourselves.

We need a broad range of emotions and periods of intensity in our lives. If we cut off the profound sadness that wells up when we lose someone we love, we will also prevent ourselves from experiencing the greatest joy. Also, we often experience a variety of conflicting feelings at the same time. These are all functional. They help us to live as fully as possible and to change when necessary. If we allow these feelings to surface and find expression we will be free to carry on our lives in the best way possible.

How to use this book

This book is intended to be a companion on your journey through grief. It is about the role of suffering and change in our lives and about the healing that change and suffering brings. It describes the common feelings, behaviors and reactions that we experience when we lose a loved one.

The book is organized according to the phases of grief and the different kinds of loss. The reader will find chapters on the particular loss he or she is experiencing, whether the loss of a sibling, a parent, a child or a spouse.

Part one, "The Experience of Grief Today," presents an overview of the grief process and includes a chapter on losses other than death, as well as a chapter on the crisis of meaning that may be precipitated by a significant loss.

Parts two, four and seven deal with the stages of grief: part two, "When Someone Dies," describes the early phases of grief; part four, "As Time Passes," addresses the later phases of disruption and disorganization; and part seven, "Reaching the Other Side of Grief," describes the reorganization of our lives after the long process of grieving.

Part three, "Losing a Loved One through Suicide or Homicide," is devoted to the loss of a loved one through suicide or homicide. These losses present some particularly difficult issues and thus deserve separate attention. Those who have suffered these types of losses may find that the narratives and essays in parts two and four may be also be helpful.

Part five, "How We Can Help Ourselves," comprises a practical guide on how we can help ourselves while we are traversing the phases of grief. Many of us who suffer grief feel that we must continue our professional and personal roles as if nothing had happened. We may be accustomed to care for others in a number of ways. However, it is extremely important to take care of ourselves while we are grieving. The chapters in this part will help us with the problems of daily living and also help us to express our feelings and to find supports.

Part six, "How Friends and Co-Workers Can Help," is intended for friends and associates of the bereaved. Often as friends and employers or co-workers we are puzzled as how to deal with the bereaved. This part provides a guide which will help us to understand the grieving person and also provides some suggestions for things to say and things to do for the grieving person. Although mourning is an intensely personal and self-regarding phase of our lives, it occurs in a context of family, friends, work, and educational institutions. We can all benefit by learning about grief.

This book is meant to be read according to our individual needs. Although we grieve within social contexts, our grief is always intensely personal and has its own course. Each of us will find a chapter within the parts which relates to our own loss and to our perception of our relationship with our loved one. If our friend who died was like a sister to us, we may want to turn to the chapter on the loss of a sibling. If our grandparent or aunt was like a parent to us, we may find the chapter on the loss of a parent helpful. As time passes, we may be ready to read about the reactions to loss that our siblings, parents, spouses or partners may be experiencing.

This book considers the loss of a partner in a heterosexual or homosexual relationship that is not formalized as being the same as the loss of a spouse. Therefore, the reference to loss of a spouse includes the loss of a partner in a committed relationship and references to "widow" or "widower" can be used in these contexts as well. While the responses of our family, friends and associates may be different in these circumstances, our life partner is a chosen person just as much as a married partner and the grief we experience from such as loss is the same.

The research for this book included interviews with a number of people who had experienced different kinds of loss. Some of these are recorded as narratives within each chapter of the book. They are intended as mirrors in which we can see some of our own experiences and which will help diminish the feeling of isolation so many of us face when we have lost someone. While we all experience grief in unique ways, there are common threads to that experience.

The taboos around the feelings of grief are complicated by gender images that may further restrict the expression of feeling. Therefore, the narratives include the stories of both men and women on the premise that they may have had different socializations and could be expected to show different attitudes towards the expression of emotion.

The narratives which appear throughout the book are the stories of ordinary people who have experienced different kinds of losses. Although they may come from different backgrounds and different family settings, and although they represent a broad range of religious backgrounds, they express feelings that all of us who have suffered loss have experienced at certain times in the grieving process. They are the accounts of people for whom the loss was not too recent and who have traversed all the phases of grief. Because a number of years had elapsed since their loss, they were able to bring the perspective of time to their experiences. Some of these stories may be similar to our own. Some may seem to have their own unique character. We hope you will find that you are not alone and that this shared experience will help you on your own path through grief.

THE EXPERIENCE OF GRIEF TODAY

It is the incomplete,
the unfulfilled, the torn
that haunts our nights and days
and keeps us hunger-born.
Grief spills from our eyes,
unwelcome, indiscreet,
as if sprung from a fault
as rivers seam a rock
and break through under shock.
We are shaken by guilt.

May Sarton, from "Of Grief"

1 • *Grief as a Personal Crisis*

Grief and the individual

We are all unique in our personalities, our family background, our cultural heritage and our genetic makeup. Therefore, everyone's response to grief, how we express it and how we cope with it, will be different. Also, the nature of the relationship we may have had with the deceased is different for each person.

Only we can define the importance that a relationship has for us. We may grieve for a grandparent as intensely as for a parent, for an aunt as much as for a parent. To have lost a child or a marriage partner is considered by many people to be the most painful kind of loss. However, sibling loss, or the loss of an elderly parent can be just as painful. When a relationship is not recognized or legitimized, such as a lover, fiancé, or partner in a homosexual relationship, loss does not elicit the same sympathy or may even be unrecognized.

Although each type of loss confronts us with its own issues of identity and with its own social problems, ultimately loss is painful regardless of age, sex, or relationship. For instance, we may pay little attention to the loss of elderly parents on the assumption that their parenting roles are no longer functional and that the primary focus of our caring may have shifted to spouse, children, or lover. However, it may be very difficult to lose elderly parents simply because of the fact that we have had a long period of time in which to strengthen the bonds of love. While others may comment that we had plenty of time with our parent, we may regard our loss as untimely. We are never ready to lose a loved one.

We expect to grieve for someone with whom we have had a close and loving relationship. However, we also mourn for those we have lost in a troubled relationship and our mourning may be complicated by the feelings of resentment and dislike we harbored for the dead person. A former student of mine had a very troubled relationship with her mother and still feels great anger years after her death. Given the nature of the relationship, she has been struggling with confusion and with the conflicting feelings of loss and relief. There is nothing wrong with feeling relief at being out of a problem-ridden situation. However, feelings of guilt and self-blame may complicate and draw out the grieving process.

There are deaths that bear stigmas: suicides, homicides, deaths from AIDS, drug overdose, abusive behavior. Sometimes, we may find ourselves blaming the victim of a violent death. It's almost as if by blaming them, we mark them as somehow separate, distancing ourselves from the reality of the violent death. In these cases, we frequently go over and over the details preceding the death. The senselessness of these deaths make the circumstances seem so important, as if they could somehow bring us closer to the meaning which eludes us.

Sometimes the death of a loved one propels us into a new situation which leaves us little time or energy for grieving. If we are widowed and left with children we may need all of our energy to care for them. As a widow, we may have to find work and to face new financial problems. If we are a widower, we may find ourself juggling the demands of work and child-rearing for the first time. If we are in the midst of working towards a college degree when our parent dies we may still have to prepare for exams. Sometimes, we are faced with important life tasks that claim our attention before we can face our grief.

There are other reasons for postponing our grieving. We may have issues that we need to work through before we can give ourselves over to our sorrow. A woman I know spent years confronting the difficulties of having lived with alcoholic parents before being able to grieve for the sister she lost. Sometimes we need to address a difficult situation before we can begin to grieve. It's not helpful to judge ourselves for postponing our sorrow while we face these tasks. On the contrary, once we have moved through these issues, we may find that we can allow ourselves to grieve more fully.

Once our new lifestyle as single parent, as student, or as someone who has addressed a difficult issue is established, our emotional demands may arise and our grief surface. Sometimes that surfacing may be triggered by an event such as another loss or perhaps the breakup of a relationship. Or we may be reacting intensely to a minor event only to realize that it was a response to a loss we suffered years ago. Because each one of us faces such unique life situations, we will all have our own calendar for beginning the process of grieving.

There are identifiable phases in the grieving process, but the duration of these phases and their sequence may vary. Everyone has his or her own timetable and while one person may have reconstructed his or her life within a year of a death, another person may need several years to complete the process of defining new roles and new identities. The most helpful remark someone made to me after my mother's death was that it generally takes three years to recover from a major loss. The emotions I was feeling at the time were so intense that I knew I could not work through them in a matter of months. Her comment relieved the pressure for a speedy return to "normality."

The phases of grief

Many researchers have studied the process of grieving and have identified common patterns. The model described in this chapter is similar to the one developed by John Bowlby and by Colin Murray Parkes (see Additional Reading, p. 245). Although the phases of the grieving process do not necessarily unfold in an orderly manner, we can nevertheless distinguish between immediate reactions to loss and long term responses. The immediate response to the death of someone we love is one of shock and protest or denial. This is followed by a period of disorganization during which the routines, habits and roles we are accustomed to are disrupted. Ultimately, we reach a period of recovery or the reorganization of a new life. It does not mean forgetting the person we have lost, but placing that relationship somewhere inside us where it's comfortable so we can carry on our lives. That profound sadness is no longer the center of our attention.

When we know that a person is dying, or when a person has been suffering from a long illness, we may begin the grieving before the event of death. During this anticipatory period, we may do some of the work involved in grieving. We may resolve some of the issues in a relationship, gain perspective on that relationship and say some of the necessary things. While we may grieve the loss of who that person was before his or her illness, we still focus our attention on that person. During bereavement, we focus on ourselves.

Shock
The initial phase of bereavement is one of shock and disbelief. We are confused and disoriented by the death and may keep hoping that we

will wake up and discover that it was all just a mistake. We keep hoping that it is reversible like a film. This wish to deny the event of death may last for days or even weeks. We move as in a dream, filled with a sense of unreality and distance. Sometimes these feelings may persist even though we may need to communicate with others about the death, to arrange for the disposal of the body and the funeral. People frequently speak of a sense of unreality, of going about daily activities in a dream-like state. This period of numbness actually gives us the time we need to mobilize our resources and to cope with the impact of the loss when we are more ready.

Being present at a death or viewing the body helps acknowledge the reality for us. Though some people may prevent this from happening, the experience of seeing and saying goodbye to the dead person helps make it possible to develop an image of that person as dead. When a friend of mine delivered a stillborn baby, the hospital staff encouraged her to hold it in order to be able to have an image of her child. When there is no body, as happens during a war, an airplane crash, or an accident at sea, feelings of unreality and denial may be prolonged. We may feel that somehow that person will return as if she or he had been on a trip. The funeral and the disposition of the body are occasions for private and public farewell. When we are denied this important ceremony, our grieving is made more difficult. This may help to explain the time and effort spent recovering the bodies of those who have been reported missing years after the Vietnam war.

After the funeral, the real work of grieving begins. We are confronted with a home that is full of painful reminders of the dead person. During these early weeks, we may be preoccupied with the dead person, continuing to converse with him or her in our thoughts. Many people report that they can actually sense or feel the dead spouse, child or sibling around them. This is not unusual and can actually be a source of comfort. There is nothing wrong with continuing this communication, with talking to or writing to the deceased. Visiting the cemetery or writing letters are a way of prolonging the leave-taking, of acknowledging the continued presence of that person in our lives.

During this period, we are experiencing the pain of separation. The sadness comes in waves and we frequently feel the need to cry. Often we are seized with a desire to cry at the most inopportune and unexpected times. We may be driving to work, reading the newspaper, or sitting in a crowded cafeteria. It is very important to allow these moments of great sadness to surface. Crying is very cleansing and will serve to relieve us. Any time when thoughts of the deceased well up is a good time to cry. Tears cannot be postponed for a more convenient time and trying to block them may cause us problems.

In our society, it is difficult for men to shed tears, especially in public. For some men, a close friend can help facilitate the flow, almost like granting permission. In Bill's narrative in Chapter 21, he describes how he was helped to shed those tears by a woman friend. They were putting flowers on his wife's grave and she told him to "Go ahead and cry." His friend gave him permission to step outside of the image of male behavior. Although younger men are becoming more comfortable with expressing their emotions, this is still a difficulty for middle aged and older men. However, both sexes are vulnerable to demands for being "brave," or "strong."

During the early weeks after a death we need to tell the story about those last hours, to go over the details of the illness, the accident, the last words spoken. It is as important to listen to these stories as it is to tell them. They are an attempt to find meaning in a very bewildering event. A friend of mine who lost his wife kept repeating the story of her death and the trip to the hospital. She died very suddenly at home, and though she had been very ill with cancer he had blocked any thought of her death. He told me the story over and over. This was very helpful to him in leading him to accept both the reality of her death and the seriousness of her illness. The person telling the story is healing himself. He is adjusting to a new and painful reality and exploring its meaning.

Disorganization

The period of numbness which is the early phase of grief shelters us until we are able to feel the very painful emotions which come with loss. After the shock wears off, the sadness wells up. Not only do we feel a profound sorrow, but other powerful emotions assail us and they may occur in combinations. We may simultaneously feel guilt and anger, sadness and depression. Also we may experience abrupt changes in our daily routines, in our own behavior and in the way we see ourselves.

The death of a loved one also means the disruption of the habits and patterns of our lives. Most of us who live with someone have developed habits for the most minute details of our lives. For instance, one of us may sleep on a certain side of the bed. One of us may wake up earlier and prepare the morning coffee. Each one of us will have certain preferences in food or music that the other will account for in a number of ways. More importantly, family members or lovers and trusted friends share each other's deepest thoughts, fears and hopes. In losing a loved person, we also lose the roles of companion, confidant, lover. We therefore experience significant changes in status.

Our sleeping patterns are likely to be disrupted at this time and many people have difficulty falling asleep or wake up with a feeling of tenseness and unease in the middle of the night. Frequently we dream about the dead person although the nature of these dreams will change over a period of time, as will their frequency. In the early period after a death, our loved one may appear in our dreams as if he or she were still alive. One of my students had a recurring dream about her mother in the months after her death. She dreamed they were having a picnic together, but when she reached out to hold her, her mother, vanished. We may continue to dream of the deceased for years, though the nature of these dreams may change. In our later dreams, the fact of the person's death may be reflected in their lack of response to us.

Some of us may neglect the need for nourishment just to avoid the loneliness at mealtimes. We may also overlook our own health by ignoring physical symptoms or missing an important check-up at the doctor. We may need to be reminded by our friends or family to take care of ourselves.

Not only are we apt to be fatigued by the great demands of our emotions, but our self-esteem may be very low at this time. In losing a loved one, we have received a heavy blow and may feel a greatly diminished self-confidence. Our close friends may expect us to pull ourselves together and resume our normal pace. Or, former friends may shy away and avoid us just when we need them the most.

Often in sudden deaths and even in deaths resulting from a long illness we tell ourselves, "If only." We think that if only we had done things differently, we could have prevented the death. When my mother died of a heart attack, I kept thinking of the flu shot she had taken and of all the studies which described them as dangerous to older people who were suffering from heart conditions. We feel responsible, as if somehow we should have prevented that death. Even under the best of circumstances, we feel a powerful sense of guilt.

Our sense of guilt may be heightened after a death by suicide as we grapple with the meaning of the act, wondering if we could have done something to prevent it. This is especially true if the suicide came as a complete surprise. Suddenly one is confronted with all the issues, stresses and problems in a relationship and also with the rejection, for suicide may be regarded by some of us as a rejection. While we move through the same phases of grief, the initial period may be prolonged because of feelings of guilt. We may feel that we have failed as a friend, or spouse, or parent. We may go over and over past events. However, these feelings of guilt are normal, and may be with us until we can see the relationship we had with our loved one in a clearer perspective.

We may go over our past behavior during this period and wish it could have been different. A mother who lost an adult daughter remembered the times she had lost her temper at her during the teenage years. She also told me that she had gone shopping with her daughter and found a very becoming coat which she then decided not to buy because of the cost. That incident kept haunting her after her daughter's death. As Maureen points out in Chapter 8, siblings remember the times they quarreled and wonder whether the deceased brother or sister really knew that they loved them. As time passes, we regain a sense of perspective and remember the good times as well as the difficult ones. But in the early months after a loss we are frequently troubled by scenes from the past.

Along with guilt, feelings of anger are apt to assail us after a death. The targets of our anger may vary, whether it is directed at the doctor or nurses for being insensitive, or at family members for not helping during an illness or during the funeral arrangements. Some of us may be angry with God for the injustice and senselessness of the death. Most of all, we may be angry at the dead person for leaving us.

Sometimes we may erect a shrine to the dead person, keeping our loved one's room in its original state or acting as if he or she were still present without making any changes in our life. We may even expect that our family members adopt this behavior and believe that we are grieving the most. It is normal to be obsessed with the our loved one in the early months after a death. However, prolonging this behavior and erecting a shrine draws out the early phases of grief and prevents us from moving on.

The emotions of anger, guilt or sorrow are unpredictable and do not necessarily occur in sequence. We may feel very vulnerable because of the intensity and unpredictability of these feelings. However, wishing to control or deny them only means a postponement. Denying these early manifestations of mourning may even push us into extreme forms of behavior such as losing ourselves in work, or turning to alcohol and drugs as a way of numbing the pain we may be feeling. Frequently, adolescents may adopt anti-social ways of behavior as a way of acting out anger. If we allow ourselves to express it, the terrible pain we feel moves and changes. It may seem as if it remains the same over a long period of time, but it is constantly transforming and ultimately will move to the margins of our lives.

Family dynamics may be changed by the death of a family member. Death means not only a crisis in personal identity but may also mean the loosening of family ties. The death of a family member will affect us all differently depending upon the nature of our relationship with that person, our involvement during the time of dying, and how close we were. Some of us may experience grief in an anticipatory manner while others may display little grief. The variety of our responses can complicate communication among family members. When both parents die in a family with a number of children, an older sibling may find that he or she is relinquishing her sibling role and assuming that of a parent. The other siblings may respond to this change in a number of ways, from adaptation to profound resentment. Couples may draw closer together after the death of a child, or they may project their anger on each other and create bitter dissension. Sometimes the death of one parent may mean the loss of the key element in keeping the family together.

It is not unusual for tension to rise in a family after a death because the magnitude of the feelings aroused leave us little emotional strength for mutual support. Each one of us may have a different rhythm in our grieving and entirely different coping styles. While one of us may wake up one morning feeling energetic and ready for new activities, another may feel consumed by pain and fatigue. In such situations, it may be helpful to seek out separate supports.

The reorientation of our habits and expectations occurs within the context of the family. Therefore, at this time of relative instability or of reordering of family relations, it is helpful to maintain stability in other areas. For instance, after the death of a parent, keeping a child in the same school environment or in the same living arrangements will give that child the security he or she needs and the assurance that her life will go on without other major changes. If we are an adult, that sense of stability may come from keeping the same job or residence. This is not a time for major changes or decisions. We are spending a great deal of energy dealing with our emotions and even the smallest chores may be burdensome. It is a time to be as gentle as possible with oneself while placing other demands in the background.

Holidays are especially difficult after we have suffered a loss. These are occasions for family reunions and we may feel a heightened sense of pain at this time. Even the expectations of others that we share their joy may be a heavy burden. Then it may seem as if time were standing still, as if all the progress we might have accomplished during the year were evaporating. Anniversaries of the death and the birthday of our loved one are just as painful. Some people have found that the anticipation of holidays and anniversaries was more difficult to deal with than the actual events. It is normal to feel a renewed sense of loss during these periods. Many people have found unusual, non-traditional ways of observing holidays, forgoing the usual rituals. Some people observe a modified Christmas, focusing on the children rather than on the social practices of sending cards, or entertaining friends and neighbors. In Chapter 24, Anne tells us about her decision to take her children to Disneyland over the Christmas holidays rather than staying home and putting up a tree. An older widower decided to take a trip to Italy to visit his relatives during this time. The important thing is to find a way to observe the holidays that is both comfortable and meaningful.

Painful as they are, the very strong emotions we experience during this phase of grieving are part of the long process of healing. Because they are so absorbing, we need plenty of time to move through them. This varies with each individual. Some people may pass through this phase in a few months, others may require many months or even years. Also, we may move back and forth between phases in an unpredictable manner. It is helpful to remind ourselves that this is a very necessary and normal part of grieving and that even though the signs of progress may not be readily apparent, we are doing some very important work. During these difficult months, we are thinking over our relationship with our loved one and our own role in the world. Although it may seem like a period of turbulence and confusion, we are paving the way for the reconstruction of our lives.

Reorganization

One morning we may wake up with a new sense of energy and a new interest in the world. We may have discovered new friends while we were in the most difficult period of our grief and now we might turn to them to share other interests. We may have changed our daily routine and take more of our meals out with friends. We come to understand that the fabric of our lives has been disrupted and have stopped anticipating the events of our former lives. As time passes, we not only change our lifestyles, we may actually enjoy these changes. We may even come to look forward to being alone at home listening to music, curling up with a favorite book and simply enjoying our own company. We begin to experience moments of contentment even though we thought we could never be happy again.

Our whole network of relationships appears in a new light. At first, we may have been disappointed in our friends, but ultimately these tensions and stresses will have helped us to make the decisions we need in order to create a new life for ourselves. It is a long process which moves in fits and starts, but there are joyous as well as painful aspects to it. While we may have been hurt at the behavior of some of our old friends, we may have discovered new friends and interests, the surprise and pleasure of being liked by different kinds of people. Or we may discover new talents. A close friend of mine who lost her mother discovered a bent for writing. She even learned another language and became a well-known translator. Another friend who was widowed decided to go to graduate school in painting and design and is now showing her work at a number of galleries. In Chapter 22, Eric describes his decision to enter the field of film-making. While we may have expended tremendous energy in the previous phase of grieving, now we may discover a surge of talents and interests that will bring us a satisfaction we could not have predicted. We are changing as we move through the grieving process, even though the changes may be slow and barely visible from week to week.

Perhaps we may still feel married for a long time, or we may still miss that best friend, or feel that our life has lost its meaning without our child, but gradually our loved one is less and less in our thoughts. We continue to feel sadness, but the intensity has diminished. Our relationship with that person is no longer at the center of our lives. We have new energies to invest in other activities and persons. New relationships or the decision to have another child are not a sign of betrayal. They do not mean that we are "replacing" the deceased. Beginning a new relationship or a new lifestyle is a sign of our recovery.

2 • Loss and Change

We associate grief with loss through death, but we also experience grief as a consequence of some of the major changes and other kinds of loss in our lives. We may experience the emotions and the disruptions of grieving as a result of these losses, just as if we had lost a loved one. This book deals primarily with loss through death. However the accounts of the phases of the grieving process and the coping styles for dealing with loss through a death may also help us to face other major losses.

As we move through our lives, we continually experience change;

and while change may be beneficial, it also may involve loss, as if one hand were for receiving, and the other hand for letting go. The important passages of life including marriage, the birth of a child, the change of a residence or a job, the growth of our children and our own aging may fill us with a sense of fulfillment while also striking us with feelings of sadness. Each of these events sets in motion a whole series of changes in our roles and status which may involve considerable loss.

When we face change such as moving to a new home or a new job, or sending our child off to college, we are apt to think of these changes in terms of practical tasks. For example, we may expend great energy in preparing for our child's departure for college, gathering packing cartons, purchasing clothing and perhaps appliances. We may even accompany our child to his or her college dormitory and spend an afternoon or a day installing her things and arranging for telephone service. But after we have negotiated all the physical changes and returned to our home, we begin to feel uneasy. Now, we may face the emotional toll of an empty nest and of the changes in our roles. We may feel a profound grief at our loss without acknowledging this.

When we change jobs, or move to a new home, there is also a myriad of practical tasks to accomplish from packing, to making new connections in a neighborhood or office. But while we are seemingly gaining a new working life or a new home, and even if we view these changes as improvements in our lives, we may be feeling disrupted. Because these changes are not recognized as also involving loss, we may not allow ourselves to feel and to express the grief that comes with loss. But for many of us, both work and home are an important part of our identity, and though we may be moving forward, we also may need to mourn the loss of the network of friends in our neighborhood, the home where our family grew up, or the job which filled our life for a number of years.

In this age of rapid technological and economic changes, some of us may be fired or laid off. While some of us may find new and rewarding jobs, others of us may have difficulty finding the kind of work we feel we are suited for or that fulfills our needs for creativity or esteem. And some of us may never find work again. It is not always possible to retrain for another field if we are in our forties or fifties. Because work may represent such an important part of our identity, we may grieve as though we had lost a loved one and we may experience all of the stages of the grieving process. Not only have we lost a career, but we have also lost our dreams and hopes for the future.

As a population, we are aging, and while there are numerous studies of the aging process and of mid-life changes, few of them acknowledge the attendant grief we experience. In the middle of our years, we may feel sadness and anger at the realization that we have not fulfilled our hopes in our work or in our personal relationships. We may experience all the emotions associated with the grieving process. It is helpful to recognize these feelings and to give them room in our lives both because of their emotional impact and also to help clear the path to changes that will address our needs.

Perhaps the aging process is almost imperceptible to many of us. But one morning, we may look in the mirror and notice that our hair is thinning, or that our waistline has expanded. Changes in our body may cause us to feel a loss of self-esteem. We mourn the loss of our looks and our vitality. We also experience changes in our sexual responses or in our physical vigor, and we may suffer an impairment of vision or of our hearing. While we may tend to think of these as "physical problems," they take an emotional toll on us. As in any other type of loss, we need to take time to express our anger, our sadness and the dips in our self-esteem.

The changes we continually face in our lives may be painful, but if we allow ourselves to experience the emotions of grief, we will find that we may grow in strength, resourcefulness and compassion.

While there are many resources that deal with the issues associated with key changes in our lives, the following sections will discuss some losses that are particularly traumatic and for which we may grieve as deeply as for the death of a loved one. The coping styles for living through grief presented in this book may answer our own particular needs even though our loss may be unique.

Divorce or a broken relationship

The loss of a partner through divorce or through the breakup of a less formal, though committed, relationship may involve all of the feelings and reactions we have after the death of a spouse. However, the person we lose nevertheless remains present in our lives in some way. In some cases we may be able to maintain an amicable relationship with our former spouse or lover. A friend of mine who divorced nine years ago still has an abiding friendship with her former spouse and the two of them are able to cooperate in raising their daughter.

However, in many cases our former spouse can remain as an ever-present threat in our lives, especially if there are difficulties with custody of the children. If we have been given joint custody or we must share the children for holidays and summer vacations, we are continually faced with the pain of separating from our children and possibly also with anxiety for the well-being of the child while he or she is with our former partner.

There are a whole train of losses involved in a divorce or separation when we have children. We may grieve for the loss of a family unit. We may grieve for what we had dreamed of and which proved unattainable, the creation of a family with our partner and the hope of being loved. A friend of mine who retained partial custody of their son after her divorce described feeling less whole after the divorce and feeling that she and her son were not a complete family.

If we did not have children, regardless of whether we were in a formal relationship or not, we lose our dream of building a life together. It is no comfort to be reminded by our friends and acquaintances that we can begin again or find a new relationship. We mourn a specific loss, the wish to have a life with our former partner.

We may also experience a profound sense of guilt for the failure of our relationship, especially if we initiated the breakup. Both sides may feel that they have failed in one of the most important relationships in their lives. We may feel anger at the situation, at our partner and also towards ourselves.

The breakup of a marriage or a relationship has ramifications throughout our extended families. If the breakup was a bitter one, it may be difficult to keep up a relationship with our former in-laws who are also grandparents to our children. Each member of our family experiences loss in many ways. Our child may lose his or her siblings if the children do not remain together. He or she may lose grandparents, cousins, aunts and uncles. Knowing that these people are there, but inaccessible to us, can be a continual source of pain.

There are many losses involved in a broken relationship. For example, we may face the loss of our home and our possessions. Many women who divorce experience a significant drop in their standard of living. They may find that in order to keep their home, they must take a new job or enter the work force for the first time. Frequently, women move to a smaller house or apartment. Both partners often face the stress of a new neighborhood and a new lifestyle just when their self-esteem may be particularly low.

For many of us, losing a partner also means losing our friends. Just as in the loss of a spouse, we may find that we are suddenly a single person in a world of couples and that we may no longer feel comfortable with or feel rejected by our former friends.

In many societies, the breakup of a relationship may be a taboo. If the members of our family had never had a divorce, we may experience a diminished parental esteem. Perhaps our parents had tried to dissuade us from initiating a divorce or breakup and we may feel the pain of their judgment. This may be especially true in an extended family which has a more traditional set of values regarding marriage.

There are particular issues that may cause us pain if we have lost a partner from a less formal relationship. People may feel that we should go out and find someone new right away rather than taking the time to integrate the loss in our lives. Many couples, homosexual or heterosexual, live together for years without marrying. They have invested the same hopes, dreams and efforts as in a marriage. Because these relationships were not formalized and because there may be fewer material, visible results, such as children or the accumulation of possessions, the importance of that bond tends to be invisible to society.

It's important to allow ourselves to feel all of the emotions of grief when a relationship ends. The importance we attach to a relationship is a highly personal one and readers may find that some of the chapters in this book which address specific losses have relevance to their own situation.

The serious illness of a loved one

When a loved one contracts a life-threatening illness or a serious illness like Alzheimer's, heart disease, cancer or mental illness, it may feel as if he or she had died although the body is still there. Perhaps our loved one was in a serious accident and remains in a coma or a vegetative state. We may experience all the emotions, all the stresses and strains resulting from a death. However, we cannot carry on a new life. We must continue to care for and to visit our loved one even though others may not understand our continuing attachment.

If our loved one has a life-threatening illness such as cancer, we live with all of the effects of treatments like chemotherapy which may weaken and transform that person. If our loved one is a parent, we may find ourselves in a new role as the provider of support and we may both resent this change and feel guilty about our resentment. If we are young adults, we may resent the fact that our parent needs constant care and is also weak. If we are middle aged, we may find ourselves caught between the demands of caring for our own children and caring for our ill parent or relation. Or perhaps our children had recently grown up and we were looking forward to having some time for ourselves after the long years of nurturing others. When we are absorbed in the care of a loved one, it's easy to forget our own needs, both physical and emotional. We may even feel guilty about wishing for time to be with ourselves and to pursue our own interests. It may be helpful to remember that we can only care for others if we ourselves are in good shape.

If our loved one has suffered for a long time from a serious and painful illness, we may find ourselves wishing for his or her death and then feel guilty about that wish. We experience a complex set of emotions in such a situation: guilt, anger, profound sadness. We are grieving for the person who can never be the same, but who is still present in our lives.

If our child was born with a mental or physical disorder or becomes mentally ill, we grieve for the child we thought we had. We grieve for the wished-for child and that grief continues throughout our lives. With each passage of life, the time for starting school, for becoming an adolescent, we feel a fresh surge of sadness and the pain of comparison with others whose children develop normally. A good friend wrote to me about her young son who is autistic: "So we keep on going, day to day, marvelling at his growth, until we see a 'normal' four-year-old."

In addition, we may have other children and other burdens in our lives. We may feel the stress of trying to divide our attention between the child who is ill and his or her siblings, and we may feel that we would like to do more for both. We may feel guilty as if somehow this illness were a judgment on us. And we may also experience a lack of understanding from other people. There is also the ever-present worry about the care of our child or relative when we will no longer able to provide that care.

Some of us have been able to confront our anger and guilt and to come to an understanding of our disabled or ill child as a rare opportunity for loving. A woman whose young son had leukemia described how she felt a special closeness as they struggled together with his disease. A former student of mine had a brother with Down's syndrome and always described the special love and support her brother had from his siblings. He had brought out a rare tenderness in the whole family.

The loss of health through illness or injury

Losing our health through illness or injury is a great blow to our self-esteem. We may be surprised at the intensity of our emotions as we grieve for the self we were. We may feel anger towards our own body for somehow "failing" us and we may even try to punish ourselves by either undereating or overeating. If the onset of our illness or the loss of a bodily function such as vision or hearing is sudden, we feel as if we were projected into a new world with few guides to help us. While others may see us as struggling with our new physical condition, the emotional struggle may be even greater as we experience waves of anger, despair, and sadness.

If we become hospitalized for a period we experience a loss of autonomy as we become subject to hospital schedules and regulations. We may even feel like an object as we are wheeled from one test to another or to treatments such as chemotherapy. If we are the breadwinner in the family, we may experience a loss of income and the sense of identity that comes with our work and our salary. For many of us, it is humiliating to have our meals brought to us, or to have a nurse bathe us and take care of our most basic needs.

Some of us who have lost our health experience a loss of our sense of sexuality. We no longer feel feminine or masculine. This can be especially true if we must undergo chemotherapy or radiation and suffer through all the side effects of water retention and the loss of hair. A friend of mine who became ill with cancer of the bone marrow mourned the loss of her long, wavy hair. It was part of her distinctive beauty. We mourn our disfigurement and, just as if we had lost a loved one, we wish we could go back to the time when we felt whole.

We may not only lose our looks, but our independence, our very mobility. Perhaps we suffer from a severe case of arthritis that makes it difficult for us to accomplish the most simple tasks. It may become very hard for us to hold on to our autonomy in the face of our family's and friends' well-intentioned desire to take care of us. A number of disabled people have confided to me that they had to struggle to keep their loved ones from "smothering" them with care, and that struggle is a daily one. When we go out, we may have to confront the stares of passersby or the assumption of some people that disabled persons are also mentally deficient.

When we lose a body part through surgery we may experience profound grief. We may be angry over the need for surgery and perhaps guilty about the role our own behavior might have had in bringing about this condition, such as smoking or postponing a medical check up. We may find that we have difficulty sleeping, that we are extremely anxious or depressed, just as if we had lost a loved one.

It has been projected that one in ten women in the United States will develop some form of breast cancer. While not all of these cases will result in a mastectomy and while new treatments for breast cancer are being developed such as lumpectomy and hormonal treatments, those of us who develop this illness and undergo a mastectomy may feel that we have been mutilated. We may feel shock and numbness for weeks and even months after the procedure.

The loss of the breast means a loss of our body image, our view of ourself, and our perception of our attractiveness to others. We worry whether our husbands or partners will continue to love us. One woman contemplating prophylactic surgery remarked that if she were alone, she would have no hesitation, but she worried about her husband's reaction—"He loves me and he loves my body."

There is also the threat to our very life which such a disease involves. A woman in her thirties who had cancer described changes in her fundamental sense of self, that she had lost her sense of eternal youth that one has in one's thirties and that she developed a phobia of being ill. Anyone of us who loses a limb, a part of our body or a bodily function has been brought face to face with our mortality. We need to be able to express our sadness, anger, guilt and especially our anxieties about our altered self and its acceptability to others.

Finding a support group of persons who have experienced similar losses may help us to express our sorrow and to receive affirmation for our feelings. Bereavement centers often include support groups for those with serious illnesses and most hospitals have begun to sponsor such groups on their own premises.

Gradually we may come to accept our different body and to develop a new sense of self. We may gain a sense of pride and accomplishment for the battle we have fought. We may have also acquired a new perspective on life.

A runaway or missing child

A close friend of mine, whose child ran away as an adolescent, kept telling me that there are some situations in life which have no redeeming sides to them. "What lesson could there possibly be in this terrible pain?" she exclaimed. When our child has run away, we may face the same welter of conflicting emotions as when a loved one is seriously ill. We mourn a loss, but the person is still there. We are torn with anxiety, with hope for our loved one's survival, and with guilt. In the first months or years, we may devote all of our energy to finding our child. These efforts may give structure and meaning to our life. We may also feel anger at our child for abandoning and rejecting us. The anger may be so overwhelming at times that it masks our sorrow.

As a parent, we may blame ourselves for our child's disappearance and we may sift our past behavior relentlessly for clues to our "failure." As parents, we want to be omnipotent, to assure our children the very best we are able to give them. It is very difficult not to judge ourselves under these circumstances. We may have been the very best of parents to our child and still find fault with ourselves. We may have recognized that our child had difficulties and have gone out of our way to do extra things for him or her, and yet we were not able to prevent that child's disappearance. It's helpful to be gentle with ourselves and to acknowledge our sadness. In time we may learn to see ourselves in perspective and to remember all we were able to do for our child during the years he or she was home.

Just as in the tragedy of a child's death, the disappearance of a child may place great strain on our marriage or relationship. Because each partner grieves in his or her own way and because each has built up a set of expectations for the other, we may have difficulty communicating in the long, painful months and years after such a loss. Some families may seek separate supports and some may turn to a counselor as a family unit. Counseling or support groups may not only help us through our grief as a family, they may also help us to respond to unhelpful comments by friends and co-workers.

There is no calendar for moving towards an understanding of the separateness of our child. We may feel that we are making progress and some incident will spark our memory and plunge us back into sadness. Some of us may feel ready to go on with our lives in a year, some of us will need more time.

As years pass, we notice the changes in our appearance and in ourselves, but the image of our child is frozen in time. Although we will always wonder where our child is and what he or she is doing, we also need to go on with our daily life. Deep within us we may harbor a hope for our child's return, but gradually we may allow ourselves to do some letting go and to move on.

3 • The Crisis of Meaning

We experience the transformations of our lives and feelings as we traverse the phases of the grieving process. However, the quest for meaning is also a part of our journey through grief. As we struggle with our religious beliefs and our views of a just world we may find that these may change radically. When a loved one dies, our belief in a benevolent Creator may be shaken as we ask ourselves, "Why did this happen to my spouse, or child, why did this happen to me? I've always been a good person." We may wonder why the good are not spared illnesses, accidents and untimely death. We may question a divine plan in which we lose a child at an early age, a spouse when we have children, a lover or a friend. We think, "unjust, unfair, inexplicable," as we examine our shattered lives.

In the early period after the death of a loved one, we are thrown back on ourselves and the ground under our feet may no longer seem solid. Some of us may find our faith a source of support and experience a deepening of our beliefs. Others may find an emptiness in religious ceremonies and we may wish to withdraw from our previous observances for a while. Even those who turn to their religion with a renewed understanding may feel angry at a Creator who allowed the death of our loved one. Death causes us not only to examine our lives, but also our place within the universe.

The death of a loved one through suicide or homicide seems senseless and defies our structures of meaning, our very sense of justice. We may feel a deep confusion and fragility, as if we were adrift in a hostile universe. One of my daughter's close friends was brutally murdered. She and her friend were very similar physical types, petite and slender. "Does that mean I could also be a victim?" she wondered.

While these questions may persist, we may gain new insight into life as we progress through the grieving process. Many of us discover that we have developed a new sense of what is important. Things that used to seem significant to us, whether success in our careers or material wealth, can now seem unimportant. We may have a keen sense of how much our relationships with family and friends matter and we may feel that we have come closer to ultimate reality. Along with a new scale of values will come a new understanding of the fragility of life. If the life of someone who is at the center of our own being can be snuffed out in minutes, everything else must seem tenuous.

Ultimately we discover that we are survivors, and as survivors we have gained new strengths and new insights. We have been able to incorporate sadness and pain in our lives and have understood how these emotions transform us. Our own suffering has helped us to feel and express compassion for others and to discover just how precious life is.

Many of us who have endured the death of a loved one through violent means or through an agonizing illness may have learned that it is possible to live without answers to our fundamental questions and that some experiences have no redeeming sides to them. Having to live with this ambivalence is not an unusual fate.

These insights into meaning can be expressed in many different ways, ranging from working to help others who have suffered from similar tragedies, to changing our line of work, or finding the ability to appreciate the elements of our everyday lives and the facts of the human condition. In Chapter 14, Margaret describes her work with Victim Rights. The search for meaning may have been a terrifying journey, but along the way we will have discovered hidden resources and affirmations we never expected.

WHEN SOMEONE DIES:
THE EARLY PHASES
OF GRIEF

One of our nephews drove me
to the cemetery.
You weren't there.

I stood in the temple
with the mourners.
You didn't hear.

I go to dinner
at friends' houses;
their silence

pins you deeper underground
than the earth
heaped on your coffin . . .

Ruth Feldman, from "Visits"

4 • When a Parent of Young Adults Dies

Jeremy:

Mom and I had gone to pick up a part at Sears and we were driving back. We drove up to the house and there was a police car at the next door neighbor's, so I thought, "Uh, oh, maybe our dog bothered them again." So we went inside the house and I was just sitting down when the doorbell rang. It was the police and that's how we found out my father had a heart attack. I can still see everything there and I can feel that moment. My sister Anne said to me that she had changed, that she's a different person. And I said that I wasn't any different, but when I think about it, she's right. That day really made me change.

I haven't cried since the funeral. The funeral, I think, was very very good for my family. We had Father Krauss come up and help with it. What we did is that each of us children picked a passage we wanted to read for a eulogy, so instead of just sitting in the pew and listening to someone read, we actually stood up and read to the friends and the family. It pulled my brother and myself much closer than we have been in a long time, and it sort of helped me because I felt that I had something to do and I felt that I was part of it. It was hard.

The summer before he died I was at home and my mother wanted me to go down with her and visit my father and I was thinking, "I don't want to go, why should I have to go?" I felt very angry at my mother. I wanted to stay home and have a good time, but I went because my parents asked me. We spent four days down there and it was great and we had a really nice time. We did a lot of nice things, just the three of us. At least I don't feel guilty about how I treated my father at the end. I feel unhappy that things were just starting to come together for my father. He had this new job that was going well.

The weekend before he died we went up to Michigan. We have a house up there that the whole family built together and this was something that he put a lot of effort in. He just loved Michigan. (My family went up there again for the first time after he died and that was really hard because a lot of him was up there.) Anyway, that was a nice weekend. He really enjoyed it. One of the reasons I feel guilty is because I didn't want to go up to Michigan. I didn't want to be there with them and I was forced to. I wasn't in a good mood that weekend. Everyone was saying how good my father was feeling and how well they connected with him and I didn't feel that way at all. I remember that I had been rude or something like that. I thought he was being a jerk, really obnoxious to me. I thought, "I don't need this garbage from him." And then when I found out that he had died four days later, I thought like, "Gosh, I know it was really minor but I felt bad that that had to happen."

Sue:

I was twenty-three when my mother died. It'll be ten years this year. It's hard to believe it has been that long. It doesn't seem like it because she is still so alive for me.

It was her third bout with cancer. I was home when she had an operation to remove her bladder. It was right after I graduated from college. A year later she was diagnosed as having cancer again. I was in Boston when she died. I had been planning to go home at Christmas and possibly stay longer if I was needed. I had seen her the previous September when I'd been home for my sister's wedding.

She died the day after Thanksgiving. I was on an island in Maine and I had a dream Thanksgiving night that I had gone to her bedside. It was a very strong dream. When I woke up, I felt very uneasy. When I got back from Maine that night my sister had called to say she had died that morning. I had dreamed that when my mother pulled down the sheet, her body was transparent and I could see the cancer through her body.

I had many other dreams about her after she died. I would dream that I would be somewhere and that I would run into my mother and she would say, "I'm not really dead, why did you bury me?" Some of them were accusatory, and some of them were joyful reunions.

I went home for the funeral. My father had taken care of most everything. There were viewings in the mortuary which I just hated. My two younger brothers refused to go. They were fifteen and nineteen. They didn't want to deal with it at all. They did not want to talk about it. My father got very closed up in a lot of ways. My mother had not wanted any extreme life-saving measures. She had wanted to stay home and she did, although she went to the hospital the night before she died.

I took care of my mother's belongings because my father just couldn't do it. I must have cried non-stop for weeks. Then, when I came back to Boston, I didn't have any family. But I didn't feel that staying home would work either, though some relatives would feel that it was my responsibility as the older daughter to stay home and take care of my brothers and father. He didn't put pressure on me to do that though there were times I thought I probably should have done that.

My mother and I had been through a very long struggle and were just resolving it when she died. My whole breaking away from the family and the church when I went away to college was very difficult, and there were a lot of things I still felt very guilty about when she died. I know I caused her a lot of pain and we really didn't talk very openly for several years. I didn't come home much during the college years. I was glad we had gotten to some point of resolution. We had some of the best times we ever had during the week I was home for my sister's wedding. Luckily, the last time I had seen her we were on better terms than we had been on for quite a while.

When my paternal grandmother died when I was thirteen, I had been at loggerheads with her and so I had some worries about that. Then my maternal grandmother died. It seems as if there was this period when everyone died. I was very strong-willed and my grandmother and I had had a lot of arguments. It wasn't the same with my mother, but there was a lot of guilt I felt along with the grief. If my mother had died a few years earlier in the midst of all that turmoil it would have been worse than it was because I really feel that we had been working things out.

As young adults we experience a whole spectrum of initial reactions to loss, such as shock, anger, and denial. Moreover, as young adults, we are more vulnerable in general than the mature adult. During this period of our lives we may be exploring new identities, and our relationships with our parents may be in a state of change. We may be forging new roles either as students or as new members of the work force. It is a time of keen sensitivity to the judgments of our friends and families.

Efforts to develop new roles may cause tensions within the family. Jeremy was in the process of a very normal "separation" from an intense dependency on his parents when his father died suddenly. On the surface, his conflicts with his parents over how to spend his time may have seemed contentious, but they were actually part of the normal process of trying to establish his own identity and seek his own separate destiny. Sue had disagreed with her mother about religion, and her decision to leave the church caused a great deal of misunderstanding between her and her family.

These kinds of stresses may cause us to feel enormous guilt when a parent dies. We may feel responsible for the tension and pain we believe we may have caused. On the other hand, both Sue and Jeremy had had positive relationships with their parents. Also, for both, not only the quality of the relationship but also the quality of the time spent together before the death were important in the successful unfolding of the grieving process. Sue had a period of warm companionship with her mother during her sister's wedding. Jeremy could look back at a harmonious and enjoyable summer visit with his father.

If, on the other hand, we have experienced bitter and contentious relationships with a deceased parent we can struggle for years with feelings of guilt and anger. We may try to deny our feelings of guilt and anger either by suppressing them, or by idealizing the parent. This will cause difficulty in moving beyond the first reactions to grief. Counseling may help resolve some of the issues in such a relationship, freeing us to feel and express sadness.

Because we are still so reliant on our parents at this age, we may have fewer significant others to turn to when a parent dies. In fact, we may find ourselves isolated from our friends as we cope with new family responsibilities. Sue faced "not having a family" when she returned to graduate school, while her friends may have been absorbed by romantic ties or academic issues.

When we return to high school or college after a loss, we may not find anyone to talk to about our anger and turmoil. Because we will be experiencing shock, we may continue attending classes and writing term papers as if nothing had happened, causing our friends and professors to conclude that we are feeling better. Our deep distress is not visible to those who could help us, thus increasing our sense of separation from the world. Sometimes we may feel conflict about returning to college and leaving behind a parent and younger siblings. We may feel that we should have stayed at home to care for them, yet at the same time we want to get on with our lives. Many young adults plunge themselves into school work and manage not only to finish their studies, but to do very well. However, we are only postponing the grieving process, and our grief may surface again later on in our lives.

When older adults experience loss, they may have a sense that others around them have had similar or even greater problems. Certainly they are more likely to have friends who have suffered loss. What we as young adults may perceive instead are friends who have "normal" families or situations. The perspective an older person develops from a life of experience and of observing others may not be available to us at this time. What we see are friends who have "normal" situations. It may seem difficult to talk about sadness or despair to others dealing with what may suddenly seem as minor issues such as grades or dates. Therefore it may be particularly difficult for us to reach out. Not only are we suffering from what seems like an unusual situation, but because we want people to like us and worry about being accepted by others at this stage in our lives, we may hesitate to make demands on others just when we need to.

The explanations of religion may not have much meaning when

we are faced with the terrible injustice of a parent's untimely death. Jeremy felt very keenly that his father died just when his job and life circumstances were improving. We may not have had any prior experience of death, or perhaps if we have, it may have happened to an elderly person with whom we had little contact. It's important to turn to a close friend whom we trust at this time. Just talking about our feelings will be a great relief. It will help us to realize that we are not "abnormal," or "crazy" but that others have similar responses to loss. A real friend won't misjudge us.

Sue refers to her younger brothers' apparant detachment during the wake and funeral. They may have been feeling the shock of mortality— their own vulnerability to death—and were therefore unable to acknowledge their mother's death. They may have feared losing control of their emotions or experiencing the negative reactions of others to their responses. Fear that our emotions might be unacceptable to our friends and family causes many of us to suppress our anger, guilt, and insecurity. The college-age son of a friend of mine reacted to his mother's death by plunging himself into social activities with his friends, suppressing his initial shock and bewilderment at his terrible loss.

There are many difficulties that complicate the grieving process during this period of our lives. We may be facing crucial choices at this time— the choice of a major in college, or a new job, or whether to continue a romantic relationship. We may have anxieties about our performance in school, about money, about our appearance. There is much to challenge our self-confidence, and make the death of a parent even more overwhelming.

The demands of our families coupled with social pressures may cause us to bury the troubling emotions that assail us after a death. Watching the deep sorrow of our surviving parent, we may not feel that we have a right to grieve. Or we may not want others to know how we feel because they might criticize us for those feelings. It is important to remember that everyone feels profound emotional turmoil after a death, and to feel free to express our anger and sadness. Our real friends will want to listen.

We are engulfed not only by waves of powerful feelings when a parent dies, but also by a host of new worries. We wonder if the illness or even the accident that caused the death may not also happen to us. We are suddenly brought face to face with our own fragility. It is normal to feel we might develop cancer or a heart condition because a parent died from that disease. We should discuss these fears with others.

My students have suggested that when a friend loses a parent or loved one, sometimes it is necessary to remind that person of his or her importance. Friends need to tell each other to take care of themselves, get plenty of sleep, or eat properly. After a death we may feel that our own well-being no longer matters. At a time like this, we need to take special care of ourselves, not only of our physical well-being, but also of our emotional well-being.

5 • *When a Spouse Dies*

Anne:

He died on January 14th. The previous Thanksgiving, he did not feel that well. His stomach was bothering him. Finally, it was bothering him so much that we decided he might as well go and see a doctor and get it over with. December 11 he went to see our doctor. We go from stomach ache on Thanksgiving to dead in January. It turned out to be cancer of the pancreas and they operated on December 23. I found out before he did because they were doing tests. It looked like it might be jaundice. They had to do CAT scans. We were assuming that it was gall stones. Then they said at the hospital that they were going to look at the pancreas. I went home and got a book about adult diseases, from Better Homes and Gardens. *So I looked up cancer of the pancreas and when I saw it I said, "I'm going to be a widow." I knew it right then. Thank God I knew it before he did. The next day after he was operated on, the doctor was back in half an hour. I wouldn't have been so ready if I hadn't read that book. So then I told him. He knew, or he was afraid of it underneath. So I said, "It's not very good news. They say it's cancer and your time will be numbered in months." Months! You think ten months. Meanwhile I am coming in twice a day, taking care of kids, working.*

The kids were in school and as each one came home, I told them he was going to die. I could have waited. but I didn't. They asked, "How's daddy?" and I said, "Well, he came through the operation and it wasn't good. The doctors said they were going to do the best that they could but they say he has cancer of the pancreas and you don't get better from that. They say he has months." That was hard, but I knew it was the right thing to do. Good news you can surprise people with. But not bad news.

Everyday I would wake up and think it wasn't true. It's as if you had an automobile accident and thought if you could just go back for three hours, like on a movie tape, it wouldn't have happened. So you have that feeling. The children cried, but they were pretty good. They went in on Christmas and we brought presents. I was strong at that time. I had the initial strength you have from adrenalin. I had people over and I thought I'll do this and I'll have insurance money. It was a little macabre because he was going to die, but he wasn't dead yet. Then he would say to me, "Well, you'd better sell the car." We always thought we had more time than we did, and that was merciful during that period of time.

You say a person is dying, but they are alive. When they are dead you can go back and say, "He was dying." When they are dead. We would talk about the fact that we hoped he would be home. It turned out that he developed phlebitis of the leg which kept him in the hospital. It was fortunate because they don't want dying people in the hospitals. Hospitals are for sick people who are going to be better so they wanted him out as soon as he was dying. The only reason that he could stay was because he needed an I.V. It's merciful that he didn't come home because the children would have had to see ambulances and stuff. He never came home. That was it. He was on morphine and cocaine mixtures. I was very pleased that everyone was respectful to him. He wasn't a casual person. They called him Mr. Ross. And we talked frankly. It was good.

Bill:

My wife Ginny had breast cancer and she was on chemotherapy and had been on radiation. Apparently she knew that she was dying but she had never told me. I suppose I should have known it, but I didn't really want to know it. We went away to Maine on the Fourth of July and she obviously knew something was wrong then, because she was very insistent that our daughter and son-in-law come down. My daughter had planned to go somewhere else. Normally she would have said, "Okay, go somewhere else," but she was very insistent that Patty go with us, which tells me that she had an omen. The whole family went and we had a wonderful weekend.

When the weekend was over, she was in the kitchen cooking and I was in the dining-room eating and she walked by me and said, "I can't get my breath." That's not an unusual thing to happen to people, but there was something that told me I should go in the bedroom and check. When I got in the bedroom, she was sitting on the bed and I sat next to her and put my arm around her. As soon as I did that, she lay down on the bed and died without saying another word. I didn't know that she was dead and I didn't check her pulse or anything. We struggled her into the car and my daughter Patty drove. We took her to the hospital. It took about twenty minutes. She was lying in my arms in the back seat. I still thought she was alive but unconscious. When we got to the hospital,

Patty ran in to get the doctors. At that point I gave her mouth to mouth resuscitation. At that moment one of the interns came out, took one look at her, rolled her eyes back and said, "She's gone." I answered, "Of course she's not gone." He was just a young intern so he pounded on her chest to get her breathing, and then they rushed her into the emergency ward.

My daughter and I went in the office to fill out the forms assuming that in a few minutes everything would be all right. The doctor came in and told us that she was dead.

I was just numb. I had heard something that didn't seem possible. We got up and left, drove down to the cottage. I just was in a numb state as if it couldn't be. I had lived with this lady for thirty-three years, known her for thirty-five, and suddenly she couldn't be dead. The rest of that day all the friends and relatives started to accumulate. I still had no sadness. I was still in a state of shock.

I still don't remember when I first had the feeling of sadness but I think it wasn't until after the funeral. Even during the funeral I had this numbness.

When I came home and everything was over with, I was alone. I can remember cooking and crying. Men don't cry of course. So many times the doorbell would ring and I would run around and get a towel and dry my eyes, stalling until I let that person in. This is the way I went on. In five or six months I started to date women and that got my mind off it. But every now and then I would think of it. Of course you can't help it. You think of the things you did together.

A difficult thing was when little by little I had to get rid of her clothes. I still find some of her personal belongings. Even today, if I come across those things, that gives me bad memories.

Eric:

Diane died in April, 1983 of melanoma, which is a form of skin cancer. She had first been diagnosed when she was twenty-one and died when she was thirty. When she was about twenty-nine she found some tumors in her stomach, so that was the first indication that the melanoma had gone anywhere else besides her skin. That was when it became very frightening, but even then it had stabilized and we thought she would really beat it. She had always been a very spirited, very energetic person, incredibly positive, full of life and energy. She didn't seem like a cancer victim. She also took a very strong hand once she realized that the melanoma would not go away. She became very active in searching out ways of dealing with cancer. She found a program at the Beth Israel Hospital called the Program of Behavioral Medicine where they teach people how to meditate and try to reduce stress. Diane worked with a woman there and became a pretty disciplined meditator.

When we returned from our honeymoon, she didn't feel well and it turned out that she had a very large tumor in her abdomen. She had surgery but she never quite recovered. She decided to stay home, although it turned out that she was in very bad pain the last two weeks. They kept giving us stronger and stronger pain killers. It wasn't working. It seemed like the only thing that would work would be intravenous morphine which they couldn't give us at home.

That process of preparing for death was really good in some ways. Diane's younger sister is a nurse so she came to stay with us and brought all these books on death and dying. Diane and I read a lot of books and we were great researchers. We had researched melanoma, but it had never occurred to us to research death.

Diane was a real stoic. She had always been very brave and it was hard for her to admit that the pills weren't working, that she was in such pain. But we had this time to talk and we did talk a lot. I had started to see a therapist and she saw a therapist too. I started to see a therapist about a month before Diane died because it was clear that I just had to have someone to talk to. Both our therapists kept telling us that the thing to do was to talk to each other about it. It was our last chance. Also if you don't talk it becomes this great unmentionable that just snowballs. When there is no future, it becomes very superficial if you don't talk about that, because you can't talk about anything else. I mean you can't make plans.

Everything becomes heightened, takes on this emotional meaning. You really lose touch with other things. There is only one thing that is important and then this person dies. She had been my whole reason for living, my whole huge effort for the past few months. Not only had I lost, but it was a double whammy because I failed. I felt that there's nothing left, that there's nothing to do. You feel you failed because this person died and you didn't prevent it. There's still a sense that you failed the person, that there are things you didn't say that you should have. It comes and goes. There's a great sense of letdown when someone dies after a long illness; it has been your whole life, then there's nothing.

Her whole family came, her parents, her brothers and sisters. They're a very close family. But then they left. There's a new life. There's a sense of adjustment, really different and foreign, unwanted and unknown.

It's hard to believe that all that energy disappears, Diane. I mean it has to be channeled. I don't have any religious beliefs and she didn't either. She had this kind of pantheistic view, nothing really to do with God. She had a sense of spirituality. She wanted her memorial service in a church done by a clergyperson. She didn't care where. Also she didn't want God mentioned or Jesus Christ.

She was very specific about the kind of music she wanted. She wanted people to talk about her, to say what they wanted. It was actually very moving. Three hundred people came, including her first grade teacher, an old woman who said, "She made a lasting impression on me." All our friends came. When I said that Diane had asked anybody that wanted to get up and say whatever they wanted, there was this pause. Then there was this woman who works with me who stood up. She had never met Diane in her life, and she got up, went to the microphone, and said what it was like to work with me for the past couple of weeks. It was just beautiful and very touching. It turned out to be the perfect way to break the ice. The last one to speak was a woman leaning over the railing in a white dress. She had been in a B.B.C. film with Diane, a documentary about mind, body, and healing. Diane was doing very well in the meditation exercises and this woman who couldn't meditate and relieve herself of stress was getting better. She said she had been in the film with Diane and asked why it should have been Diane who died and not her.

She was cremated. She didn't want her body there or in a casket. In a way that's hard for people. Seeing a body makes you realize that it's the end. When there is no body, it's harder. It helped to have these people talking about her.

I remember she died at the end of April. You get so absorbed in the funeral arrangements and the mail and the people who come, all the details, which is good. But it has to end and it does end. And there you are. I was still in shock, still not all there.

I went to get my hair cut one day, and this young girl asked me, "What do you do?" I answered, "Oh, I don't do anything because my wife just died." This was a few days after she died. Then I was running at Fresh Pond and I saw this girl who looked like Diane. I mean there was probably a very vague resemblance to her. I went running up to her and said, "You look just like my wife who died." This poor woman. She must have thought I was crazy. You do things like that and they're irrational. It is a sense of shock and numbness.

The death of a husband or wife is a devastating event, one of the most stressful occurrences we face in our lives. There are as many different kinds of marriages as there are couples and though the intensity and strength of ties may vary, all marriages contain powerful emotional bonds. Some marriages consist only of sharing household management and daily routines. Companionship and the sharing of intimate lives characterize other marriages. But in all types of marriages, loving or troubled, the partners function as one. Losing a partner leaves us feeling incomplete.

Couples who are living together in a committed relationship, whether heterosexual or homosexual, experience these powerful emotional bonds. This is also true of elderly couples who may have already been widowed and who have chosen to live together rather than to remarry and lose their social security. Their relationship is functionally a marital one, yet these relationships do not have social status. This complicates the grieving process because while the sadness and pain of loss may be as intense as the pain of losing an "official" spouse, these feelings elicit no response from others and we may believe that somehow we are not entitled to feel so strongly. Because of this, we may want to hide our emotions. However, it is important for all of us to realize that the loss of a life shared with another is as overwhelming to those who have not had their living arrangements acknowledged by society.

When we have lost a spouse after years of marriage, we lose the years of growth in intimacy and companionship. The dreams we may have shared for the future become memories. Even if the relationship was a troubled one, we miss the presence of our spouse. If there were difficulties, we have lost the opportunity to try to solve the problems and strengthen the bonds. We may be burdened by regret as well as guilt.

If we are young when we lose a spouse, we are robbed of a life of sharing growth with its joys and difficulties. We will never have the children we dreamed of bringing up together. We have not only lost a life in common but we have also been robbed of our future. Some people may try to console us by saying that since we are still young, we will find another partner, but this is hardly a consolation. The future we are cheated of is a future with our loved one and we may feel that it cannot be replaced.

Many people are not used to encountering widows or widowers in their twenties or thirties and don't know how to respond. These years are years of building, of beginning new relationships, or bearing children. People feel uneasy when meeting the newly widowed because it reminds them of their own mortality and also because they may lack experience with this occurrence at an early age. This may make us wary of burdening others with our feelings. However, as Eric's narrative in Chapter 25 show us, expressing our feelings when we are with our friends is actually helpful to them. It not only relieves us but also teaches them. It's important not to worry about burdening others at this time. We are carrying enough of a burden ourselves without adding additional guilt. A real friend will treasure our openness and will learn from our experience .

The way in which our spouse died will have an important effect on the nature of our immediate response to the death. In the case of a sudden death such as an accident or a heart attack, the initial shock is much greater and can be overpowering. We are seized with a sense of unreality. How can a person be with us in the morning and not in the afternoon or evening? We expect him or her to return, keep thinking that he or she will eventually come back. In the narratives we can see that Bill experienced a feeling of numbness for a longer period of time than Eric did. Although Bill's wife was also ill with cancer, he either did not admit it to himself or was unaware that she was not going to recover.

If our spouse had a terminal illness and we knew that he would die in the near future, we might have begun to prepare ourselves for this event. Often however, we may have hopes that our spouse might survive or that a new cure might become available. Our expectations may change throughout the illness, bringing sharp mood swings in their wake. Sometimes we may entertain unrealistic hopes that cause us to resist thoughts of death. This may add to the pain of our adjustment after the death.

We may have mixed feelings as our spouse is dying. Imperceptibly, we begin to think about our future alone and may start to plan for it. However, as Anne's narrative points out, it is troubling to think of preparations for our future when our loved one is not dead. We may feel it to be a betrayal, as Eric did when he admitted feeling guilty about applying to law school. How does one deal with a spouse who has no future? We may want to talk about these arrangements with our spouse and to share our thoughts with him or her. The dying person may have some wishes and concerns to share at this moment and we may wish to have their own thoughts on our plans.

Watching a loved one suffer and feeling powerless to help that person is an emotionally draining experience. We may feel anger at our helplessness or at the demands placed on us. We may feel fearful of losing our spouse while wishing that his or her suffering will end. We may be assailed by a whirl of conflicting emotions at this time. These are all normal reactions and we should not burden ourselves by feeling guilty about our responses. These emotions are the rafts that will carry us through these stormy times.

How to deal with children and relatives at this time is a very important issue. As Anne's narrative points out, it's best to be open with children and tell them exactly what is happening and what to expect. Sooner or later, children will find out that a parent is dying and they will feel betrayed if we keep that information from them. The mother of one of my students died of cancer when my student was ten years old. Her father didn't tell her how seriously ill her mother was, and when she was finally hospitalized, he only brought her to the hospital at the very end. By then, her mother was comatose and swollen with cortisone. She felt she should have been prepared for this and was shocked and terrified at the sight of her mother and the sudden revelation of her impending death. Children need our guidance in preparing for death. Our silence can be interpreted by them as helplessness or as a sign of more dire things to come.

After the shock of the death wears off, we are apt to feel confused by the storm of emotions that assail us. Many people speak of waking up in a panic during the night and especially of feeling terribly lonely.

Our spouse may have provided us not only with a sense of identity, but also with a reason for living. Therefore we may feel an anguishing emptiness in our lives and a loss of meaning. We may wonder why we should get up in the morning, why we should work or carry on our daily routines.

In fact our daily routines have changed dramatically. We may not know what to do with the loneliness in the house. The pain may be so intense that we wish to make changes in our life, perhaps to move to a new location or take a new job. This is not a good time to make an important decision that may affect our lives. Rather, we should concentrate on taking care of ourselves, trying to get as much rest as possible, eating properly and communicating our needs to those who are close to us and to other members of our family.

There are many practical problems and tasks to be accomplished at this time, arranging for the funeral, informing friends and relatives. We need to fill out the death certificate and deal with wills and with financial issues. Some of these tasks may actually provide an order to our otherwise disrupted life, or for someone unfamiliar with financial and legal matters this may be a very difficult period. This is a good time to seek appropriate help in dealing with these matters. A retired woman who was suddenly widowed turned to the association of retired people in her town to help her file her tax return after her husband died.

Most marriages are characterized by a division of labor. When a spouse dies, we acquire a whole new set of chores in addition to accustomed ones. A woman will have to deal with repair people, with lawyers and bank personnel without the protection of her husband. Frequently, women experience sudden changes in status with respect to credit and financial situation. These are not small burdens considering the depth of our distress at this time. In more traditional marriages, a widower will be faced with learning to shop or cook, especially learning how to be in an empty house. The organization of a household may seem as complex and difficult to a man as learning to deal with tax forms and bank statements for a widow. In addition to learning how to function emotionally without our partner, we are tackling new tasks every day.

Besides the allocation of chores, spouses collaborate in making important decisions about household and child rearing. As widow or widower we may be left with the sole responsibility for earning a living and for bringing up children. If our marriage has been ridden with conflict, we may find rueful gratification at being able to make certain decisions alone. However, we all feel the difficulties of having to shoulder responsibilities alone. We may feel anger at the sudden increase in responsibility for decisions and the number of tasks we have to handle. We may ask ourselves "Why me?" We may be angry at everyone else who still enjoys being a couple and at a world in which everyone seems to have a partner.

If we have children, we are faced with the necessity of being both father and mother to our children, acting as provider and source of emotional support. It is difficult enough to accomplish this when one is feeling well, but this great responsibility when we have just experienced the death of a spouse may lead us to postpone our own grief.

When our spouse has died, we step out into the world with a different identity. As a widow, we may be perceived as a "sad" person, reminding others of the fragility of life. We may also be considered as a threatening sexual rival. The social supports we enjoyed while still married may no longer be available. People whom we considered our friends may avoid us, intensifying our feelings of loneliness and confusion. On the other hand, we may be surprised by gestures of friendship from members of our family or acquaintances who have suffered from loss themselves and who therefore may be sensitive to our needs.

While a woman may experience special difficulties in facing the world after her husband has died, a man may experience problems with living alone. He may take his meals out or go out every night, just to avoid being in the house without his former wife. He may even avoid spending time with old friends, knowing that after a round of golf or a drink, they will be returning to their wives. This is especially true for men whose children have grown up. Children may not understand their father's need for company and new friends at this time and may regard their father's behavior as a betrayal of their mother's memory.

However, although it is just as stressful for a man to "re-enter" society as a single man again, he is not likely to be perceived as a threatening person. It seems to be easier for men to establish new relationships a few months after the death of a spouse than for women. However, our family and friends may misunderstand our efforts to develop new ties as a betrayal of the former marriage, while we may see no conflict between a new relationship and a commitment to our deceased spouse.

After the death of a spouse we experience feelings of emptiness and incompleteness. Perhaps it is not possible to reach out immediately for comfort or for new friendships. However, added to our deep pain is the stress of adjusting to changed social roles and status. Our standing within the family may have changed drastically. We may find our role changed from that of giver of advice to recipient. Perhaps we were used to host family dinners during the holidays and now this ceremony is taken over by an adult child, or another member of the family. We are already experiencing low self-esteem from the blow of the death and these additional changes may diminish our self confidence.

If our partner in a lesbian or gay relationship dies, we may find ourselves suddenly cut off from our partner's immediate family, or we may find ourselves denied access to the extended family. Often we are so affected by society's reaction to our situation that we may hesitate to seek outside help. However, one woman who had lost her partner in a lesbian relationship joined a support group of widows and found both help and acceptance. Just because society may minimize a relationship doesn't necessarily mean that we have no right to our grief or to outside support.

The weeks after the death of our spouse are not only very lonely and confusing ones, but also a time of gathering in. We may feel very private, not ready to reach out. During this period, we should be kind to ourselves and avoid taking on any unnecessary burdens. Even if we are responsible for others, we need to take special care of ourselves, to make sure that we have periods of rest and times of privacy for the tears to flow. We need to think about the deceased and to continue our communication with our spouse in our thoughts or by our attention to his or her affairs.

6 • *When a Child Dies*

Phil:

When I first heard about it, I was in the classroom. I got a phone call from my best friend who told me that there had been an accident. I jumped in the car and drove I don't know at what speed. In the next few days when my daughter was in the hospital I learned what really happened. An elderly man not attending to his driving caused the loss of life of my daughter Jenny. She was walking her bicycle across the street. She had stopped at the crosswalk just like she had been taught to do. This is a quiet little town where we lived. It was in the Fall. It was the afternoon, three o'clock, a nice clear day. She was waved across by another person. Then she saw this man who wasn't looking while he was driving. He stepped on the gas instead of on the brakes. What happened after that wasn't very nice.

That has always been difficult for us. The injustice of it all. Afterwards he didn't behave in a manly, human way. The legal proceedings were terrible. The worst thing is that he continues to drive his car. That's always been a thorn in our sides. In addition to the loss, we've always had to deal with that other aspect of it, the conduct of that person. As a Christian you don't want to harbor hard feelings, but I have those feelings because it was an injustice. This man is in his late seventies and does not belong behind the wheel. It causes my wife a tremendous discomfort. Society doesn't have a resolution for the victim.

For three years we've had constant news bulletins about the case. And each time we have to relive this thing. It opens those wounds again. It also opens up that feeling about how unnecessary it all was.

Jenny was one of our three children. She was the middle child. For us, Jenny was the catalyst in the family, the source of energy for us. For me, she was my ever-present shadow. My older daughter and I had a wonderful relationship. But when I would come home from meetings, Jenny would always be waiting for me. I would run after work and she would always go with me. When I went to the ball park, she always wanted to go. She was a big baseball fan. She went to about nine or ten games with me, and every time the Red Sox won. The last time we had a lot of difficulty in getting in and finally got some standing-room tickets. We were standing way in the back. We could hardly see. Then this gentleman walked up to me, looked at me and at Jenny and said, "I've got some great seats. You know, I have to go back to work. Stay right where you are and I'll come get you." She was just enthralled. I can remember seeing her expression and I have just memorized the whole thing. She had a very magnetic personality. She was a tremendously alive person and had a great deal of hopefulness about her. It's not a case of making someone bigger than they are. When your daughter and your companion and your friend goes, that's very very difficult. We didn't know how to deal with that.

Marilyn:

The quick summary of what happened is that I had a stillborn child, a little girl. I didn't know it was a girl until I gave birth to the child and I went through a regular labor and birth. I held her after she was born and we named her. Subsequent to the birth we found out that it was due to a genetic problem that my husband and I have, and subsequent to that we tried again. The second pregnancy was problem-ridden. I didn't get to the point of genetic testing as I hoped to and we terminated the second pregnancy because of problems. Then the third pregnancy miscarried.

My own physical health was very much a problem through all of this because between pregnancies I had to be operated on for a fibroid and that fibroid was a problem during the first pregnancy. The second pregnancy was mostly a problem with stress, not knowing from moment to moment what exactly was going on with that one. It was not clear from the beginning whether we would ever get to genetic testing and to term. The third one miscarried. After the miscarriage we found out we had problems with the pregnancy. I have had to have blood tests since then.

One of the problems throughout this whole thing is that I began to see myself as unhealthy, and in some ways I was. It was a tremendous physical as well as emotional drain. I'm only really feeling myself again now after several months.

My reaction is also very much colored by the second and third experience. The great tragedy was not only the first time and the others were not minor losses. I had hoped after the first one that I would try again and someday have a child. I lost hope. I've really given up, which is very hard to do and it sounds very negative, but I see it as positive and so does my husband.

A friend of mine was a member of the Resistance to the Nazis during World War II. She was caught and spent the war years in concentration camps. Who can imagine a worse fate? Yet years later, her son Peter was killed in an automobile accident. In the epilogue to her book on the holocaust she wrote about her son: "The wound is deeper than Auschwitz." No matter what age the child is when he or she dies, no one anticipates such a loss. We expect to lose our parents through old age or illness, but no one expects to survive one's own child. It seems contrary to nature, a blow which is barely comprehensible in its cruelty.

Although there are differences in the grief we feel for the death of an infant, the death of a child or of a young adult, as parents our role is to protect, nurture and love. As parents we have a desire to be omnipotent, to arrange the child's circumstances so that he or she will be as happy and healthy as possible. When our child dies, we may feel as if we have failed in our role as parents. Our helplessness in face of illness or an accident compounds our guilt.

If our child died through illness, we may have had to watch the child suffer for a long period of time and experience the pain of the progressive decline. After that death, we may go over and over this period, reviewing it. We may wonder if we should have done things differently, whether we might not have done just a little bit more. Even those of us who spent all of our time in the hospital at the bedside of our child may agonize over our care while our child was ill.

Some forms of cancer account for many deaths of children. This may mean that the child who died had to endure chemotherapy or radiation treatments with all their painful side effects. One of my neighbor's children died of a brain tumor when she was eighteen. The chemotherapy and cortisone caused Julie's hair to fall out, and her face swelled and puckered like a newborn's. Eventually she became partially paralyzed. Looking back we may wonder whether we were sufficiently loving and reassuring at these times. Children worry about how their peers and others will react to them, whether they will still be accepted and how, finally, they themselves can accept this transformed self.

When we look back on this period, we may see ourselves as so caught up in the physical side of our child's care or in our own sadness that we may wonder whether we were sensitive enough to our child's reactions to the illness. Children will react differently to these disfigurements. Because of Julie's age, she felt more comfortable being bathed by a visiting nurse than by her mother. However, this may have been difficult for her mother, who was already experiencing grief over the impending termination of her parenting role to that child.

As Julie's condition worsened, she stayed at home. Although every effort was made to organize family life so that she would be as comfortable as possible, family activities continued. Her mother's friends stopped by once a week for a game of bridge and her sister continued to pursue her own activities at school. Trying to keep home life as normal as possible is helpful both for the parents and the dying child.

Children of any age will have anxieties about dying. Parents who are already experiencing the difficulties of facing a child's death may not find it easy to address the questions and fears of the child. The child may want to know whether he or she is going to get better or not. Pretending or side-stepping these questions leave children feeling confused. Or trying to maintain a stoic attitude before a terminally ill child may make that child feel that he or she must behave in the same way. Children are very sensitive to our behavior. They know when we are lying. When we are trying to cover up something, they can read our body language with great acuity and will be bewildered if our words and non-verbal signals conflict. They take their cues from us so that if we feel free to express our sadness and pain, they will be able to share their own grief with us.

Children grieve not only for their own impending death, but for the separation from family and friends. A child's age, personality and coping styles will determine how he or she grieves. His or her way will not be our own way of grieving and we may have difficulty reading his or her cues. A child may express regret over not being able to attend a graduation, a school dance, a basketball game. We may not have seen the child's own mourning over death in these regrets. When we are burdened with the care of a terminally ill child, it's not always possible to have the perspective that time and distance may bring. We shouldn't blame ourselves for not having the wisdom that only hindsight can bring.

When a child suffers from an illness, we try to seek out superior care, to do everything humanly possible to assure the child's recovery. We ourselves often become absorbed in the physical care of the child and when we are not actually caring for that child, we are thinking and worrying. After the death, we are suddenly cut adrift. It's as if we had lost a large part of our life and the very meaning of our life. Even if we have other children, each child is unique. Each child has his or her own place in our hearts and lives. Even if our days are filled with other responsibilities and concerns, the emptiness after such a death may make us feel as if we were living a nightmare.

Because our role is one of giving care to others, as parents we may have great difficulty, not only with the brutal termination of our parental role, but with our own need for nurture and support. It is confusing and disorienting to find ourselves suddenly in the grip of the overwhelming emotions of anger, guilt, and sadness. It's as if we were propelled out of our nurturing role and into our deepest selves.

Living together as a family may be especially difficult after the loss of a child. For instance, a wife may not wish to go out to a movie or dinner with her husband because she is having a bad day, but that doesn't mean she doesn't want to be with him. If a mother is sitting on the living-room sofa crying when a child comes home, the child may have a sense of not being important to her. It's very difficult to be a parent after the death of a child because we are so caught up in our emotions we have little to give. But we need to level with children, let them know where we are. We can tell children that we are feeling bad that afternoon, but that we still love them and that they are still very important to us. Surviving children need to know and to be constantly reassured about where they stand, even though our energy for parenting may be drained and we may need to be nurtured ourselves. They are often better able to understand our needs than we imagine.

We may feel that not talking about the death will protect the child, but the child may respond by withdrawing and engaging in anti-social behavior. If we show our own tears and sadness, while assuring surviving children that they are very important to us, they will feel more free to express their sorrow. The tears we shed do not necessarily cause others to cry. When our crying seems to spark tears in others, it is only because we have tapped the tears which were already inside that person. We can think of it as liberating those tears. We may not realize how deeply children grieve, or that silence or withdrawal does not indicate the absence of sadness. The contrary is the case.

When a child dies, everyone within the family is affected and everyone grieves in his or her own way. This places a tremendous burden on the nuclear family. We have built up expectations over the years, and at such a time we may not be able to live up to them, to be the strong supporting, nurturing parent or the well-behaved child. It is extremely helpful to seek outside supports at this time, not only for our own relief and but also for the health of the family. In the narratives, Phil mentions going out with an old friend. Both he and his wife saw a counselor. Marilyn turned to a counselor and to close friends.

Other members of our family do not so much expect us to be strong or invulnerable at all times, as to communicate with them. As family members, it's important to recognize that we can't control each other's feelings. The emotions of grief are so powerful and unpredictable that it may be difficult to communicate clearly after a loss. However, if we can be patient and tolerant with each other and not expect too much, that in itself will be helpful to our family life.

While we may have had a chance to prepare ourselves for the death of a child during an illness, losing a child by accidental death seems more difficult. The shock is more intense and lasts for a longer time. The feelings of guilt are apt to be stronger. As parents, we may feel that we should have prevented the accident. We may go over and over the details as if we were replaying a film. Phil's daughter was killed as she was crossing the street. She had wanted to come to work with him that day, but his schedule was too crowded. After the accident, he felt that if he had not been so busy, his daughter would still be alive. We blame ourselves for not being able to prevent accidents, for failing as protectors.

Our anger may be as intense as our shock and guilt and may be directed at the driver of the car if the child died in an automobile accident, at the policeman who informed us, or at the hospital personnel who had to give us the news of our child's death. Most of all we may feel angry at the sheer injustice of such a death. In addition we will have the added anguish of dealing with courts and lawyers and having our distress prolonged as the legal battles drag on.

As parents we believe that the worse thing that could ever happen to us would be if one of our children were to be killed. We want to die on the spot ourselves. We don't see how we can possibly continue. We may wish it had been ourselves and may be stunned at the senseless way in which a precious life can be snuffed out in just a few minutes. Losing an adult child by accident has its own particular difficulties. The married daughter of a middle aged couple decided to sail across the English Channel with her husband. The parents felt this would be taking a risk, given the poor condition of the boat. Nevertheless, the young couple decided to go ahead with their plans. The boat did capsize and the young woman, who was pregnant at the time, was drowned. This family not only lost a daughter who showed great promise, but also a grandchild. It's as if their future had been canceled. When we lose adult children, we are not only robbed of future generations, but also of watching a young person unfold and develop a new identity. We see a terrible waste of a life.

My great aunt was eighty-five when her only daughter was killed in a head-on automobile collision at the age of sixty. "Why couldn't it have been me?" she wept. "My life is over." Frequently, and this was certainly true in my aunt's case, there is a role reversal as mature adults assume the parenting role for an elderly mother or father. It is not only difficult to deal with such a shock physically and emotionally, but also to comprehend the enormity of such an event. Friends kept telling my great-aunt that she had grandchildren. But though one may love one's grandchildren, they do not replace a daughter. I held my great-aunt while she cried and told me how terrible it was to survive one's own child. One has to respect the fact that an elderly person does not have a long future in which to heal and move on to a new life.

It is extremely difficult to let go of a parental role. Therefore, for some of us, the preparation and the event of a wake gives us the opportunity to prolong that role for a short while. However, for parents who lose an older child, the funeral can be a trying experience. Young people generally have lots of connections and we may be meeting many of our childrens' friends and acquaintances for the first time. While some of us may derive comfort from this experience, others may consider it an invasion of their privacy. For others, the presence of large groups of people at the funeral may serve as an acknowledgement of their loss.

After the funeral our needs will be different. We are faced with all of the physical reminders of our child: an empty room, the clothes, toys or books which make the absence more poignant. Our child's friends may stop in and that may make us experience fresh waves of sadness as the full reality of the death takes hold of us. Some people may eventually want to redecorate the child's room or give away some of his or her personal things, keeping only a few mementos. There is no absolute calendar for this. It's a matter of feeling ready deep within.

In the case of an accident, some people decide to move to a new house or a new town, far from the site of the collision or drowning.

This may actually help us to move to a new place inside ourselves as well as help us to avoid painful reminders. The timing for such a decision will be similar to the timing for decisions about the child's personal effects. During the first few months after the death we may be experiencing periods of great confusion and sadness. We may not be ready to let go of those particular memories.

The death of a child leaves us feeling as if our lives were shattered and our emotions were in chaos. Maintaining a sense of continuity in our daily routine, especially maintaining our outside connections through work or friendship, may serve as stepping stones to our eventual recovery.

However, in the early weeks and months after the death, we should be careful about burdening ourselves with too many tasks. Just getting through the day after such a tragic loss is a great accomplishment and may require considerable energy. Initially, we are grateful for the day's passing. Then we can traverse weeks. Then gradually we can begin to think of other things. But those weeks of seeming inactivity are actually periods of hard work for our emotions. It is helpful just to allow our sadness to well up and our tears to flow during these times.

Everyone fears and imagines the loss of a child and therefore people may be unwilling to see us or to talk to us after the death of our child. We need to be especially responsive to our own needs at this time and not to worry about those who avoid us. We need to be able to talk about the death, to weep, and to find time for ourselves, as well as to turn to friends who will be sensitive and supportive. Different family members may need to have separate supports because we all grieve in different ways and experience different needs.

Couples generally have expectations of mutual support within the family. However, when both parents are affected by a tragedy, the relationship may be subjected to great strains. Men and women may have different coping styles, and this may be the cause of irritation, friction and misunderstanding. A woman may express her grief through tears and through talking. A man may seem as if he is being stoic by maintaining silence and plunging himself in his work. Although he may be in great pain, his wife might conclude that he's not feeling anything. It may be difficult for a man to act in a nurturing or supportive way with his wife, holding her, or putting his arms around her. Or conversely, the same may be true of a woman, or each may expect responses when the other is having a bad day. It's important to communicate with each other as clearly as possible, regarding both our own grief and our feelings for our spouse.

If we are a single parent, we may feel the additional pain of handling all the burdens alone. It may be helpful to reach out to supportive friends and special programs. We need to talk about the sadness we feel for our child and to be accepted in our grief.

7 • *Stillbirths and Miscarriages*

Although the grief over a child lost through miscarriage or a neo-natal death is not recognized by society, it is nevertheless very complex and profound. Because no one else really got to know our child, and because it didn't seem real to others, there is a tendency for others to deny our grief. In years past, some hospitals may have discouraged a mother from seeing or holding a child who died after or before birth.

The death of a newborn is in truth the death of a wish and the death of our dreams. During the months of pregnancy, both parents have invested their energy, not just in painting a room or buying furniture and clothes for the new child, but also in planning for their life with that child. After a death, the focus of that hope is gone and we are left with an emptiness, a feeling of having been cheated. We grieve for the child we didn't know. Just because we never did see the color of their hair or get to know them doesn't mean that we will stop thinking or wondering about them or that we will stop caring for them.

In the case of a miscarriage, we may examine our own behavior or the state of our health during the pregnancy, searching for causes, wondering if we were careful enough. A friend of mine who lost a child through miscarriage worried for months afterwards about her responsibility for the loss. Even though she had taken good care of herself during her pregnancy, she kept looking for possible causes. Because we identify so closely with a child during pregnancy, we feel responsible for the development of that child. After all, during pregnancy, a baby is part of a woman's body. If we lose that child, we will not only face physical and emotional adjustments, we may feel that we have failed.

Sometimes, comments by other people about our pregnancy may reinforce our belief that we ourselves were somehow to blame for the miscarriage. Because of the meaninglessness of such an event, we are particularly vulnerable to veiled suggestions that we were somehow at fault, or got what we deserved. We should be especially protective of ourselves during this difficult period after a loss, and seek out friends who will be supportive.

In the case of a stillbirth, the way the news is communicated by the doctor may influence our reactions: whether it was communicated with regard for our feelings or in a very dry and clinical way without eye contact. When I was in the recovery room after delivering my first child, a doctor came in and in a very brief and terse way told the woman next to me that her child's lungs didn't function properly and that it had died. He expressed no regret or concern for her feelings and left immediately after he delivered his news. The woman was left to cry quietly by herself. It is important for us to be able to hold the child, to name it and then to say goodbye.

A local hospital not only gives bereaved parents the option of holding their dead child but also provides them with a "memory envelope," with the baby's hospital bracelet, a lock of its hair, a set of footprints, and photographs. Keeping these mementos, and also sharing them with others, is an affirmation of our baby's brief passage. Society may deny the importance of such a young life, but we are entitled to our feelings for that child and to our grief.

There is a tendency to consider this kind of loss as one that only mothers suffer. However, we need to remember that even though the father's body is not at issue, his dreams and hopes are, in addition to his concern for his wife. It may seem doubly difficult for him to lose a child and then to have his own pain ignored. Condolences and words of sympathy should be addressed to both parents.

The loss of a child through miscarriage or in stillbirth is a difficult topic to talk about with others. Some people may wish to know the details. However, if they are too painful for us to talk about we may want to simply respond that because it is difficult for us, we would rather not talk about it or limit our answers to the simple facts. Some people may try to minimize our loss by saying "You can always try again." These are not exactly comforting replies. After time had passed, Marilyn learned to respond to these comments by saying that she didn't feel that it was for the best and that it was a painful loss.

Many people have made repeated attempts to have children without success. In the narrative, Marilyn makes very clear that each of the three losses was significant to her and her husband. When each pregnancy ended, they experienced the loss of hope and the denial of a deeply felt wish. They were also filled with anxiety about Marilyn's health and their own future as a family. Marilyn is seeing a counselor and she and her husband are thinking about adoption. She discovered that after such a difficult loss, she had to be very selective about friends, and spend time only with those who responded to her and her husband's pain with tact and sensitivity.

When our child dies, the grief we feel is apt to be with us for a long time. Even though we may eventually move on to new concerns and occupations, and even though the pain moves away from the center of our lives, it will always be part of us. Whenever we enter a new social situation and people ask us about our families, we will experience the pain of having to say that we had four but lost one, or that we lost an only child in stillbirth. We will always be a parent to the child we lost.

8 • *When a Sibling Dies*

Jim:

As I look back at it, there were two very very difficult times for me: the time right after she died and the anniversary of her death. I found myself writing poetry as the anniversary of her death approached. Her death in some way was an expression of a lot of the pain and emotional distress in our family. It was a drug abuse related death. She was a nurse. She was three years younger than me, the middle of three children. She always felt that she was different. When we were kids she used to insist to my parents that she was adopted. There was something in our family that produced that feeling in her. All three of us escaped the house as soon as we could. One of my avenues for escape was college. Ellen never felt that she could go to college, so she went to nursing school. She always felt that she didn't have a lot of ability. The first guy she ever dated she was very attached to, and when he graduated and went to college, he cooled it off and that devastated her. As soon as she got to nursing school she met another guy, and married him after she finished nursing school.

For some reason, she started taking Darvon and then started to take it on the sly and gradually got more and more involved in drug abuse. Initially it was drugs that she would only pilfer from the hospital. Eventually she got caught, and lost her job. But she had figured out the system, and called pharmacies pretending to phone in prescriptions. About three years before she died, it first became apparent to everyone how serious the problem was. She went through several periods of treatment. She developed epilepsy, secondary to drug abuse.

They still don't know what happened. She was working in a nursing home and apparently had a massive seizure, and fell down the stairs. One of the strangest things that happened was this incredible need I had to find out how she died and the anger and frustration at the coroner who took so much time in finding out what had caused her death. But they ended up saying the immediate cause was undetermined, that it was probably related to this seizure which was secondary to chronic drug abuse. It happened at a time when she had appeared to be doing much better. My mother and sister had just seen her the week before, which was significant because there were often extended periods when we wouldn't be in touch with her.

There was a very miserable and tragic period that led up to her death. It was very difficult for me because my relationship with her had grown strained. But there was this intense period when her drug problem surfaced and we became very close. She came out to visit us, supposedly having gone through a residential treatment program and having improved. We wrapped up all the medicines and hid them away. We had a visit and it was reasonably good although she still seemed pretty depressed, and we talked a lot about our parents. My father is currently a recovering alcoholic. My parents have a terrible relationship. For the most part my father drank heavily and my mother is an extremely devout, an almost pathologically devout Catholic. Though if I think hard, I can remember some happy periods in my childhood. I was trying to provide as much support for her as possible in that drug thing. When she left, I found that she had taken all the medicines that I had hidden. I called her on the phone and at first she denied it, and finally she acknowledged it. Then I got involved in this role I always played in the family, this role of "I was going to save her." I tried to set up another admission for her. I flew to her home to try to get her into a program, and when I got there, she refused. Her husband was not helpful. He said that it was just a problem of will power, that if she tried to stop she could. After, she went into another treatment program and during this time I stayed in touch with her.

The last time I talked to her was about a year and three months before she died. She had just gotten divorced from her husband. The last thing I said to her was that this was a time when she should really be careful. She should try to meet a number of new people, and just take time because she was still young and there was no need to rush into anything. She seemed receptive to that. I think that when she took off with a guy, she couldn't face me. Then I couldn't contact her when she was moving around the country. And then I got angry at her for not contacting me. I stayed angry for at least a year. About three or four months before she died I was feeling less anger and more of a sense of missing her. By that time she and this guy had come back and were living in New Jersey. I knew now that I could contact her and I had gotten the address and phone number from my mother. It was one of those things I kept putting off, and I didn't do it before she died.

That was very horrible for me, to have had that period when I was not in touch in with her. I know it is normal to feel guilty and responsible under circumstances like these. I felt, and still have not really worked through, a very pervasive sense of guilt that I was treated more favorably than she was in the family, that I did a lot more crazy things with drugs than she did, and yet I survived. But it pulled her down and destroyed her.

Maureen:

I'm twenty-five now. My sister was nineteen when she died. I was in the ninth grade; I was fifteen. It happened so fast. One summer she became sick and went to the doctor. Then her right side was paralyzed. Her hair started to fall out. I didn't see much of her that summer because I was living down at our Cape house and she was home working. She had just finished her first year in college. She spent a couple of months in the hospital having tests and taking medicine that made her cheeks look like chipmunks' cheeks. Her speech slurred and you could only understand her if you were living with her. She was at the Children's Hospital with young kids and it was hard because she was nineteen years old. When she came home from the hospital, she was in bed all the time.

The worst thing about it was that I didn't know what to ask or who to ask about what was happening. I didn't want to ask my parents because I was afraid of learning the truth and I was afraid of hurting them by making them talk about it. It was really hard.

One day I was driving to the hospital with my father and I asked him what was wrong with her. My father told me that he didn't want to lie to me and pretend she was going to get better. He said she had a brain tumor and that it had probably been dormant all her life. He also told me that it wasn't inherited so there was no way that I would get it.

My sister and I always used to hold hands until I was about twelve years old. When she became ill, we started to hold hands again. At least we could do that. I think that was our closeness. When my parents would go out, we would just lie on the bed and watch television and hold hands. I wish I could have said things.

In the end, she was in a coma for about a month and then my parents said that she was in God's hands. That was the toughest time to go and see her. She was in a nursing home for retired nuns and there were all these old, whacked-out nuns. It wasn't my sister. She wouldn't respond. I'd just go there and hold her hand and hope that she knew that I was there. That was the hardest time to go and see her because I didn't want to remember her being that way.

The day she died I was coming out of an art course. They had been paging me all through class. Finally I answered the page and they told me to go down to the guidance office because my mother was there. I saw my aunt's car outside and and when I got to the office my mother was there. She looked at me and said, "Honey, Joan died. We loved her, everybody loved her. God loved her so much he wanted to take her." That's how she justified it. In my mind I was saying, "That's just bull." I didn't know what to do. I went to get my books. I just wanted to walk out and get away, just leave and cry. I stood alone at my locker and then I went to the classroom and grabbed my books. My teacher asked me where I was going, but I didn't answer. I was crying and I just walked out and got in the car with my aunts and my mother. We went to pick out flowers and a dress for my sister. Then we got home and I got on my bike and left.

I went to a field and cried and smoked cigarettes. I was thinking, "Why her? Why my sister?" She was the sweetest girl and I'm a tyrant. She wasn't very smart, but she tried. She was beautiful, but I always saw her as very insecure. Losing her hair and having her her face all puffed up was so terrible for her. I wondered, "Why her and not me?" It should have been me. I'm stronger than she is and I could deal with the things that she had been going through. She was such a sweet person and she shouldn't have died. I wondered why God did this. I remembered all the times I had been a jerk to her. I felt so guilty the day she died. I kept hoping she knew that I loved her, and that she'd forgive me for all that I pulled on her.

I cried all that night. I thought about my parents and how much they were hurting. I tried not to cry in front of them.

I remember the funeral and the wake. My friends came to the funeral. Some of them came to the wake and they went through the line. I wasn't even there. I was in the bathroom crying. There were so many people there. I cried when my friends came, especially when one of them came up to me and hugged me. I began to wonder what I was doing there. I didn't want to be there. I didn't know what to say. Nobody knows what to say. I met a lot of people that I'd never seen before or that I'd met but never talked to, and I tried to make conversation. It sounded so insincere. I thought they weren't coming for me, but for my sister. I was the one who was getting the pity, but I wasn't the one who died.

At the funeral, my mother cried. My father cried. I think my brother was crying. I was walking down the aisle in church following the casket when I saw one of my mother's best friends and then I started to cry. I realized that I was saying goodbye for the last time.

We went back to the house for coffee and doughnuts. I had to sit there and be phoney and talk about things I didn't care about. I had to pretend and say to everyone that we were glad it was over. We almost had to pretend it didn't happen.

Losing a sibling is particularly difficult because the other people in our family may be considered as the primary mourners. If we lose a brother or sister as a child, all the attention will be focused on our parents and we may feel invisible in our sadness. If we lose a sibling as an adult, the sympathy will be offered to the spouse and children of our sibling. Our own loss is a very wrenching one and yet there may be no acknowledgement of it.

As in all relationships, the quality of ties, whether we identified closely with our brother or sister or whether we felt rivalry and resentment towards each other, will affect our reactions towards a loss. However, we may feel guilty even when there were deep feelings of mutuality with a sibling. We may remember the times we quarreled, or think of things we wish we had done. We may feel that our brother or sister died because of something that we did or said. It's helpful to remember that a sibling's death does not represent a judgment on us.

Perhaps we may feel survivor's guilt and wonder why our brother or sister died instead of ourselves, as Maureen did when she asked "Why her and not me?" This is a question that many of us ask after the death of a sibling. We may identify so closely with our sibling or admire him or her so much that we wonder why we were spared.

The quality of our relationship during the time before death is also going to affect how long we feel guilt and anger. The fact that Jim did not have the opportunity to be with his sister before her death affected him profoundly. However, this was a relationship in which he had made years of significant contribution and this positive side will become clearer as time passes. But even though he had made all these contributions to her well-being, he was unable to save her. Often we feel powerless in the face of death .

In Jim's narrative, we see the relationship he had had with his sister carried over into their adult years, as Jim became almost like a parent to his sister in assuming responsibility for her health. Often when parents are unable to function as such, an older sibling assumes that role. In a sense, Jim is grieving for the loss of a child as well as for the loss of a sister, with the added difficulty of not having either the status or influence of a real parent. In acting as the conscience of the family, he bears a heavy burden.

There are differences between losing a sibling as an adult and as a child. When Jim's sister died, he was already established in his career and had a family. These were available to him as supports, and he also relied upon the wisdom of his accumulated experience. When Maureen's sister died, she was still a teenager facing all the turmoils of adolescence. Her behavior towards her sister, which troubled her so much after her sister died, was the normal acting out of adolescent stress. When we lose a sibling during our teenage years, we may not have the perspective to remember all the nice things we did, and the loving thoughts that we had for our sister or brother. This can be a difficult burden to bear. It's helpful to remind ourselves of the good moments we experienced in our relationship with our sibling.

If our sibling died after an illness we may have been very confused by the illness as Maureen was. She saw her sister's face swollen from the chemotherapy but did not understand the acute nature of her illness and the implications of her symptoms. A friend of mine who lost her sister when they were both teenagers remembers not realizing the seriousness of her sister's condition until she heard her father weeping during a telephone conversation. As her sister was taken to the hospital she recalls her saying "Goodbye house," as the stretcher carried her away. Even when her sister died shortly after, and she was sitting by the body at the wake, she still couldn't comprehend the fact of her sister's death. As young adults we are not apt to understand the nature of our sibling's illness until it becomes critical. Therefore, we may be very confused by the death.

As younger people we may not find solace in the explanations of religion or in so-called systems of justice. We may see religion as part of our parents' world and as having little meaning for us. Perhaps our parents tried to explain the death of our sibling as "God's will." This may be small comfort to us when we resent our brother or sister's absence. We may feel turned off by religion and angry at a God who could have taken away our sibling.

As Maureen did, we may resent the funeral for its "phoniness," for all the people present at a time when perhaps we would rather be alone with our parents. Ritual which can be a source of comfort for our parents may seem like an empty charade to us. We may not have been included in or even consulted about the funeral arrangements and we may be feeling left out. Some of us would rather be with our family at this time or we would rather not participate in the funeral. However, even if we would prefer not to go to the funeral, we would like to have the choice of taking part or staying home. Maureen's disgust with the funeral is not unusual. We may feel uncomfortable with other people's display of feelings at this time and we may not wish to have others see our distress. There are times when we may wish to express our sadness in the privacy of our room.

Our parents may react to the loss of our brother or sister by being over-protective or demanding of us. A colleague of mine who had lost her sister as a teenager had to contend with her mother's anguish every time she went out. At the time she couldn't understand why her mother always wanted her in sight. It was difficult for her to understand that her mother was afraid that something would happen to her. All she could see was that her freedom was suddenly restricted. It's not unusual for parents to change their behavior towards us after the loss of a child.

Because our parents miss our deceased sibling, they may idealize him or her. It usually takes many months or even years after a death before we can see our relationship with the deceased in perspective. Parents will remember above all the good qualities of their child and the joy he or she brought them. They may seem overly concerned with the memory of our brother or sister. A friend of mine remembers asking her parents in frustration some months after the death of her sister, "Do you still love me?" Her parents were astonished by the question, believing that their deep love for her was obvious. In their grief, it was difficult for them to see that their surviving daughter felt left out.

Not only may our parents be absorbed in their grief over our deceased brother or sister, the whole atmosphere in our home may have changed. A friend of mine who lost a brother when she was young remembers her home as a place of gloom she wished to escape from. Eventually she went off to college and a new life and later on was able to have a close relationship with her parents. However, the year after her brother's death remains in her memory as a very unsettling time. As children, what happens in our home after a death affects our sense of security. After all, our home is our universe when we are young and we are likely to be deeply upset by changes in our daily life, our routines around school or friends or the way we spend our free time.

When we lose a brother or sister, our grief may be ignored in our parents' preoccupation with their own sorrow. We may feel terrible loneliness in face of our parents' sadness. Our parents may seem overly preoccupied with their feelings and with guests who may be pouring into the house. This is a time when we may want to have the attention of our parents and we may resent the intrusion of outsiders.

In the face of such difficult circumstances, we might feel that we must avoid any behavior which might cause our parents further pain. It's terribly upsetting to see our parents grieving and we may feel that we must do everything possible to avoid causing them further sorrow. We may try to keep our room as tidy as possible, to be very quiet and not to make any demands on our mother and father. However, it's important to recognize our own grief and to realize that expressing our own sadness will not add to our parents' sadness. It's normal to want to assume responsibility for our parents' pain. However, it might be a great relief to realize that their sadness has nothing to do with our own behavior. Feeling free to be sad or angry over a sibling's death will not hurt our parents and will help us on the path to healing.

Frequently we must face an empty room if we shared a room with a brother or sister. For some of us, it may be a comfort to be near our sibling's things. Some of us might find this a fearsome experience. If we were one of several children, our sibling's bed might be taken by a younger brother or sister and we may resent the intrusion. Besides the reminder of the room, there are all the places we may have gone together, the drive-in, the park, the family excursions which are occasions for sadness.

Many of us who lose siblings when we are teenagers or young adults may find that all the attention is focused on our parents and that we have no one to turn to with our own sorrow. Sometimes our parents' friends or our own relatives may even urge us to take care of our parents. They may tell us to "be strong" for them. It may seem as if our own grief is invisible and somehow inappropriate. It's helpful to remember that while everyone grieves in different ways and that while our own grief is different from that of our parents, it nevertheless deserves our attention. There may be friends at school who will share our feelings with us and who may have experienced loss through a divorce or a death in their own families. Perhaps we feel ashamed of or uncomfortable with the depth of our feelings. But a true friend will want to share our sadness as well as our happier times.

Our friends and perhaps even our family may not want to mention our deceased sibling because of their own pain or because they may be afraid of hurting us. We may interpret this silence as an admonition not to grieve. But losing a sibling is like losing a part of ourselves. It touches the core of our identity. As survivors, we need to express our sorrow and our anger in a way that feels comfortable for us.

9 • When a Parent of Mature Adults Dies

Writing about a father who had just died, an author referred to middle age as the "final orphanage." This may seem like a paradox. People in their thirties, forties and fifties usually have families, careers, lives of their own. We hardly think of them as children. Yet we are still the children of our parents, and we carry this relationship with us as long as our parents are alive, no matter how old we may be. A friend of mine who teaches psychology described this situation very simply. He told me, "I had teenage children when my father died, but even though we never communicated very well, I felt lost without him. But I still had my mother. When things got tough, I could say to myself deep inside, 'Ma.' Then when she died, I really felt abandoned. There was no more calling out to Ma when things got rough." Even though we are adults with responsibilities for others, we still have powerful feelings and relationships with the people who nurtured us and raised us from infancy.

In middle age, we discover in a new way what we had perhaps always taken for granted, our parents' unconditional love. As my friend so aptly described, they are the ones we may think of or turn to for acceptance and support in the truly difficult periods of our lives. Even if they do not fulfill these expectations, we may nevertheless continue to have them. If we have had poor relationships with our parents throughout our lives, we may experience this legacy with renewed impact as we age.

Our parents also give us a sense of belonging and of identity. Even if we may have rebelled against them when we were young adults, in later years we may discover traces of that parent in ourselves. Writing about his father in the *New York Times Magazine* column, "About Men," Clark Blaise mused that "As I enter my perilous years, I find that he is inside me, we are becoming one." Having confronted our own failures and weaknesses, we are now ready to accept the parent we may have found wanting or we may be ready to accept the love we feel for that parent.

By the time we reach our middle years, we have had a long period of time in the parent-child relationship, time for it to grow, perhaps to transform into one of friendship or at least mutual understanding. We will have had plenty of opportunity to think about these ties. Men may often think about the issues of their professional identity, either doing better or as well as their fathers or perhaps wanting their approval.

Both men and women may gauge their accomplishments according to their fathers, either by trying to measure up or perhaps by trying to compensate. However, women also may develop closer ties with their mothers as they age. A psychologist who studied marriages found that frequently a woman's mother may have provided the closeness and support or companionship missing in a partnership. Mothers often provide moral support and advice during periods of change associated with childrearing. A woman who loses a mother in middle age may not only mourn the end of that relationship but also the loss of an intimate friend, someone who knew her better than anyone else. Sometimes men experience a closeness and communication with their mothers that they couldn't achieve with their fathers. They may suffer great loneliness and a sense of being abandoned after a mother's death.

As we grow older, we may tend to think about who we are, over and above the roles we play. Inevitably, rumination about our identities involves our parents. In a society which is non-traditional and highly mobile, our sense of rootedness may come not so much from place or lineage as from our nuclear or our chosen family. When we lose our parents, we lose that sense of belonging. Even though we may have families that we created ourselves, we may still feel a terrible emptiness after the death of a parent.

If we have children when our parents die, we also lose grandparents for those children. Our parents may have shared important events with our families and may have spent holidays with us. During these celebrations we may feel a renewed sense of grief. After our parents die, we become the older generation. As a friend once described, "After my parents died, there was no longer any shelter from my own death." Just as our parents provided a buffer against life's problems and hurts, they were also a buffer against our own deaths.

Many people live with their parents after they have become mature adults. If we have remained single, our parents may have become our chief emotional tie. We may have experienced with them not only the sharing of a household, but also the intimacy and companionship others find in a partnership or in marriage. Perhaps our parents were in poor health and we provided them with physical and financial support. When our parents die, we are left without the resources that our married friends may have. I remember talking with my unmarried cousin after the death of her mother. When I told her that I also lost my mother and understood the pain she felt, she looked at me and said, "But you had a husband and children."

Sometimes a single person may feel burdened with the responsibility of living with an elderly parent and may resent the loss of his or her own separate space. It's not unusual for the member of the family who has remained single to be expected to shoulder this responsibility by his or her married siblings. Or perhaps we may have given ourselves the permission to have separate housing and arranged for our parent to live in the neighborhood or in the same town. After our parent dies, we may feel guilty for not having shared a roof with that parent. Even though we are entitled to our own lives and our own space we may be torn between a sense of responsibility to our parent and the desire for privacy. This is not an easy conflict to resolve. The death of a parent under these circumstances may leave us feeling confused and complicate our grieving. It is helpful to remind ourselves that it's all right to have made our separate lives and that we did care for our parents.

As mature adults, we are not expected to grieve over the loss of a parent or parents. I remember the silence that greeted me both at work and from acquaintances after my mother's death. It was as if the pain I was feeling and the importance of the ties I had with her were completely invisible. Also, because older people are not as highly valued in a society which places so much emphasis on productivity, consumption, and health, their loss is not considered in all its fullness. There is a widespread perception that it is easier to let go of a loved one when they are older. "It's all for the best," or "He had a full life," we hear. But that is small comfort when we are grieving for one of the most important relationships we may have had in our lives.

Our age at the time our parent or parents died, the quality of the relationship we had with them, and the way our parents died will all affect our grieving. We will react differently to a death after a long illness than we would to a sudden death through accident or a heart attack. A troubled relationship with a parent may complicate our experience after his or her death. Even if we may believe that we had come to terms with the difficulties and frustrations in relating to a father or mother, we are struck by the finality of death. We may know intellectually that somehow we couldn't bridge the distances and misunderstandings between us, yet there was always the possibility and the hope for change. After a death we may suffer years of bitterness and regret for what we did not have or were unable to achieve. Even though we may continue to feel responsible for our parent's failings, we needn't blame ourselves or feel guilty about resenting negative qualities in a parent. We can love someone we have difficulty liking. It's not unusual to feel anger at the inadequacies of a parental relationship.

If we are younger adults in our late twenties or thirties when we lose a parent, we may lose a very important emotional support just at the time when we are establishing our own identities, either getting married or starting families of our own. A former student of mine who had lost both parents went through some major events in her life with great loneliness and yearning. Although friends and siblings came to her college graduation and to her wedding, they could not replace her parents. Years later, when she had her first child, she suffered a depression. This is a period when a mother's guidance and support is very important in helping us to face new responsibilities. The birth of Andrea's child filled her with a resurgence of grief and a renewed sense of the dimension of her loss. A young mother whose own mother died of cancer just before she had her first child told me, "There's not a day that goes by that I don't think of my mother and how she would have loved seeing her grandson."

As adult children, we want to share our accomplishments and our important passages with our parents and may suffer deeply from loneliness during these times if we have lost them. We feel the same sense of abandonment if we have lost a father when we were young men establishing ourselves in a career or a family. A father often provides us with advice and guidance when we are establishing our professional identities. Even in our twenties and thirties, we need parental approval to assess our journey in life.

If we are in our forties and fifties or older when our parents die, we may have had a different relationship with them. We may be facing the dual responsibility of adolescent children and parents whose health is declining. While it's possible to resolve these responsibilities without conflict, often the challenge taxes our patience and stamina. Often we face the agonizing decision of having to place a parent in a nursing home and may find ourselves running between visits to the home, errands for the children and our jobs. In addition we may be burdened with the financial costs for our parents' support.

If we are caring for elderly parents, we may find ourselves in the uncomfortable position of role reversal, parenting our own parents. We may feel anger towards them for not being able to fill their parental role and conversely they may resent their helplessness. Much as we may love our parents, these conditions may cause mutual resentment and misunderstanding. Quite naturally, we may feel emotionally and physically drained by the responsibility.

Caring for an ill parent often means juggling this with our jobs and attention for our children. In some instances, we may be making frequent trips to another city to visit our ill parent. A friend of mine whose mother suffered a stroke found herself dealing with her family, her job, and her own painful arthritis as well as repeated flights to New York City from Boston. These are trying circumstances, and after a death we may feel great anger over the burden we carried as well as for the suffering of our parents.

An illness such as Alzheimer's disease or a stroke may transform our parent to such an extent that we may feel we are caring for a stranger. Losing the parent we knew through such circumstances is almost a separate grief. We feel as if we had lost our parent before they died. We may have very complex reactions to such a difficult situation, wishing our loved one freed from a life which hardly seems like a life, and then feeling guilty about this wish. Or we may even wish for the relief of being able to grieve for the death of a parent rather than living in a twilight area where our parent may be in a coma, or totally inaccessible. We are spending our time, energy and emotion in caring for our parent, but he or she is not the person we knew.

When a parent dies after a long and difficult illness, we may experience guilt, relief and regret as well as great pain and sorrow. We may go over and over this period, wondering if we made the right decisions about care, whether we did the best we could. Even the most conscientious son or daughter may find reasons for guilt. This is a time to be easy on ourselves and remember all that we did do in the face of many competing claims for our emotional resources.

Our reactions to the death of a parent will be different depending on whether our parent died suddenly or after a long illness. If our parent had been ill, we may have had time to prepare ourselves for his or her death. We may have been able to grieve in anticipation of the loss, to experience denial, disbelief, anger and sadness though in a muted way. If our parent died accidentally, we may suffer from a more intense and prolonged shock immediately after the death. We will also be coping with the meaninglessness of an accidental death.

My aunt was a very active woman. She lived on a farm and was always on her feet, milking the cows, making jam, tending the vegetable garden. It seemed as if she was never still. While she was driving into town, exactly one mile from home, she was killed in a head-on collision. Her family reacted with extreme shock and disbelief. When someone we love dies suddenly, our sense of shock is usually heightened and lasts much longer than the shock we experience after a death from a long illness. How can we take in the reality of being separated forever from someone we had just spoken to hours or minutes ago? It is too much to assimilate in such a short period of time. This is especially true in relations characterized by close dependency and deep love.

Sometimes our shock is expressed by a feeling of numbness. My cousins methodically prepared for the funeral, setting up tables on the front lawn, trimming the flowers, arranging for the reception. Then, shortly after the funeral, one of my cousins came down with pleurisy. After such a shock, we may be overcome with sadness and pain and may develop acute physical reactions as a result. When a death is sudden we are not only brutally cut off from a loved one, but we are also faced with a whole new set of circumstances at one blow. Not only do we have to deal with lawyers and wills but with a whole new set of responsibilities. The period of shock is actually a protection for us until we are psychologically ready to accept the fact of death.

When I was in my thirties, my mother died of a heart attack while she was reading in bed. Because she was alone in her apartment when she died, a neighbor called the police. I flew in from Boston and found a police officer in the apartment and my mother's body covered with a sheet. The image of her body remained with me for weeks and the eerie unreality of going to a police station where the air was thick with mace. The circumstances surrounding her death added to my shock and bewilderment. The night before, we had spoken on the telephone planning for a family celebration. In her bedroom there was a pile of unwrapped gifts. I felt as if I were left hanging in mid-air.

I dealt with the lawyers, with calling relatives and arranging for the funeral as if I were in a dream. It took me weeks to allow myself to feel the full intensity of my pain, and months for the anger to surface.

My mother and I had a close and loving relationship. The period of horror and the images of her death faded and I was able to retain the joy of our time together. However, if our relationship with our parents was conflict-ridden, a sudden death may heighten the guilt and resentment we feel and we may struggle with our grief for a longer period of time. My father also died suddenly while traveling in Europe. We had had a distant and difficult relationship and had not spoken to each other for years. My reaction of shock was a curious one. I interpreted my numbness as a sign of not caring. But, even though I knew intellectually that there was no possibility of reconciliation, I was haunted for years by our unfinished relationship. A sudden death can be like a door slammed shut in the midst of a quarrel. There are no more opportunities for resolution.

The grief we feel after a sudden death may be more complicated and problematic than our grief after a long illness. Immediately after such a death, we may feel as if we had gone insane, may hallucinate the smell of our dead parent's pipe or feel a presence around us. This is a perfectly normal reaction. We have been thrust headlong into a new reality, as if we were hurled into the deep end of the pool for our first swimming lesson.

10 • When a Lover Dies

Couples who are lovers, whether heterosexual or homosexual, experience the same powerful emotional bonds as those who are living together or those who are married. However, while living together without marriage is becoming a more accepted practice, homosexual relationships and extramarital affairs are not sanctioned by society. When we live outside prevailing social norms we suffer the difficulties of discrimination, hostility and rejection. Often the relationship between lovers in extramarital affairs or with homosexuals is known only to a few acquaintances. When our lover dies, we may find ourselves without the usual support of family, friends and co-workers.

A friend of mine who had had a married lover for ten years handled this relationship with great discretion and very few people outside of her family were aware of this connection. However, he was very close to her children and acted like a father to her younger daughter, taking her to college interviews, keeping in close touch with her during her years at school, and attending her wedding when she married. Although her lover participated in events with her family, only a few of his friends and acquaintances knew about the relationship. Then he was diagnosed with terminal cancer and immediately hospitalized. All of a sudden my friend was completely cut off from her lover. Because his family was constantly at his side, she was unable to visit him. By disguising her relationship to him she was able to call the hospital and find out how he was. After an agonizing few months in which she managed to get bits of information about him, he died.

My friend received the news of his death while she was in another city on a business trip. Because she was excluded from his company during the period of his illness and because of the way she received the news, she reacted as if she had just received news about an accidental death. Under the circumstances she was not able to attend the funeral services or to go to the cemetery. Even though she felt widowed, and even though she lost not only a friend and lover, but someone who was like a spouse to her, she was unable to experience the solace of a funeral ritual. Her exclusion from the support these events provide added to her sense of loneliness and grief.

An elderly friend of mine experienced the same situation when her lover died. Since she was denied all the socially sanctioned outlets for her feelings, she designed her own memorial service for him. She invited a few close friends to a service in which she gave the eulogy. After this event, her friends felt as if they too had been given permission to comfort her and to talk about her lover with her. No matter what our relationship was, the loss of a loved one is a devastating blow and we are entitled not only to our own grief, but to share this grief with others and to receive support.

Although gays and lesbians have received more understanding in the past few years as a result of our political and educational efforts, we may still experience or may expect discrimination. Because social hostility may be so painful some of us may conceal our relationships from family, friends or co-workers. When a lover dies, we may have no one to turn to.

If our partner died of AIDS, we may experience a deep fear of social ostracism as well as fears for our own health. This is a difficult moment to face alone. We are as entitled to our own sadness and anger as we are to the love which gives meaning to life.

The process of grieving can be a very lonely one, but this is especially true in these kinds of relationships. Our friends may feel that we shouldn't be experiencing such a depth of sorrow, or people may be surprised at our response. These reactions may confuse us or make us wish to hide our feelings. It is important for everyone to realize that the loss of a lover can be as painful as the loss of a spouse. This is not a time for others to judge our relationships, our identity, or our behavior.

11 • When a Friend Dies

A friend of mine who recently lost a close friend after a long illness told me ruefully, "Water is thicker than blood." Her comment revealed the importance of friendship in a society where nuclear families or fragmented families rather than extended families are the rule. In a society with an increasing number of singles, friends may frequently function as family. But even when a family has all of its members living together, we may share our more private selves with a friend.

The importance of friendship may vary with our age and with the length and intensity of the relationship. While friendships are significant to us at all ages, this is particularly true when we are at critical periods of our lives. When we are adolescents and young adults, friends are supports as we develop our own identities and begin the long process of separation from our parents. When we are bringing up young children or are newly married, friends may share the stresses and difficulties of parenting. As we age, and our children become independent, and our careers and marriages no longer seem so absorbing, friends answer our needs for emotional bonds and companionship. The elderly may have had friends throughout their lives who know their history and who have shared important life events with them. In addition, for the elderly, friends are the carriers of the values and culture of an entire generation. Losing a friend in old age is like losing a large part of the world.

In a highly mobile society in which the circumstances of our lives are apt to change frequently, a friend is one who knows our history and who may have shared our most private thoughts and feelings. A friend not only has known us over a period of time, but will also have shared with us the high or low points of our lives. Because of that, we may continue to feel deeply about such a person even if we no longer see each other frequently or even if we live in distant cities. If that person dies, it's as if we were losing a part of ourselves. The death of someone with whom we may have identified closely may leave us with a feeling of emptiness.

When a close friend dies, especially if that friend is the same age and sex as ourselves, we are brought face to face with our own mortality. Especially if we are adolescents or young adults, we may be made suddenly aware of our own fragility and vulnerability. We may tell ourselves it could have been us who was struck by a car or who died of cancer. Even if someone who was not a close friend, but an acquaintance dies, we may feel intense grief. As young people we do not expect anyone in our age group to die. A woman in her early twenties explained to me, "You mourn for anyone you know, who shared your space, whether you liked them or not."

A student of mine who lost one of her friends kept writing poems for her as she struggled with the finality of that death. A young person may agonize for years over the horror and injustice of a death at an early age. As adolescents or young adults, we are less likely to find people in our age group who have experienced the death of friends. We may think we are unusual or abnormal because of the pain and confusion we feel and therefore we may keep the pain of that death inside us.

When a friend dies, we do not experience the same wrenching changes in status and role as when a member of our own family dies. However, while we will not necessarily have to face major changes in our lifestyle, we still experience all the phases of grief, the shock, the waves of pain and sadness. Watching our friend's family grapple with their own sorrow, we may feel that our sadness is of little account. Yet we are entitled to our own feelings of loss and need to give ourselves permission to mourn. Love is mysterious and complex. It exists in its own right and transcends the roles which hold us together in the web of our lives. Anyone we have truly loved is irreplaceable, and the loss of a cherished person will always cause us to mourn.

When I was in my late twenties, my closest friend became ill with cancer. We both had two very young children and the six of us used to spend many hours together every week. Once the tumor was discovered, my friend's condition deteriorated rapidly. In less than a year she died, leaving a mother, siblings, her husband and children. During her illness, I had taken care of her children. Being so close to her family during that period, I felt as if I experienced their own feelings of pain.

However, in the difficult period of disruption after her death, when the family struggled with the problem of childcare as I returned to my teaching, I was surprised by the depth of my grief and the anger I felt at my friend's suffering. Although my own life didn't change outwardly, I felt shaken at the roots. I was outraged that such a young and vibrant person should die when she had just begun her life as a wife and mother. She seemed to have everything, a very happy marriage, two beautiful children, and an intense enjoyment of life. "Young people shouldn't die," I thought to myself.

I carried this sadness and pain for many months but felt unable to discuss it with anyone, as if I had no right to mourn for someone who wasn't family and who had left a grief-stricken family behind her. I have since learned that it helps to discuss and to express our pain over the loss of a friend. It is important in our own lives and merits sharing.

Losing a friend when we are middle-aged has its own complexities. We lose friends with greater frequency as we become older, and therefore death may not be such a shock to us. However, at this period of our lives, as we see more and more of our friends die of cancer or heart disease, we perceive our own mortality not so much as a revelation, but as a daily reminder. We may be grieving the evanescence, the short span of our lives. "A life passes so quickly," my uncle said after the death of his friend.

As elderly persons, the loss of a friend may add to our increasing sense of solitude, a grief in a long string of griefs, as we let go of our jobs, change our places of residence and our lifestyles, and experience changes in our health. Losing a friend means losing yet another thread which connects us to the world. When our parents have gone, a friend may be the last person who shared our memories and histories.

Losing a friend sometimes causes us to look at our own lives and perhaps to rearrange them in some way. When my father's close friend and colleague died of a heart attack leaving a large family, my father changed his highly charged lifestyle and began to take better care of himself. Because I found no "recognized" place for my grief and my newly awakened sense of mortality after the death of my friend, I began to write. We can be carried to new places inside ourselves by the shock of death.

When we lose a member of our family, whether spouse, sibling, child or parent, we are hurled out of our roles and status. For a period after the death, we feel as if we were without moorings, so closely do we identify with these roles. The changes we experience after the death of a friend may not be as disruptive, but they are significant and painful. Our perceptions of life may change, our views on the meaning of life, our sense of our own mortality. Ultimately we may change the way we spend our time.

"I care too much about my friends," someone commented bitterly when telling me about the death of a friend. To love someone is indeed to take a great risk of loss. However, not many people would want to trade the poverty of a life without friends for protection against the pain of loss.

12 • Love and Grief

Love is one of the most powerful emotions that we experience throughout our lives. However, if we dwelled on it constantly, we would have difficulty functioning. We express our love for others sub-consciously in the hundreds of small chores and routines of the day; driving our children to school, filling out insurance forms, preparing supper, or repairing a bicycle. But when we lose someone close, we suddenly feel at one blow the depth and magnitude of our love for that person. A poet once wrote that whoever was struck by the shock of love would return to his work with an altered face. Along with the shock of loss, we may feel the depth of our love for the person we have lost. We need time to be with that discovery as much as we need time to let our anger and sadness surface.

If we had a troubled and difficult relationship with someone close to us, a parent, a lover, or a sibling, we may be surprised by our grief. We do not expect to feel so deeply about someone who disap-pointed us so often or with whom we were in conflict. However, the death of such a person strikes us by its finality. There are no longer any opportunities to improve the relationship. This may leave us with a burden of bitterness and regret. Also we may discover how much we loved someone whom it was difficult to like, or who taxed our patience time and time again. If we feel responsible for the difficulties in a re-lationship, this is the time to forgive ourselves.

If the depth of our love catches us by surprise, so may the extent of it. Love is one of the freest emotions. It transcends the many roles and categories that hold us together as families, friends, church members. Literature is full of stories of love that moves across social barriers. Therefore, we may grieve profoundly for a grandmother, for a friend's child, a neighbor. If we had loose social connections with the person we are grieving for, we may feel as if our sadness is unwarranted. We may either try to minimize it or to hold it inside. We seem to have an endless capacity for loving different people. It is a truism that the more one loves, the more one is able to love.

Perhaps we also need to realize that each person we love has a unique place in our feelings. When my mother died, I felt the loss keenly, even though I had a wonderful family of my own. She was my best friend, and seemed more than a parent to me since our relationship was one of equality. We had such a quiet understanding and such a sharing of each others' burdens that I felt as if I had been widowed when she died. Since there seemed to be no place to discuss the love between parents and adult children, I found myself reading articles about widows. We are the only ones who can define the importance of a relationship to ourselves.

We take our cues from society and the larger culture. However, when someone we love dies, our emotions and feelings may be at odds with society's expectations. We may feel bewildered and confused by the welter of emotions assailing us. However painful our emotions may seem, eventually, they will help bring us to a new place in our lives and within ourselves. The core of ourselves which feels the shock and hurt of loving fully is one of the most valuable parts of ourselves, the very essence of what it means to be a human being.

LOSING A LOVED ONE THROUGH SUICIDE OR HOMICIDE

Let us not speak of the unspeakable;
Let us not dwell on the inferno that enveloped him
and turned the golden days into leaden nights.
Let us remember the wonder of him,
the quiet radiance that warmed our lives,
the questing nature ever seeking the perfect way
and measuring the clues with churning hope.
Let us speak of the lover of foods and children,
and music and books
and all that is sensitive and kind.
Let us say that in a world which festers year by year
he was the tender plant that never could survive,
but in the flourishing the leaves gave out
a touch of beauty that will never die.

Eugene T. Maleska, "The Tender Plant"

13 • When Someone We Love Commits Suicide

Merryl:

In 1982, my husband committed suicide. He was thirty-three at the time and I had just turned thirty-four. Carl had been in a doctoral program at the University of Chicago for eight years. At the time of his death we had been married for six years although we had lived together for a few years before that. We had been trying to have a child for the past six months. In a way I really felt that I lost two people. There was the potential child that was very much a part of my life at that time. That's been one of the harder griefs to deal with. It's still an ongoing grief.

Carl had been in a doctoral program for child development. It's very difficult to find a job in that field in academic teaching. For three years he sent out letters, but many weren't even answered. He met with lots of rejection. Meanwhile his dissertation was taking longer and longer and his vita was always being updated. In spring of 1982, a part-time job that he had at Childrens' Hospital was ending and he just didn't see what was ahead. He discovered what he thought was a serious flaw in his dissertation. He went into an agony of despair, believing he was worthless. He perceived the world saying no to him as his own failure.

The last week of his life he did speak of suicide. He had never spoken of it before except once, a year before ,when he woke up one morning and said, "If I ever have to go through another job search like this, I'll kill myself." At that time I didn't pay much attention. There was no context for it. He never mentioned it again. A year and a half later, I thought of his having said that. But even his supervisor at Childrens' Hospital who was herself a psychologist said that she saw Carl as someone who was very much in control of his own life. I was the only one who knew he had these conflicts inside. His parents didn't have any idea. He had been tops in his class at the university. He was very good-looking. He was president of the honor society. On the outside he looked like Robert Redford. On the inside he was like Woody Allen.

The last week of his life he was immersed in a kind of despair and I could not reach him. I stayed home to be with him. I called a psychiatrist. He did see a psychiatrist, but the doctor said that Carl would not have the courage to commit suicide.

Carl left the house on Friday of that week. He was to meet me at my office at six o'clock. He never showed up at my office. I got home in a frenzy because I knew that there was something very wrong. In eight years of being together he had never left the house like that without telling me where he would be. I noticed his suitcase was gone. The nightmare weekend began.

I called my parents and his parents. We had a vigil, his parents and I. We just waited by the phone. We had no idea where he was. He had taken the car. I reported him as a missing person.

I knew in my heart of hearts that there was a danger of suicide and we talked about it that weekend although I tried to imagine that he might be in Atlanta looking for a job. He had always talked of the South. A policeman came to the door on Sunday night. He gave me a phone number to call. I think he knew that something had happened but he wouldn't tell me and just walked away. I ran to the phone and called that number. It was a New York city number. The man at the other end of the phone said "Medical." I asked, "Is this a hospital?" desperately hoping that this was a medical ward. He said, "This is the morgue, lady."

I threw the phone down and ran and jumped off the porch. I started screaming. I didn't care if I broke all my bones. The police came because my neighbors had called them. They really didn't know what was happening. The police came and brought me in the house and said I needed some kind of sedation. I remember talking about killing myself and they said, "If you talk like that we'll have to put you in a hospital," so I just said nothing and they went away. That really was the beginning of the worst. The reason I jumped off the porch at that moment was that I had total and intense knowledge that I would never see Carl again. I had no illusions. It hit me in one solid moment that I would never see this man again whom I totally loved and with whom I wanted to have a child.

He hanged himself. He was in a hotel with a closed door. A chambermaid found him. It wasn't this cry for help that people talk about. It was this final act when Carl decided to die. There was no way to help him.

It was the christening weekend for my sister-in-law's baby. They named him for Carl. The very moment he was found dead was the christening of this little baby which was assuming his name.

The suicide person is really a victim of his own crime. Sometimes I felt as if Carl had committed murder, and in a sense he did. He took the life of the person I loved the most in the world. In a way I did get angry at him for murdering the person I loved. You start to feel angry and then you short-circuit it with the feeling that somehow you could have saved the person. You were responsible.

Although I don't think so now, at the time I found every single way of feeling responsible for what happened. I had three categories of guilt. One was our marriage, that I wasn't a good wife. Or that because we had returned here to Boston where I had found a good job that may have limited opportunities for him, and therefore I was the cause. The third part of the guilt was the last week of his life. I really was the only one involved in his life at that point in terms of knowing his suicidal feelings. I would circle around with those guilts like a mad person for a long time.

I kept short-circuiting my anger. It's slowly that the anger will come in. You make a lot of excuses for the person because you keep feeling how they suffered. It took me a long time to realize that you can have understanding of the person that they did something terrible and you can be furious at them for what they did to themselves and to your life, but that doesn't change the fact that you loved them. Sometimes you feel that you'll stop loving them if you are angry, but that's not true. Anger is a tricky emotion with suicide.

The "if only" syndrome with suicide is one that can almost drive you crazy. You have these scenarios in your head: if I had gotten home earlier, if I had listened harder. You can find a million of them waiting in every single fact. I've spoken to many people who have had suicide deaths in their family and it's a universal reaction. It's natural and necessary in the beginning. You need to rerun that movie in your head. I even had myself in the hotel room in New York. You need to exorcize that guilt to work it through. No one can speed it up for you. But if you go on like that for years, something has gone awry. It could take over your whole life.

I'm going on with my life and I'm living with another man. But there is still this issue. When do I bring Carl up? He's still part of my life. I still think about him three times a day even though it's been almost three years. It's been slowly getting easier. Telling people that I had this whole past other life isn't such a problem anymore. I feel I can bring it up when I want to.

In the first year, I used to go around hunched over. I had lost weight. I was like a totally different person physically. I hardly spoke to people, and usually I am a very outgoing person. I took a month off from work and then I went back on a part-time basis for a while. I didn't look or act like myself for eight months. I was crying all the time.

I went to Safe Place for survivors of suicides for two years, every other week, and that really helped. I had a lot of support in my mother and one very good friend and a therapist. You have to make a network for yourself. If you're isolated, it's worse.

After I got through the first year, I thought, I survived a year, but he's still not here so, so what? The anniversary of his death was okay. I made a memorial for myself. I went to a beach and I just watched the waves, and I really felt peaceful. But the next month was horrible because there was that backlash feeling of: so what, who cares? He's not here. That's the absolute fact of death.

For me it was talking that helped, a great deal of talking. I really feel that when you do communicate the pain, it does ease it. It's a long, slow process. I would talk to anybody about it. My mother was wonderful. She was there night and day whenever I needed her. Right after Carl's death, I lived with my parents for three months, being taken care of. I had no children. In an odd way that was a blessing because I could be totally selfish with my grief. This woman I worked with offered me her home. I needed a transition between my parent's house and getting back into a normal life in our apartment. She offered me a room in her house. She has a family. It was a wonderful place for me to go. She was my dearest, closest friend, suddenly. Then there was a therapist I saw three times a week. Those three things, in addition to the strengths I found inside myself, are what helped.

I was lucky in the sense that I could scream. My parents have this place off on the water and I could just go there and scream. If you live in the city, you can't do that. There's no other reaction.

I've imagined the scene of Carl hanging himself. I've read about asphyxia. In the beginning I read everything I could get my hands on. I remember my mother saying, "At least it's a merciful death." Well, I read about suicidal hanging. The person is suffering at least seven minutes before they die. I knew all the details. I was spared that agony of finding my husband. Many people are not spared that, and have terrible stories to tell and nightmares recurring for many months. I'm happy that Carl was not in the home. Any kind of violent death like that, you suffer with the person. With empathy you want to take it away but you can't.

What I didn't find and what I wanted to find was a young widow two years down the line looking normal in her life. When I went to the Safe Place, all I really found were people in agony and terrible suffering. Even if it had been two years, they weren't the ones that had put it together. I didn't have any role model, and that is one of the reasons that I would like to go back. It is very important to see someone who has been through it and who has managed to move on. The nature of a self-help group is that when people start to feel better they don't come anymore. Slowly, in this miraculous way, I became one of the ones who was making it. People would come in who were worse, and I would measure myself and say, "I'm better off."

When someone dies through suicide, it doesn't come out of nowhere. I really feel that this came out of Carl. It came out of the person he was, for whatever reason. It did come from him, and therefore it might have happened again. He had in him that terrible sense that he could get to those black depressions that are the feeling of worthlessness. That had happened to him when he was eighteen, as it turns out, and it could have happened to him when he was thirty-nine or fifty. Perhaps he might not have gotten tenure later on, when everyone around him was getting it. I have envisioned that it could have *happened later on in his life. From my reading and from my therapist I feel that I have learned a lot about what makes people people, the comparisons between me and my husband, him and other people. There isn't this sense that a random act took him away. In an odd way that's been a kind of a good feeling for me. For the spouse of a suicide, a way of understanding is to see the person as a whole person, and that they came to the relationship with certain problems.*

Because of the therapy, because of really facing the worst of it, I kind of moved on from it the first year. I did face it constantly for almost a year, and that's what freed me up to feel as much love as I do for the man I'm now involved with. I don't feel that that's in any way a lessening of my affection for Carl. One of the first things I told this man on our first date — about fourteen months after Carl died — was "My husband committed suicide and you really need to know that." I thought if he can't handle this, this is not going to be a relationship. He was able to talk to me about pain. We don't talk about Carl a lot but I know that he understands.

Writing about his experiences during World War II, the Italian author, Primo Levi, claimed that some events are unspeakable and some wounds are so deep that there are no words that could possibly console. Sometimes language is inadequate to either express or acknowledge our pain. As the narratives make clear, people who have lost a loved one through suicide or homicide tell of screaming when they heard the news. Merryl jumped off the porch and screamed until the neighbors called the police after she heard of her husband's suicide. Weeks later, at her parents' home by the ocean, she sat on the beach and yelled out her anguish. When someone we love commits suicide, the shock, pain, and all the emotions associated with loss are heightened. They are not only more intense but may occur simultaneously. The struggle to find meaning, which may be postponed in other types of death, assails us immediately after a suicide. We can anticipate the death of a terminally ill person. We may be periodically aware of the possibilities of death by accident, but how can we ever imagine a loved one or a friend taking their own lives? How can we possibly include it within our frame of reference? The meaninglessness of such a death prolongs the period of shock we experience afterwards. The utter mystery of human motivation and of suicide baffles and overwhelms.

Not only does suicide defy our sense of the meaning of life, it also calls into question our most profound social beliefs. Society considers suicide offensive. We may regard it as a blot on our family name and as a source of personal failure. Many families try to cover it up and are deeply ashamed of it. Two close friends of mine attempted suicide without success, one a single professional woman, the other a mother of three, yet a year passed before they could tell me even though we were trusted friends. The brother of one of my daughter's closest friends committed suicide years ago, yet neither my daughter's friend nor his parents ever speak of it. It's as if they had sealed a door forever, as if by this means they could push away the torment and shame. Suicide elicits both a deep sense of guilt on the part of survivors and a sense of shame before what is perceived as a social stigma.

Yet suicide touches so many of us. Although it is rarely discussed in any social setting, it would be difficult to find a person today who did not know someone afflicted with such a tragedy. Like any other kind of death, suicide knows no differences in age or economic or social circumstances. Perhaps because suicides among the young are so widespread and such a source of social concern, newspapers frequently carry stories of such events. Yet suicide afflicts many different types of people, not only the young or the chronically depressed.

Among those who commit suicide are people with a history of mental or emotional illness. Perhaps they may have attempted to kill themselves without success before or perhaps they had had repeated hospitalizations. If we have had a troubled person in our family or as a beloved friend, we may have struggled through the illness with him or her for years, but always we had hope for an eventual recovery. Often, just before the suicide, our loved one may have seemed better. But even when the person we love has suffered from mental illness for a long period of time, we never expect a death from suicide. Such a possibility goes against our very sense of what it is to be a human being.

Perhaps the person who died by suicide had suffered from depression for only a few months or weeks and had had no previous history of depression. As friends or family of such a person we may have suffered through the depression too and sought psychiatric help for that person. Sometimes, the suicide may occur just when that person seems to be finally emerging from his or her depression. It may have been that the decision to end life was the source of relief which accounted for the turnaround. Yet perhaps the person who committed suicide had expressed some kind of hope, talked of a new job, or changes in life. One man who had been suffering a depression made plans to do something with his son during the week, yet in the preceding weekend he committed suicide. In all these cases, as survivors we are left with a mystery. We look desperately for clues, but clues are most evident by hindsight and are frequently ambivalent.

Many people take their own lives who have had no previous episodes of depression. It may seem to us as if this terrible tragedy had simply come out of the blue. The perfectionist who imposes very high standards on himself, who expects himself to perform with equal brilliance in a number of areas, may be masking deep feelings of worthlessness. Some persons who commit suicide are solitary, not given to talking with others, or would prefer not to impose on other people. For most people who take their own lives, suicide is a solution to a deep and searing inner pain. They may leave notes behind saying, "It hurts too much," or "You'll be better off without me," or "Life is too hard." A person suffering such anguish is unable to see any options to cope with his or her pain. Suicide seems the only way out. As survivors, we can see other ways to cope, but no matter how much love or help we may have provided to our loved one, we could not prevent the suicide, and that is difficult to accept.

We may try to enter into those last moments our loved one experienced in order to understand his or her point of view, but how can we possibly imagine a pain so profound that suicide seems the only way to end it? A woman whose husband committed suicide had a sudden revelation of his own inner logic when she was lying in his study one morning among his books and papers:

A primitive awareness took me over. The pain he had spoken of weighed itself against the failure and worthlessness of his life as he saw it at that time. To trade away such pain—and the only thing required, to give up a worthless life. When I lived through it as I did that morning in the absolute terms that had gripped him, it appeared to me for a moment as it had to him: there was only one choice.

How and where we discover the suicide may affect our grieving. The discovery of a suicide in our own home shakes us at the core. We may relive that discovery through nightmares for months afterwards, or we may have great difficulty going into the room where our loved one killed himself, or even in following the same path we took when we found him, whether opening a certain door, or going up the stairs. Our house may seem tainted or changed.

Miriam's husband had been depressed for three months. It was the first time during their married life that he had been through a period like this. He was a person who was always concerned about being healthy and physically fit. He seemed very contented with his life and his living arrangement with his brother and sister-in-law and their children. There were four parents and four children, living in harmony and enjoying their closeness not only in everyday life but also during vacations and weekends. When Miriam's husband became depressed, all three adults rallied round him. They showed their support in a number of ways, by talking with him, offering him the option of taking a trip or stopping work for a while. Finally Miriam arranged for a visit to a psychiatrist. He did go and he made an appointment for another visit. Before the second appointment, he hanged himself.

That fateful morning, Miriam had stayed in bed a little late because she wasn't feeling well. Her husband got up around seven and when he came downstairs to the kitchen he met his mother-in-law who was staying with them at the time. They greeted each other and then his mother-in-law went out for her usual morning walk. When she returned, Miriam's husband had hanged himself in the kitchen. Her screams sent Miriam racing down the stairs.

When the suicide occurred, Miriam's two children were away for a weekend with the rest of the extended family. She telephoned them immediately and then had to face the terrible burden of telling the children. She did this in stages. First she told the boys that their father had died and as they asked questions about how and why, she gradually told them. As a family, they had always had a very open style of communication and were used to leveling with each other. Although the door where her husband hanged himself was eventually taken down, the family continued to use the room and the children were soon coloring and playing there again.

The family arranged the funeral rites so that everyone could participate. The father's body was cremated and his ashes were scattered over the sea. The children included messages and letters of farewell with the ashes.

Some families have much greater difficulty coping with the shock and horror of discovering a suicide in the home. One family, whose fourteen-year-old son committed suicide, arranged for a cremation and private funeral within twenty-four hours of the death. They were trying to push the horror of it away as soon as possible. Eventually, they realized how precipitous their planning was and with great difficulty rearranged the ceremony to allow the participation of close friends. Sometimes the shock of such a death makes us want to deny it, and it is easy temporarily to lose sight of the many years of joy we experienced with the deceased. We want to get the body away fast, and above all we do not want anyone to know what happened.

For some of us the discovery of a suicide comes at the end of a painful search for a missing person. Spouses and parents may have a premonition of the possibility of suicide when a child misses the usual schedule, or as in Merryl's case when her husband failed to show up at her office as planned. Then follows what Merryl referred to as her nightmare time, when the family reported him as a missing person and began the long vigil by the phone. Even though the way the news was conveyed to Merryl was heartless and impersonal, she was grateful that she didn't find her husband herself, in their own home. But those of us who receive news of a suicide by telephone may experience a phobia of phone calls for months and years afterwards.

How our loved one killed himself or herself, whether by hanging or slashing the wrists, for example, is also a continuing source of anguish. We relive both the mental and physical pain he experienced in the months before the death and also the seemingly endless minutes of dying. In our images and in the replay of events, the mental and physical anguish our loved one suffered reinforce each other. Knowing how painful such a death can be, we can only imagine the depth of emotional pain which could have chosen such an ending as a relief.

Because taking one's own life is so difficult to understand, we go over and over the last moments or hours we spent with our loved one. We examine our last conversations and the final events in order to find some sort of explanation. We spend many waking hours going over the details of the time before the death as if we could find a reason for what happened, some cause to blame. In this type of death we are apt to be haunted by these details because our beliefs have been undermined. While we may dwell upon the last months or weeks of suffering that a loved one may have endured during an illness, we are nevertheless able to return within a few months to the better times and the joys we may have experienced together. We can let go of that time of suffering.

We need a much longer period of time to get through the terrible significance of suicide. More than for any other type of death, we may be obsessed with trying to pinpoint the specific circumstances which might have led our loved one to such a tragic ending. We may focus on difficulties and pressures in our loved one's working conditions, or perhaps his or her struggle with alcohol. In some cases, we may request an autopsy, or we may spend time talking to hospital personnel in our effort to comprehend that question which cannot be answered. However, it is only many months or years later that we can separate the immediate circumstances of our loved one's life from that decision to end it.

Behind the details we sift like the ashes after a fire is the feeling that we are completely responsible for the suicide. We feel that somehow we could have prevented it. We may say to ourselves, "If only I had heard what he was saying, if only I had been there at the time, if only we had not made the decision to go away." Our imagination can unfold an endless list of "if only"s. This is one of the biggest issues we face as survivors of a suicide. We need to go over our roles in our loved ones' lives and we need to be allowed the months and even years it takes to examine our own conduct. We have a powerful sense of responsibility to those we love and this feeling of responsibility is closely related to conscience. It is simply not possible to sidestep this process. Even when we begin to be able to perceive that perhaps we could not have prevented our loved one's death, this may be a purely intellectual perception. The heart and the stomach are slow to follow the mind's reasoning.

In the period of disorganization following our initial shocked reaction to a suicide, the feelings of guilt and anger predominate. Our sense of guilt can be paralyzing. We know that we need to continue our lives, turn our attention to our jobs and surviving family and friends and yet, just when we feel it is finally possible to move on, the guilt returns and pulls us back. We may think a lot about whether our loved one had planned the suicide for some time and may look for evidence such as failing health, or perhaps paying bills and attending to financial matters far ahead of schedule. Then we think of ourselves living with the person who had made that decision and wonder what we could have done to prevent it had we only noticed and paid more attention. We may be able to function, to go through the motions of our lives, but we are caught in an internal struggle as we face our sense of guilt and the unfathomable nature of such an event.

This feeling of guilt continues during the bereavement period until we are finally able to let go of it. At one point, Merryl realized that she would never become whole again if she didn't let go of the feeling of self-blame. That realization has to come from within. However, we may gain a sense of perspective from friends who listened and talked to us during this period. Our friends will remind us of all the things we did do to help our loved ones and which we may have forgotten in our agony of searching for causes. Our friends will remind us that we are able to see clues and symptoms only by hindsight. A good friend will keep repeating these insights to us and that will help us internalize them and ultimately to see our loved one in relation to himself or herself and not only in relation to ourselves.

After a suicide we are not only shaken by guilt, but we also experience a profound anger. We may not necessarily be angry at the person who died, given that person's extreme pain. However, we may feel angry at the pain we are left with after the suicide. "She took away her pain, but left us with it," or "How could she do this to us?" we may ask ourselves. Some of us have found it helpful to think of the deceased as two people; the one we love and the one who murdered that person. We can be angry at the murderer while loving and accepting the victim. In some cases we may also perceive the suicide as a rejection of ourselves. We may be angry that our wife or lover didn't consider us important enough to live for. We may be angry at our loved one for leaving us in this way. In a moment of humor a member of a support group for survivors of suicide exploded, "If I could have him back for just five minutes, I'd kill him."

A suicide in our family or among close relations may arouse fears that other members of the family or even we ourselves might be prey to suicide. Perhaps the person in our family who killed himself was the one member who always seemed in control of things. When the unlikely person commits suicide we begin to look at the more fragile or vulnerable members of our family with new concern. Or we may experience a terrible fear that we ourselves might be vulnerable to such a tragic end. After the death of someone we love deeply, it is normal to feel that we don't want to go on. But there is a big difference between feeling that we don't want to live and feeling that we shouldn't live. A suicide can be a terrifying precedent to confront.

The brother of a young man who committed suicide became depressed after his brother's death. Unlike his brother who had had mental difficulties, he had always been balanced and had felt positive about his own life. Then he began acting like his dead brother. He dressed like him and took on some of his characteristics. It was his way of taking responsibility for his brother's death. Ultimately, the young man regained his health and stability after attending support groups for survivors of suicide and after seeing a psychiatrist. However, as family members of a suicide, we may be vulnerable to the thought that we don't deserve to live.

As survivors of a suicide, living in a home where the suicide occurred may be especially difficult. We may feel that our home is somehow marked, and yet may have few options for alternative housing. Merryl found it helpful to live with her parents and then with a friend until she could confront her own apartment again. It may take some time until we can see our home as a place where we and our loved one had a very full life together as well as a place with painful reminders.

Holidays, which are always difficult for those who have lost loved ones, are especially trying for survivors of a suicide. When Thanksgiving arrived, Miriam didn't feel like getting out of bed. She wished the whole day would disappear or that she could ignore it. This is not a possibility for families with children. Miriam gave a special reading for her husband at the beginning of the Thanksgiving dinner and that helped her through the day.

There are also painful daily reminders that make our passage through this period a difficult one. Our children may continue to ask us questions or they may express their pain and confusion in their play activities, by the pictures they may draw, or by acting out the suicide with a stuffed animal or toy. Not only do we have to answer our own questions which revolve in our thoughts, but we have to address the pain of those around us.

If it is awkward and sometimes seems impossible to talk about the death of a loved one, it is even more so to talk about suicide. Some friends and acquaintances may be willing to listen to us talk of our deceased, but it is very rare to find someone who is able to listen sympathetically while we air our pain over a suicide. Survivors of suicide have found that support groups where they can discuss the particular issues around suicide are extremely helpful. Many people stay with these support groups for two and three years and then return as helpers for those experiencing recent loss. It is good to talk about this kind of death, to share our experiences with others who have had similar ones, to see people in various stages of the grieving process and especially to see those who have left the most difficult phases behind them.

It is hard to admit that we can't control the circumstances and fate of our loved ones. As a society we put a great deal of energy into the prevention of suicide and therefore we feel like failures when someone we love takes their own life. However, even when we may have known what was troubling a spouse or a child or a sibling and even when we may have done everything humanly possible to help that person, ultimately we could not make contact. Only the passage of time can help us to accept our powerlessness to save those we love.

It is always difficult to explain a death and our grief over that death to our friends and co-workers. But it is particularly hard to tell people about a suicide. We feel protective of ourselves and our family because of the powerful social taboos against suicide. We may feel a sense of shame and dread adverse social reactions. Consequently some of us may try to cover it up by telling others that our loved one died of an accident or a heart attack. We may feel protective of some members of our own family, the elderly, very young children or the emotionally fragile.

The way we deal with the problem of facing the outside world depends on our own style of communication and our own way of coping with events. When she returned to work, Merryl sat down with her new secretary and explained to her that her appearance and withdrawn behavior was due to the recent suicide of her husband. Some people are able to speak of suicide, others want to play it down. However, many of us experience a deep sense of isolation on returning to our lives as workers, students, or parents. It's as if such a terrible tragedy seems to set us apart from others. As survivors of the suicide of someone we love, we are also victims. We carry the burden of it our whole lives.

14 • When Someone We Love Is Murdered

Margaret:

My story begins on June 9, 1978. At that time I had three children, a son aged seventeen and two daughters aged fifteen and ten. My son John was learning to drive and drove me and his friend to a graduation party. He was happy, in love and looking forward to a great future for himself. I was very happy. He had caused me a lot of problems when he was in his early teens but now he was turning seventeen and he had seen the light. It was wonderful.

At 12:30 on June 10, I was awakened by a doctor calling me from City Hospital telling me that my son had been stabbed. Since I was alone, he arranged for the police to pick me up. There were three policemen in the car. They didn't speak a word to me but chatted with each other as if I weren't even there. The first hospital that I was taken to was the Cambridge City Hospital. Looking back, they were really great. They had a crisis center counselor there and she put her arm around me while the doctor told me what condition John was in. They had decided to move him to the Massachusetts General. When I arrived there I was immediately asked whether I had Blue Cross/Blue Shield and put in a room by myself. I remember saying the Hail Mary out loud. That was something I hadn't done in a long time. My heart was pounding.

A doctor came into the room, and matter-of-factly told me, "Your son has expired." I ran outside the hospital and I screamed and screamed and screamed. Thank God I was able to do that. Then my defense system took over and I was anesthetized. From the moment he died, I was consumed by the loss. I just couldn't be concerned about how he had died, it was just that he had died. I didn't know what was happening to the person that killed him. I didn't want to believe that John had suffered and that he knew he was going to die. I wanted to believe that he had been stabbed in the back and never knew anything. I couldn't bear to feel that he had suffered, so I didn't ask any questions.

I was told by my brother that a Probable Cause Hearing was being held and that later a Grand Jury hearing would take place. During this time, the person who had stabbed my son was in custody, and had been since the night of the murder. I read in the paper that sufficient evidence was found to have him stand trial. I was under the delusion that I would be notified when the trial was to begin. Not so. I found out the date of the trial when I contacted the prosecuting attorney just to find out what was happening. At the trial I was totally ignored. I was the person who was the most deeply affected by the crime, and yet I was treated as if I didn't exist. Perhaps the attorney could have told me how things were progressing in the case before the trial or even talked to me during the trial. It was humiliating to be ignored.

The person who killed my son was convicted of second-degree murder and was sentenced to life in prison. He will be eligible for parole in fifteen years. I'm lucky because somebody is paying some price for the crime. Many people don't have that luck, if you want to call it luck in this situation. At least I had somewhere to go after the trial. I could get on with my life.

I felt nothing except pain in my head for the first month. At some point somebody said to me, "You must be angry at God." That gave me permission to feel angry. I hadn't felt angry until that moment and then I was totally enraged.

I feel lucky that I had had some therapy before John died. I got some of the other stuff out of the way. During 1972, I had had a love affair that ended and my father died. I was suffering terribly. The psychiatrist kept mentioning grief. Now this was thirteen years ago. I thought grief was some psychiatric term. I really didn't know that grief was something that everybody experienced when they lost someone, because people didn't talk about grief. I kept wondering would I ever feel better again. I kept asking people whether anyone ever recovered from it. No one was able to give me an answer and that was one of the reasons I thought I would write a little of what I felt when John died so that someday I could say to someone, "I felt this bad and I got better."

The week after John's funeral was just a blur of pain. I ran around looking for someone, for anything that I could find out about grief. I called people. I looked in the death notices to see if I could find someone whose child had died and I wrote letters to people who had lost children. Nobody responded and I believe now it was because my son had been murdered. Their children had died from illness or accidents. Even people who are grieving can't relate to homicide.

My son died on June 10. On June 29 I wrote in my journal, "I can't imagine parting with John's clothes. I feel like this will never heal up. It's so awful I can't believe it. Everything I do reminds me of something I did with John. I love him so much. How can I have a decent life without him? What a terrible pain to have to bear for the rest of my life. There's no consolation. I keep picturing John, so full of life."

On August 15 I wrote, "I feel a lot of anger towards a lot of people. They are so smug in their security. Everyone except me and my daughters seem to be getting over it. I feel like everyone has forgotten it. I feel like I'll never stop crying."

On September 27, I wrote, "I feel so bad I just can't comprehend it. It's so horrible. All I can say is, 'Oh my God, oh, my God.' I feel as if I'm going to split into pieces. Why did God ever let this happen to me? If there's a God, I hate him."

The trial took place that November and lasted for two weeks. At that time, I felt as though John had just died. I was back to square one. People couldn't understand why I had to attend the trial. I had to. He was my son. I had to complete that journey. When the defendant was found guilty, I was elated, for one day. But then, so what? John was still dead.

The months of December, January and February were the worst I experienced in the whole mourning period. There was no relief from pain. The only way I could tell people how badly I felt was to say that I didn't want to live. I didn't think of suicide but that was the only way to express my feelings. Paradoxically, it was just at this time that people were letting go of me, feeling that I was now able to stand on my own two feet.

On January 2, I wrote, "I'm in agony. My son is dead and I will never see him again. For the first time since he died, I feel as if I can't stand it. I can't get him out of my mind. I feel like screaming all the time. I feel very angry towards people. I guess I'm not getting any special treatment any longer and I think I should. What I'm contending with is so intense, I can't believe I can go to work. It almost feels worse now than before. People ignore the facts of my life. They expect me to be happy."

People who have lost children agree with me that one's public grieving is over in eight months. After that people are no longer interested. They don't want to know you are still feeling bad.

On April 3, I wrote, "I looked at pictures of John growing up today. I thought I was up to it. I wasn't. It broke my heart. I know I've healed somewhat because I don't think about John all the time. I think I'm letting go of him a little, through no choice of mine. I don't want to. The space in the house is filling up a little."

After the first anniversary I wrote, "I've survived." I think there was a high in getting through the first year. Now I'm stuck with it. I have to live with it day in and day out.

I hardly wrote in my journal after the first year. I was reinvesting in life. I took some courses. I continued to attend Compassionate Friends for two more years. After three years, I had recovered sufficiently so that I started doing some work on victim rights.

I had a good support system, but they were all grieving too. My mother was *very upset. Looking back, I got little, but my children got nothing. I wish they had had some supports in the school system. If I feel guilty about anything, it's about my daughters, because I was totally unable to help them. No one mentioned it in school. They went back to school, nothing was said about it. If only people would acknowledge what happened or at least say, "I'm sorry." People feel that you might cry. You probably will but that's okay.*

I met Charlotte Hollinger shortly after her daughter was murdered. She started a group called Parents of Murdered Children. She said, "The church was no help. I was getting platitudes: 'It was God's will.' Or: 'God wanted Lisa so badly he took her early. She's much happier now with God.'" There's nothing more maddening or patronizing then to be told this. Another thing I hear from other homicide victims when they talk about the clergy is that they are told they have to forgive. I don't know how you get around to forgiving. I haven't even thought about it myself. I think it's asking a lot to ask people to forgive someone who murdered their loved one.

I went to Compassionate Friends, a support group for bereaved parents. I did not talk about the fact that my son was murdered there. I used what I had in common with these people. I didn't feel as if they were comfortable with the fact that John was murdered. Maybe it was in my own head. I never did have a lot of opportunity to discuss the fact that John was murdered. I think what happens to homicide survivors is that they constantly relive the murder scene. I could be drying my hair and I will suddenly picture John getting stabbed and staggering across the street screaming, "I've been stabbed." Even now I think more about John than my children who are alive because all I have are memories. There are things from John's childhood that will pop up. I drive a long distance to work and that's when I'm by myself and that's when I'm very sad.

If I hadn't gone to a group, even though I didn't meet anyone who at that time had lost a child through homicide, I would have thought that I was the only person in the world who was suffering. At least when I went there, there were other people who were suffering and it helped somehow. You hate everybody else who is having a good time. You're totally obsessed with this death experience. It's just on your mind morning, noon and night.

I was lucky because I was in pretty good shape when this happened to me. Not everyone is in good shape when something like this happens to them. I had suffered before, so I knew something about suffering and that helped me.

It's been seven years since my son died. I feel I have recovered to a certain extent. It's below the surface. I live above it all the time. I'm very sad and very angry. I can talk about the rights of crime victims without crying but when I talk about my own son John I can't do it without crying. I don't mind but it's very hard for other people to deal with. One of the things that's very hard about losing a child is that people won't let you mention his name. It's like he never existed.

To me the best thing that could ever happen is that somebody would say, "Do you have a picture?" When it's your child you feel like you want to talk about them. But when I talk about John, I will cry. Then there's this thing about murder. If I tell people that John was murdered, then I have to take care of them. It's hard to decide whether or not to mention it. In fact one person did say, "Why did you mention it?" I say well, I did have three children. I hate to leave him out of my life. I had him for seventeen years and I was very proud of him. I still want people to know that he was very good-looking and that he had a good personality.

I don't know what this experience has taught me. I've had other grieving experiences to which I could look back and know that I've learned something. I can't say anything good about this experience except that I didn't lie down and die myself. I have learned that the human spirit is amazing. We don't know what we have inside us, no one knows. You live, you survive.

Though murder is the focus of so many television shows, movies and newspaper articles, we never imagine that it could possibly happen to someone we love. Although we may belong to a group whose members are less likely, statistically, to be murdered, we are all vulnerable to drunk drivers when we are on the highway and we may all be prey to wanton murder.

Murder is commonplace in the pseudo-reality of the mass media. However, the drama of murder which we witness on our television screens focuses upon investigations, arrests, and courtroom scenes. On these programs we rarely are given any view of the terrible emotional impact on the survivors of a murder and often even the victim is given little attention.

When a loved one is murdered, the emotions of grieving, such as anger, are more intense and long-lasting than in other kinds of loss. The element of horror and cruelty in such a crime throws us into acute turmoil. Our initial reaction may be shock and confusion and that period of shock may last for weeks and even months because it is so difficult to comprehend such an event. Frequently we are obsessed by an overwhelming need to know about the details of our loved one's death and the depth of his or her suffering. We replay the event both because we need to know the extent and nature of the victim's suffering and because somehow, gathering the details is a search for understanding what seems like an incomprehensible event.

We are caught in a kaleidoscope of emotions: rage at the murderer and a very normal desire for revenge, sorrow at the pain of our loved one, intense anxiety about our own safety and the safety of the world we live in. We feel we should have been able to prevent that death and may be tormented by guilt. We may have great difficulty sleeping and when the sleep finally comes we may experience terrible nightmares. We feel out of control in a world which seems arbitrary and unpredictable.

The father of one of my students, a policeman, was killed while he was on duty. He was killed by an inmate who had been temporarily released to take part in a new program of study initiated by a nearby university. After the murder, the university offered my student a scholarship which she refused. Within the same year her uncle, who was also a policeman, was murdered. During the next two years of her college career, Doris was disruptive in class, would frequently interrupt her professors during their lectures and would storm out of a room at the slightest difficulty. Her anger was a heavy burden for her to carry. Eventually, she joined the police force herself when she graduated. The violence which shattered her family life had a profound effect on her life choices.

It is not unusual for the survivors of a murder to want to kill the murderer. We may simultaneously feel sorrow for our loved one, and a deep rage towards the person who killed him or her. We may be obsessed with a desire to avenge that death. Amy's husband was stabbed in a quarrel after a hockey game and then dumped outside and left to die. The killer was never charged, but Amy feels that she knows who did it and fantasizes killing him herself. When she blurted out this wish in her support group, instead of chiding her, the members remained silent. They understood this feeling and may have experienced it themselves.

When someone we love is murdered we feel victimized ourselves. The stigma of murder in the family is greater than the stigma of suicide because we feel marked in a more public way. If the crime occurred in our town or city we may wish to move away. We need to be assured that there is nothing wrong with us. It is normal to feel helpless and to feel as if we ourselves have been violated, after such a horrible event.

For many of us, the anguish of surviving a murder is compounded by the way we were notified. Margaret's experience of being driven to the hospital by three policemen who were absorbed in their own small talk and then being matter of factly informed by the doctor that her son had "expired" is not untypical. Some of us are notified by telephone, or are given inaccurate and incomplete information. We are entitled to know what happened, when and how. Some of us discover the news through the media and that causes additional pain. Being notified by trained policemen with the aid of a crisis counselor can make a great difference in helping us deal with our initial shock.

A violent death presents us with its own special demands such as identifying our loved one's body, dealing with medical personnel and ambulance bills, notifying our friends and dealing with the media. We may be subject to the intrusiveness and insensitivity of newspaper reporters who seem more concerned with the "story" than with the suffering of our loved one. And if our loved one died in a sensational or "newsworthy" crime we may feel harassed by the constant presence of the media even as we leave the funeral services.

The type of murder and the way in which our loved one was killed will affect our grieving reactions. If the victim was a woman and was sexually violated before she was murdered, the assault may cause us as much anguish as the murder itself. As fathers, brothers, or boyfriends we may have difficulty even thinking about such a horrible event or we may feel guilty that somehow we were unable to protect the victim. As mothers, sisters, or girlfriends we may have difficulty continuing to have normal sexual relations. We are caught in our images of the terror and degradation our loved one must have suffered.

In many murders, the body has been violated by repeated stabbings or other mutilations. Viewing the body for identification and prior to burial is an excruciating experience. We wonder whether our loved one was unconscious while the act took place. We fantasize that he or she was, but that question nags us. Like Margaret, we may want to avoid knowing because that knowledge can be unbearable. My aunt was killed in a head-on automobile collision which resulted in an explosion. Her children and husband could not bear to see the body and made arrangements for the funeral and burial without ever viewing it.

If our loved one was killed by a drunk driver, we may suffer additional outrage and a sense of isolation by the manner in which vehicular homicide is viewed by society. We tend to excuse drunk driving and to refer to deaths as a result of drunk driving as "accidents," not as criminal homicides. Assailants are generally given light sentences and may have caused deaths before the one that took our loved one. If the assailant is young, we may be urged to forgive and forget, to consider the assailant's life. This may leave us with a sense of deep bitterness, a sense that justice has not been done.

Elaine's twenty-year-old daughter Susan was killed in a motor vehicle homicide. She was driving home from a party with her friend Marie who had had too much to drink. The car crashed into a pole and Susan died in the car while Marie survived. The absence of skid marks near the pole attests to the level of alcohol Marie had in her body.

Marie was charged with motor vehicle homicide but this was by no means the end of Elaine's efforts to deal with the crime. This type of homicide is not a priority in court and Elaine arrived at the court

four times, ready to make her statement, only to have the trial postponed. When the trial finally took place, Marie was given a very light
sentence, six months in an alcohol clinic, five years' probation, and
the loss of her license. Marie appealed to have the sentence cut in half
and eventually after a rehearing, she did get two weeks off the
sentence.

To Elaine, this seemed like an extremely light sentence. But in
similar cases, some sentences are never served and often the person
charged is placed on probation. The results of the case heightened
the anger that Elaine already felt over the death of her daughter. And
along with the anger, Elaine was left with the profound grief over her
daughter's absence. When she returned home after the trial, she felt
that nobody had won. Her daughter was gone forever and even
though Marie got off with such a light sentence, and was presented
with a new car by her father, she didn't win either.

Because murder is such a distasteful subject, we may suffer additional pain from the reactions of our friends and even of the religious
community. Some of our friends may be distant or may even try to
avoid us. Some members of the clergy may try to relieve our anguish
by saying that "your loved one was called by God," or by advising us to
forgive the murderer. When someone murders a loved one, we may
feel as if we wish to avenge ourselves. That is a perfectly normal response. Not only is it difficult to experience such profound rage, it is
difficult to see ourselves as vengeful people. We need support in our
struggle with these emotions rather than what often seems like a
cavalier dismissal.

Sometimes, members of the clergy may receive the murderer in
forgiveness and ask the murderer to forgive himself. In 1977, when
Richard Herrin murdered his girl friend with a hammer, he gave
himself up to a Roman Catholic priest. The priest embraced the killer
and told him he must immediately begin the process of self-forgive-
ness. In a more recent case, a young man choked his girl friend to
death in Central Park. At a bail hearing the accused killer presented
a letter from a Roman Catholic archbishop testifying to his character.
As victims' families, we may be alienated from our faith just when we
need it the most.

People not only wish to avoid the very painful subject of murder
but they may try to distance themselves from the event by blaming the
murder on the victim or on the survivors. When an aspiring young
theater student was brutally stabbed in New York City in a much-
celebrated case, many people blamed the young woman for struggling with her assailant. Women are taught that remaining passive
might save them in such a situation. Others blamed her for not being

more cautious, ignoring the fact that she was attacked in her own apartment building by the son of the superintendent. Often people feel that if somehow they can place the blame on the victim and on the victim's family, they can feel invulnerable to murder themselves.

When someone we love is murdered, not only is our view of the world as a safe and predictable place shattered, but our view of the system of justice is also called into question. One of the fundamental grounds of our belief in the social and the political system is that these communities provide us with the protection of our basic safety and also with justice in our mutual relations. However dealing with the criminal justice system in our society may exacerbate the pain and stress of facing the murder of a loved one and may leave us feeling disillusioned with the court system.

Frequently, as survivors we are kept at a distance from the cases involving the accused killer of our loved one. Margaret was not even notified when the trial of her son's killer took place. She read about it in the newspaper, and then the burden of finding out the trial date and the development of the case rested on her. At the trial, she was completely ignored. Often we must learn firsthand that the criminal process is lengthy, that many murders are never solved, and that the killer can be acquitted or receive a very light sentence. Even if the killer is convicted and receives a life sentence we may be surprised that we do not feel the emotional relief we expected.

When the suspected killer is arrested, we may feel relieved that the process of justice has begun and we may feel that things will be all right. However, then we may learn that arrests do not always result in prosecutions, that prosecutions do not always lead to convictions or convictions to stiff sentences or sentences even served. Further, what seems like a clear instance of murder to us may be understood by judges and juries as manslaughter, negligent homicide or accidental death.

If the case goes to trial, the trial may be postponed or delayed for months and years, leaving us suspended in our grief and outrage. We may have a strong desire for closure, for an orderly process that corresponds to our sense of the injustice of the murder, only to realize that the process has its own calendar. When the trial occurs, we may find that we are prevented from attending because it is felt that our attendance might prejudice the jury. Imagine how we feel when we discover that relatives of the defendant are permitted in the courtroom.

In the jurisdictions where survivors are allowed to attend the proceedings we may either be completely ignored or hear our loved ones maligned by the defense. If our loved one happened to be a young woman and if she was raped during the killing, the trial may focus on the victim's reputation, not the question of whether she was assaulted. A professor of evidence and ethics at New York University School of Law has stated that not only is it not unethical to try to question or malign the character of the victim, it's the defense lawyer's duty to do that if it will succeed in a not-guilty verdict or a conviction on a lesser charge. During the trial, we may find that public opinion and the media seem more concerned with the suspected killer than with the victim whose life was cut short. Added to our profound grief over the loss of our loved one may be a sense that we are living in a world in which the very concepts of right and wrong, of accountability and social good are discounted in the system of justice.

If, after the lengthy and often alienating court proceedings, the suspected killer is found not guilty, we may feel an intense sense of outrage and disillusion. Or we may even fear retaliation by that killer. In some cases a convicted murderer may appeal and have the case thrown out on a technicality. We as well as the jurors in the first trial may feel unsafe as a result. If the suspect is found guilty but receives a sentence that we consider trivial or inappropriate, we may feel as distressed as if a not-guilty verdict had been handed down. We can readily understand how the parents of a child killed by a drunk driver must feel when the person charged receives a minimal sentence even though this might have been only one in a whole series of similar criminal acts.

Even if the killer receives what we consider a just sentence, we may be surprised at our response. We might have expected that the end of the trial and an appropriate sentence would help to lessen our pain. As Margaret discovered, her elation at the defendant's sentencing was short-lived. After all, her son was still dead. When the trial is behind us, our emotions may surface with full force because we are no longer focused on that external event. We are left with the terrible emptiness created by the murder and the knowledge that we will have to live with it.

The sentencing stage in a trial is of great concern to us as survivors. Because of recent legislation providing for "victim impact statements," survivors in some states have a right to have a say before sentencing. Sometimes this may take the form of a written statement of how the murder affected the survivors. In some states, survivors are allowed to speak to the judge at the sentencing hearing. If we are permitted this opportunity, we may at least feel that our participation has made a difference.

Those of us who see the killer sentenced after a trial rather than after a guilty plea may be faced with the prospect of endless appeals and a possible overturning of the conviction or even of an acquittal in the second or third trial. If the act of homicide causes us to feel a deeper and more prolonged sorrow than other kinds of losses, our dealings with the court system may also draw out our suffering. Margaret felt that she was lucky because someone was paying for the crime and she felt free to go on with her life.

One of the difficulties we face as survivors of a murder of a loved one is a sense of isolation. As Margaret commented, when she tells people her son was murdered, she has to support them rather than the reverse. It is very difficult to talk about the pain we suffer because of a murder. People may be frightened and repelled. And yet we need to talk, not only about the sorrow and anguish of our loss, but about the person we lost and how much we loved him or her. While we may feel pressure to move on and pick up the threads of our lives, as survivors we never forget either the murder or the victim. Margaret had a good relationship with her son and many happy memories. Thinking about her son's life is healing for her and the times of privacy she has are devoted to his memory. What other people may consider as an unhealthy focus on the past may be the route to our own survival.

There are few support groups that focus specifically on the needs of survivors of murder. Sharing our anger and sorrow with others who have had similar experiences helps to break down the sense of isolation we may experience, the feeling that we are the only ones in the world who are suffering this grief. Margaret attended The Compassionate Friends, which provides support to parents who have lost a child by any cause. She also attended a local support group sponsored by a bereavement counseling center, called Empathy. Empathy is for survivors of the victims of homicide or motor vehicle homicide. In addition to sharing each others' feelings and experiences, participants may also practice their impact statements in preparation for court appearances. Parents of Murdered Children, Mothers Against Drunk Driving, and the Violence Project of the National Gay Task Force also provide support for the bereaved.

Not only may we find that our friends have difficulty in dealing with the fact of murder and our own distress, but our families may be subjected to stressful changes. Margaret faced the problem of continuing as a parent to her daughters and of keeping the family together as a single parent. This is a heavy burden, because after the murder of a child, we are obsessed with the child we lost, and this may make it difficult to attend to the needs of the siblings. The emotions and turmoil of grief may leave us with little energy to devote to our other children.

A two-parent family may experience differing reactions to the murder. It is not unusual for marriages to end in divorce after such a traumatic event. Those of us who survive a homicide death become different people. We may think and feel in new ways and this may cause tensions in our marital relations and in our relations with other family members.

As survivors of the homicide of a loved one, we are also victims. Many of us feel that we never recover from such a blow. However, some of us not only reconstruct our lives, but also become involved in volunteer efforts on behalf of victim rights and other causes in the memory of our loved one. Three years after her son's death, Margaret helped to establish support groups and started working for victim rights. She has lobbied extensively for legislation on behalf of families affected by homicide.

The murder of a loved one changes our lives irrevocably. Nicholas Gage, whose mother was murdered in a European village during a civil war, shaped his whole life in response to that event. He emigrated to the United States and became a reporter for a major newspaper. When he reached middle age, he took time off from his job to return to his village, unearth the details of his mother's murder and write about her life. It's as if his whole career as a reporter was shaped by his desire to find out what happened to his mother. After a year's painstaking research, he tracked down the name and also the address of his mother's killer. Armed with a gun, he paid a visit to the killer's home. He had been waiting for this moment his whole life, but when he finally confronted the man, he put the gun away. Face to face with the murderer, he finally understood the futility of his thirst for revenge. What ultimately resulted from his pilgrimage home was a book, *Eleni,* and then a movie about his mother and the events that led to her death.

The reconstruction of our lives means remembering the murder victim, not just the murder. Margaret's son is very much a part of her life. She was very proud of him, and talking about him and sharing her memories of him with others is a way of acknowledging that precious life that was cut short. Recovering does not mean either forgetting or the end of our pain. It may mean that we have found something positive to do with our sorrow. It may mean simply that we have more good days than bad days, and that we have learned to separate the horror of the act of murder from the victim's life. We may discover the depth of our inner resources and what it really means to live.

AS TIME PASSES:
THE PHASE OF
DISORGANIZATION

A gray stalk in water
sends out a flower:

nothing is lost forever.
The ones who sleep underground

come back in dreams
wearing the faces of strangers.

We have to learn again and again
what to keep, what to throw away.

Beatrice Hawley, "Grief"

15 • *The Disorganization of Our Lives after the Death of a Loved One*

"It's been ten months and I'm still in such pain," a young widow exclaimed. We may be surprised by the length of time we spend grieving for a loved one. Somehow we may have expected our pain and sadness to dissipate sooner, and we may even be impatient with ourselves as time passes and we don't appear to be making any progress. Although the length of time we need to work through our grief varies with each individual, some of us may need not months but years until the burden of pain and our absorption with the loss moves away from the center of our lives. While the period of shock we experience immediately after a death may be measured in weeks or months, the phase of disorganization which we experience as a disruption of our lives may last longer.

Grieving is not only a long and gradual process but one that moves unevenly and sometimes in reverse. We may have several good days in a row and then some event, or something we may see, perhaps a person that reminds us of our loved one, can trigger those painful feelings again. These swings in our feelings are normal and it is best not to subject ourselves to timetables for moving through this phase. Even though our progress may not be clearly evident, we will find that we can see real differences in what may seem like small things. A friend of mine who lost her husband remarked that some days she is able to think about other things besides her own pain and even to talk with others about their own interests, to move away a little bit from that intense focus on her sadness.

During this period, the friends who gathered around us for the funeral and in the early weeks after the death may have returned to their own lives and concerns. Or we may find that our old friendships are unsatisfactory. We may reach out to our friends for support and find that they are unable to be there for us when we need them. We may learn that not everyone is willing or able to deal with our pain. We may even conclude that the only ones who can really understand what we are experiencing are those who are grieving themselves. Not only have we lost a loved one, but it may seem as if we have lost some of our friends.

Some of us may find a new friend in someone we have known only casually but who may have experienced loss also and who therefore understands us. Perhaps this is the time to turn to a professional helper or a trusted member of the clergy. We may feel ready to join a support group where we can talk about our feelings and our loss without feeling that we are abnormal.

At this time we may be receiving subtle messages that we should be pulling ourselves together and returning to our normal activities. We may be faced with the expectations of our co-workers that we should be resuming our work at our usual pace. We ourselves may think that we should be able to do more than we are doing. Many of us may find that on the contrary, we need to spend time on other things. Perhaps if we have lost a spouse, we may find that we need time just to be alone and to withdraw for a few hours from the demands of work and children.

Most women have been socialized to assume nurturing roles and the self-regarding aspects of grieving may be especially difficult. Children, friends, spouses and co-workers build up expectations that cannot be fulfilled during this period. Perhaps we cannot be as good a parent or spouse or friend as we would like to be, but it's important to recognize the very legitimate need to withdraw. "I feel selfish sometimes," a widowed friend confided. But taking a weekend away from the children or other responsibilities is far from selfish under these circumstances. It's a matter of our own health and well-being. We can hardly take responsibility for others if we ourselves are not in good shape.

In fact, we may feel the need to reach out to others for support. This may seem like a very difficult step for us. However, we may be doing our friends a favor by requesting specific types of supports such as talking over coffee or picking up a child after school, or simply discussing the new issues we face. By asking for help, we may be providing the structure our acquaintances need. Many people may want to help us, but don't know what to do. Those around us may be as baffled by our emotions as we are.

As the numbness of our shock wears off, we face the full intensity of our pain. We may experience a loss of energy and find that we need more rest than usual or we may discover that we are unable to maintain our usual pace at work and at home. Some people tell of working a few hours a day and then returning home because of fatigue, or of working only a few days a week. It is not unusual for people who have some savings to take off a few months from work after the loss of a loved one. We may be surprised by our diminished energy level. Even though it is invisible, the work of the emotions is very consuming. While we may feel drained for a period of time, these profound emotions are helping us through the process of healing.

Some people may plunge into activity as a relief from pain. "I try to keep busy to keep my mind off it," a bereaved parent confided. Some people are helped by trying to pursue their regular activities. It may give them a structure or provide them with meaning. Yet sometimes we need to give ourselves more space to allow ourselves to grieve.

During this phase of grieving we may feel depressed. The death of a loved one is like receiving a stunning blow and we may experience a consequent lack of self-esteem. We may not feel good about ourselves in our various roles of parent, spouse, friend or sibling. Just getting out of bed in the morning may seem like an enormous chore and if we had the choice, we might prefer staying in bed. If it seems hard just to get up and face the day, we may also encounter difficulty at work or at home. We may be unable to concentrate on our tasks or to remember small things and we have a very low tolerance for the countless frustrations the day brings. These are all symptoms of depression.

Instead of forcing ourselves through our chores, it is helpful to slow down the pace of our lives, to be easy on ourselves. This is a good time to do small favors for ourselves, to take a long walk or to take the day off for a drive to the country. There may be things we have wanted to do for a long time but postponed because of all our responsibilities. Now is the time for perhaps taking up skiing, sitting in on a course, or reading that book we have always wanted to get to. Some people who have suffered a loss have even referred to their new situation as a blank page which they will enjoy filling, and they have been able to say this without feeling as if they are betraying their loved one.

Along with depression we may be feeling angry. We may be angry at the person who died and who left us with so much responsibility. We may think that our loved one is in a good place now while we are left with all of the problems of family and work. We may be angry at God for the injustice of the death. "Why me?" we may ask ourselves, "I've been a good person. What have I done to deserve this?" Or we may have a more diffuse anger which erupts at everyday things, a simple demand by our co-worker, or some small thing which occurs at home. "I've been rotten in the office lately," mused a woman who lost her mother. We may express this anger in hostile reactions to minor events or in the bitterness of our tone.

We may feel guilty about our resentment, but it's all right to feel anger and to find appropriate ways to express it. A friend of mine who lost a child stayed home alone one morning and just let her anger surface. She screamed and pounded against the bed. A woman whose lover committed suicide went to his grave and yelled at him for leaving her. It was a great relief. It is not a denial of our love for the person who died to feel angry about the difficulties that death imposed on us.

Even though months may have passed since our loved one died, we still miss that person and may become increasingly aware of the significance of our loss as we struggle with our responsibilities and our loneliness. We miss the companionship and emotional support of our loved one, miss the physical side of love, being able to hold a child, sleeping close to our spouse. We may feel a fresh surge of sadness at special times of the day such as the time our spouse returned from work or the time we used to talk to a parent over the phone to discuss the events of the day.

Our sadness is often occasioned by a new event that our loved one would have been part of, the birthday of one of the children, a special holiday we used to enjoy celebrating together. The smallest thing, the fragment of a song, the sight of someone who resembles our loved one, may trigger waves of sadness. Or we may feel like crying for no apparent reason and in the most inappropriate place.

In time we will be able to move that sadness to a more comfortable place inside ourselves. However, the life events we all share in, graduations, birthdays, anniversaries, are both a reminder of what might have been had our loved one survived and also a fresh source of pain. On the anniversary of the death of our loved one we may feel the pain of loss as intensely as we did at the time of the death. It's a common experience to relive those events over again. These feelings may take us by surprise by their intensity, yet it is a perfectly normal experience.

Some people have designed ways to handle these events so that they can be comfortable with them. A young widow I know usually takes the day off on the anniversary of her husband's death. She drives out to the beach to be by herself and reflect. Others may call members of their bereavement support group on that day. Some bereavement centers have memorial services in which members of various support groups participate. Perhaps our family members may not want to join us for these services. We can find alternative ways to spend time with them on that day, perhaps just getting together over dinner. Some of us may prefer a more private observance such as bringing fresh flowers to a grave. It's important to recognize the effect anniversaries may have on us and to help ourselves through these difficult moments in a way that is meaningful to us.

Immediately after the death, we may have accepted feeling out of control, being swept along by our emotions, but it seems more disturbing to experience these strong emotions after the months have passed. However, this period of inner turbulence is perfectly normal. "I feel crazy," a woman who had lost a parent told me. It's frightening to be shaken by such strong feelings, yet they are part of the grieving process. They may occur when we least expect them, but allowing ourselves to feel them in all their intensity will actually help us move through them.

Some of us may have been obliged to postpone our own sadness because of family responsibilities. Perhaps we were the member of the family in charge of the funeral arrangements and the subsequent disposition of the home or business. Or perhaps we were the father left with children to care for, and the demands of work and parenting gave us little time to think about ourselves. Months may have passed without our awareness of our feelings. Then our buried grief may be triggered by a seemingly casual event. We may be watching a television show, or perhaps another loss may affect us and we may find ourselves finally weeping for the loved one who died many months ago.

A woman who lost her mother was so busy in her role as head of an extended family that she didn't even have time to think about her loss. Some months later, she attended the funeral of a co-worker whom she barely knew. All of her colleagues were astounded when she broke down and wept uncontrollably during the services. She was finally facing her sorrow over the loss of her mother.

Because our emotions are heightened after a loss, we may look for that level of emotional intensity in others and may be very disappointed when it is not reciprocated. Other concerns may seem superficial to us and we may feel that most people are only interested in trivial matters. We may want to scream out, "Can't you see that I just lost a child!" Our sorrow seems invisible at a time when our need for acceptance is particularly strong.

Frequently we may find ourselves engaging in unusual behavior during the long months of grieving. We may find ourselves having difficulty concentrating and may shift from one activity to another. We may wander through our home in seeming aimlessness and be unable to focus on anything for more than a little while. This kind of restless behavior is a normal expression of our intense emotional activity.

We may also engage in different kinds of "searching" behavior such as following someone on the street who looks like the loved one we lost. We may wear our dead parent's clothes or we may find ourselves taking on personality traits of our loved one. One woman who lost her only sister when she was in her late teens found herself assuming many of the attributes of her sister. From the more reserved member of the family, she became the outgoing and exuberant one, like her sister. This behavior reflects our desire to perpetuate our loved one's role in the world, to guarantee him or her some measure of immortality.

Even though we all experience grief in our own unique ways, our grief occurs within a family setting. The death of a family member places great stress on the family structure, both because of the new demands placed on it as roles change and because we grieve in different ways. Some of us may be very practical and logical, dealing with the disposition of effects and financial arrangements, while some of us may respond by withdrawing from practical tasks and focusing on our emotions. Just at a time when we may expect a drawing together of our family, we may experience the opposite.

Because men are more likely to conceal their feelings, their spouses and friends may conclude that they are uncaring and that their lack of expression means a lack of concern. A young woman who had a miscarriage grieved openly, weeping and expressing anger and despair. Her husband seemed to become more and more absorbed in his work and she concluded that he didn't care or couldn't understand what she was feeling. For some men and women, it is difficult to express their feelings openly or verbally. In such cases we can find ways to do things together that will be an expression of caring. We might ask our husband or wife to stay home with us an evening or an afternoon. We can hold each other without talking or expecting a verbal response or we can even watch television together as an expression of our closeness. As family members we all may need separate supports and we might need the help of a counselor to help us communicate with each other.

Children may withdraw in silence before their parents' grieving, and they may feel that their sadness is less important than their parents'. The son of a recently widowed woman told his mother on his birthday, "It's okay. I've known Daddy for much less time than you have, for only eight years and I can't remember some of them because I was a baby." The way we handle our own grief will give cues to our children. If we are able to grieve openly, they will feel free to do so, and if we try to hold everything inside, they will feel constrained. The important thing is to keep the channels of communication open and to try to reassure our children that even though we are not always able to be available to them, we love them.

Not only do we handle our emotions in different ways but we will respond differently to all the issues that arise around the death of a loved one, such as decisions about financial and material matters. As a result, the handling of wills and the distribution of personal effects may take on more significance than they really have and may even start disagreements. As siblings we may find ourselves quarreling over the distribution of furniture and personal possessions of our parents. These disagreements may reflect competitions and rivalries that are too hard to address right now.

During this phase of grieving our family dynamics are under great pressure and may be severely affected. Some families may draw closer in response to a death. Many become estranged because of the sheer burden of the grief each one experiences. It is not unusual for couples to separate after the death of a child. The nuclear family is very vulnerable to the demands placed on it. It's not always helpful to place more guilt upon ourselves for failed relationships during such a stressful period.

As time passes in the grieving process we may find that we are forging new roles for ourselves and creating new identities. This is a long and often painful process, yet there are unexpected moments of reward. We may have found some new friends, may have discovered new sides of our personality and new strengths. We may taste the new triumph of what it means to survive.

We are aware of how much we have changed although the world around us hasn't changed. The death of a loved one is a searing wound. It alters our perspective on everything in our lives. Our values, friendships and roles appear in a new light and we may feel that we are living closer to what is real in life than most people who have not suffered loss. While we may have suffered a crisis in meaning as we tried to understand the death of our loved one, why our loved one and ourselves were singled out, we may also have gained a new understanding of what it means to be alive.

In some instances we are able to move through this phase of disorganization and create new lives for ourselves within little more than a year. A middle-aged man whose wife died of cancer was happily remarried and settled into a new life a year after his wife's death. However, a man or a woman with small children to care for will need much more time to rebuild his or her life. A couple who lost a child may decide to move into a new house or begin a pregnancy or even adopt a child. A person who has lost a sibling during the teen years may decide to attend college in a distant city or move to a new town to start his or her own life.

These decisions may take years to implement. Usually we make important life decisions incrementally. A young widow moved into a smaller, but similar house a year after her husband's death. It took her two more years to move into an urban setting which reflected her change in career and lifestyles. The changes were accomplished gradually as she got to know and understand the new person she was becoming. It is only after we are able to handle the shock of death and the terrible disruption of our lives that we can even begin to think about making changes in other parts of our lives.

16 • Facing the World without a Parent

Sue:

The whole structure of our family changed after my mother died. She was the central force and then everything spun away after that and we all ended up planets in separate orbits. Most of the communication had been through my mother. My father didn't write letters very often. I don't see my youngest brothers. I hardly know them. They hardly have anything to do with the rest of the family. They left home as soon as they could after my father remarried. The pattern in my family for handling any big issue was instead of coming together and talking about it openly, we would just retreat into silence.

It was a very lonely and isolated period for me that year. I was living in a basement, in exchange for child care and housework and I was also writing. It was my garret year. I wondered at times if I was too wallowing, too self-indulgent. It's hard to know. There are no guidelines saying this is how much you should mourn: this long for a friend, this long for your mother. I read at some point the Elizabeth Kübler-Ross book, but there's no timetable for those stages and different people feel different things. I don't think I went through a denial stage. It hit me like a sledgehammer immediately and I knew she was gone. I didn't want her to be gone. There were times when I couldn't believe she was, but I wasn't suppressing it or denying it. For me it was just something raw and open for a very long time. I just walked around in a general state of vulnerability. I would see maybe a bicycle and car coming very close. Everything seemed death-filled, a hair's breath away from death.

By the summer after that November I was in much better shape to do things. But for the first six months I was in very bad shape. Then in summer I was able to work in an art gallery. In the next fall I went to graduate school. I was writing in my journal all during this period but I couldn't write poems about it. It was the next year after that that I started shaping them into poems.

I remember I had an incredibly strong anniversary reaction that November. Every Thanksgiving since has been hard. It's not so much the date but Thanksgiving and the day after. It's a very difficult time for; me for one thing it's a family time. I just always associate it with her death. November is kind of a bleak month anyway. On her birthday I always feel bad. Her birthday is June 21, which seems so appropriate for her. She was such a warm and generous and loving person, just so very open. There's the two poles of the year, her birthday and then six months later the death date. I think of the year as having those strong moments for me ten years later.

Part of dealing with my mother's death is just a sense of not having any family. She was such a link for everyone in the family. My father moved to Arizona a few years ago and that makes things even more difficult . That means I have my three brothers living in Seattle, my sister living in Oregon, my grandfather, and aunt living in Salt Lake City. The logistical problem of trying to visit everyone is so hard.

I saw my father in September. We had a small family reunion at my sister's. That was the most we've been together in several years. My father has made an effort in the past years to be more open and establish more contact with each of us; because of getting married and getting involved with a new family, things had kind of dissipated. He'll be sixty, and I think he's feeling that he doesn't want to get older and have the family be this separated. He's a very private man and my mother was a much more open, public kind of person. He didn't express his feelings in the same way my mother did.

Jeremy:

I think that the way I deal with it is just to deny my own grief, just to put it aside. Right now I'm working two jobs, and I think one of the reasons I'm working my second job is just to have more time away from my house. At my own house my mother is mostly always unhappy. I want to comfort her but at the same time I want to be far away from her grief. The other day I was sitting in the living room and she just broke down and started crying. I was correcting papers for my students and I just went on correcting. I didn't even look up to comfort her because that would have been too much pain for myself.

I have one brother and he's older. He's married and his second kid is *coming. He took it very very hard. He's not a talkative person. We don't talk about it. The things we talk about are like, "Wow, it would have been nice to call him and tell him about this," about things that happen. We really haven't talked about how much each of us feels about the loss. I've talked to his wife. Sometimes I'll stop by after work and she tells me how he feels and tells me that he feels sad about it. It's just not something that Michael and I could easily talk about. I've talked to my two younger sisters about it but I haven't talked to my older sister about it or to my brothers. I definitely think it's a gender thing. I think guys feel a lot that they have to play the roles that society sets for them.*

It's not true that I haven't cried. I just cried the other night. It's always been hard for me to cry. I sort of feel sorry that I'm feeling sorry for myself when I'm crying. You see I get a very nervous stomach. It's the same with my father. I was weighing 137 when my father died and now I'm down to 127. I know everyone's giving me shit about it. My mother's constantly giving me nonsense. I think by not eating I was trying to punish myself. And I've decided that it's enough and I've got to put it beside me, not behind me, beside me. I think if I tried to put my grief behind me I would be more negative and it would block me more. Instead I should just try to acknowledge it.

Oh yeah, I was furious at my father for dying. I was really, really pissed at him. I felt that he abandoned my mother and that he really made her life a lot harder by dying when he did. I felt very sorry for my father. I think he had a hard time. He had a really bad drinking problem when he was younger. I had a lot of anger towards my father when I was young, but over the last two years our relationship had changed a lot, became more positive. Last January I spent every weekend with my father. This was the first time that we were really together alone. He was the most intelligent man I ever met in my whole life and we would go to museums and we'd talk about history and about politics. Talking about it right now, this is hard. My father had a big problem with his weight. Before he died, he was very very skinny, very fragile. I think that actually because I wear his clothes and drive his car and that now I'm the only man in the house, I think that subconsciously, I've been trying to become him, that I've actually become him and that my weight problem is just part of the whole thing.

Did you ever see "A Christmas Carol"? When Scrooge dies, people rifle through his clothing. My sisters and brothers were arguing with each other over his things. When I went through my father's clothes, that's exactly how I felt. My father was a very private person. I had to go down with my brother two weeks after he died to close his apartment. I felt that I was violating my father. Every time I go through his study at home, through his own room, I feel like I am violating him. I remember a couple of times when I was younger — my father and I, we have the same body shape — and everyone would say, "You know you guys, you look exactly alike. Jeremy, look at your father, that's how you're going to be."

I dream a lot. I dreamed about my father being alive again. I was sitting in a tree with my sister and he was with us. He was happy and we were talk-ing about how he had fooled death. My mother was on the ground looking up at us and she was worried. She was upset at Susan and myself for talking about death and my father in such a humorous fashion. We asked him how he was going to live and whether he would have a heart attack again. He denied that anything was wrong. The week after my father died, I kept having these dreams.

I can't talk with my mother because her grief is so overwhelming. A parent is one of the most important things in your life, part of your birth, your past, your heritage. It's not the same thing for a wife. He was part of her life plan. The plans I have don't really deal with my parents. If I tried to express my grief to my mother she would be very angry. She would think, "Your anger is great but my anger is greater." I don't have the right to expect any compassion from my mom about my grief because her grief is so great that I don't think I can turn to her for sympathy or compassion or understanding. If I wanted to show my grief to my mother, I think she would welcome me and we could both grieve to-gether. But I don't think I'm ready for it. I don't think I can deal with it. I have just too many other things. My job is new. I've never taught before. I don't think I could take the time off to grieve really properly. I would lose a lot of my control on what's going on around me.

I got a letter from a friend the other day and she's really enjoying herself and doing a lot of things and I thought, "I really should be enjoying life and not having such a hard time." I can see grieving but I can't see being mad. I was mad at God for a while, but it was just half a day. I don't think that even if there is a God that he really would bother himself with making my life difficult.

I really have tried my hardest to reject what happened because when my mom talks about it I shut her off. Thanksgiving we had some people over and I tried not to think about this being a holiday and how holidays are for family.

The death of a parent may have a far-reaching impact on our family lives. Many of us who lose a parent may have to face the world with a host of new responsibilities and without the protection we have been accustomed to. For some of us, our deceased mother or father may have been the focus of our family life and our siblings may go their own ways without that unifying force. Or perhaps our parent may decide to remarry and that might either draw us together or create dissension among us. Living with a single parent has its particular problems, as Jeremy's narrative points out. When a parent dies, we're not only faced with our own broken lives but with the issues of our family members and the survival of the family itself.

The father of one of my students was left with a large family and remarried a year after his wife's death. His new wife was a woman of great tact and understanding. From the very beginning she assured Lisa that she had no intention of replacing her mother and that she wanted to be friends with her. She went to the cemetery with Lisa and helped her plant flowers at her mother's grave. Although she had a daughter of her own who was Lisa's age, she showed no preference for her own daughter and gave them equal and loving attention. Lisa was pleased to see the change in her father after the marriage. He had been moody and withdrawn after her mother died and she welcomed his new sense of contentment.

For every success story like that of Lisa's family, there are families who experience great difficulty when a widowed parent remarries. Often we may resent the person who moves in with our father or mother and we may feel left out as they focus on their new life together. We may feel as if we no longer mattered to our parent and that his or her new partner is trying to take our deceased parent's place. Perhaps it's difficult to say these things to our parent or even to admit them to ourselves and we may feel it's just easier to withdraw into our own lives and spend more and more time with our friends. It may be difficult to realize that our parent's new husband or wife may be feeling the same resentment and insecurity that we are and that our mutually hostile attitudes may be hiding our discomfort at the new situation.

Facing our own grief over the parent who died is a tremendous burden and may leave us with little energy or inclination to face the long and hard work of forging a relationship with a step-parent. It's not always possible to deal with such demanding issues simultaneously. Our anger over the death of a parent may be mingled with anger over a new situation which we neither expected nor wanted. We may feel that we have to compete for our parent's attention just when we needed him or her the most, and perhaps our resentment at the new situation may distance us from that parent. It's difficult enough to communicate with a new family member, but when we are experiencing sorrow and anger, it's that much more trying.

Perhaps this is the time to turn to a counselor for help. When our daily lives, with the demands of school or work, and family constraints, press in on us, we should be especially careful with ourselves and remember that we are entitled to our sadness. As young adults, we may often wonder whether we really deserve to devote attention to our own needs, given the pressures of our lives. We may not want to burden our friends with our troubles and we may worry that people might shy away from us if we express our pain. However, we don't have to wait for others to give us permission to grieve. We are entitled to pay attention to our feelings, to think about the parent we have lost and our own needs.

Sometimes we lose both parents through illness and must face a life of great loneliness and uncertainty. We may find ourselves living with grandparents or an aunt and uncle or with only our brothers and sisters. In some families, surviving sisters and brothers may draw closer together. In others, they may drift apart and we may experience two crushing losses at once, the death of our remaining parent and the end of our family life.

In families that manage to stay together, the older brother or sister may be confronting responsibility for his or her younger siblings and be propelled into the role of parenting at an early age. The older sister of one of my students found herself facing the care of her four younger siblings while she was trying to finish school and handle her own grief at the loss of her parents. In taking up this responsibility, she found herself in a very lonely position. Once she had taken up guardianship of her siblings, she found that she had lost her relationship with them as brothers and sisters.

Such new demands may lead us to postpone or minimize our own grief. And while we may feel very strongly about the importance of keeping the family together and may feel proud of what we are doing, we may still resent the heavy burden we have to bear. If we are in this situation, we may need to make a special effort to remember the importance of our own lives. Perhaps we are trying to finish school or we may be in the midst of a relationship that might lead to marriage. It may be difficult to arrange our priorities, but it's helpful to remember that we may not be able to care for others if our own lives need attention.

Even if we have no responsibility for our siblings, it may still feel as if our lives seem less important after the death of our parents. Because we have lost the emotional support and the motivating presence of our parents, we may have to devote extra effort to keeping up our ambition to finish college or to find a job which really challenges us. One of my students who had lost both parents attended her classes only sporadically and eventually left school although she had great promise and although facing the working world without an education would make her life more difficult. The loss of parents leaves us with a diminished self-esteem and it is only too easy to settle for choices that are much less than we deserve.

Being left with a single parent has its own particular problems. Perhaps our mother died and we are suddenly thrust into the role of caring for our younger siblings and doing household chores. One of my students was faced with caring for her teenage siblings after her mother died. She resented the fact that they rebelled against her efforts, and even though her father was a loving presence, the demands of his job left her with too much responsibility for her age.

Perhaps we felt closer to the parent who died than to our surviving parent, or perhaps the parent who died smoothed over the differences we had with our other parent. We may be faced with conflict and with a difficult competition. Our surviving parent may want to interpret our deceased parent's wishes for us and we may disagree. The discord which had been softened by our father's or mother's presence now comes to the fore, strengthened by the pain of the death. We may be feeling very resentful at our surviving parent and also guilty about this resentment. It's helpful to turn to outside support when we are faced with such a complex situation.

It's not unusual for the surviving parent to turn to us for support and comfort. We may find ourselves taking care of our parent and neglecting our own needs. Like Jeremy, we may feel that our parent's grief is greater than our own. Even if our parent does not turn to us for comfort, we may feel obliged to help make up for our parent's loss. "I try to call as often as possible and visit often, but my mother seems so lost," a young woman confided. When I told her that while her mother appreciated her efforts no one expected her to try to replace her father, she seemed relieved. Sometimes we can't fix things and that's all right. We can also act as a parent towards ourselves and see ourselves as deserving of attention.

The emotions we experience after the death of a parent may overwhelm us and we may wish to push them away. We may feel angry at the disruption of our lives, at our abrupt passage into the responsibilities of adulthood. We may be angry at our friends for having parents, for being able just to have a good time while we are struggling with our own sorrow and a difficult home situation. We may even be angry at the parent who died and left us. Or we may feel a more diffuse resentment that may surface in a general irritability.

What seems the most trying, as Sue points out in her narrative, is that there are no guidelines for the sorrow we feel. We don't know how long or how intensely we should grieve because we have had such limited experience with death. Perhaps we remember grieving for the death of a grandparent when we were young. But nothing has prepared us for the storm of emotions we feel when a parent dies.

If we are a young adult, we are concerned with our image, with what others think of us as we try to make a place for ourselves in the world. Too often we are afraid of being self-pitying in our grief. Jeremy was afraid of his own sadness, that it would not be manly. He also experienced the very real fear of losing control.

We often confuse sadness with self-pity and try to deny these feelings. We may also feel that our own sadness is of less significance than that of our surviving parent. While it's normal to feel this way about ourselves, it's helpful to remember that everyone's sadness is unique. We are entitled to our feelings and to express them in a way that seems comfortable for us. Perhaps we may want to withdraw to the privacy of our own room to shed those tears or we may want to just get in the car and drive or take a long walk by ourselves.

Parents give us a sense of rootedness and provide us with emotional support during key moments of our lives. Their love strengthens us in our daily lives even if we are only dimly aware of that love. Even if our relationship with our parent or parents was a troubled one, they were still the source of our identity and gave us a sense of belonging. When we lose a parent we are filled with loneliness and a sense of isolation. We are facing the world without a buffer or protector and we may feel very unsure of ourselves as we confront life.

It may seem as if this loneliness is invisible to others in our daily lives. We may feel that our friends who still have both parents take their good fortune and their security for granted. This loneliness and longing for our parents may surface when we least expect it. We may be out with friends having a good time when something reminds us of our loss and we may feel a fresh surge of grief.

Perhaps we missed our parent intensely the first year after he or she died and then were able to put that loneliness aside. However, the sadness may overwhelm us as we experience important events in our lives such as graduations and weddings. We may be surprised by the depth of our feelings after so much time has passed, but it is not unusual to experience these profound reactions at the key moments of our passage.

Like Sue, we may have strong anniversary reactions at the date of our parent's death or at the time of their birthday many years later. It's as if a wound reopened and we were faced with all the sadness and pain we thought we had put behind us. This is a reaction many people continue to have as time passes.

While there are support groups for many different kinds of loss, groups for those who have lost their parents are much rarer. On the other hand, we are apt to have close friends we can turn to who will support us and listen to us when we need to talk. With the high rate of failure of marriages, many of us will have friends who have lost parents through a divorce and who understand the pain of our loss. For those of us who feel comfortable talking, it's helpful to air our feelings with a trusted friend. Some of us who are more reserved may look for a shared activity such as a sport rather than conversation. A good friend who accepts us regardless of our moods can relieve our sadness.

Making contact with other members of our family, whether a

cousin or a great aunt may help give us the sense of belonging that our parent or parents used to give us. No one can ever replace our parents. However it is comforting to have a member of our parents' generation to turn to, whether to exchange letters or to visit with us from time to time.

When we lose a parent or parents, especially at a young age, we experience a sense of isolation that few of our friends may understand. Because we have been through so much, we may feel that we know a lot more about life than they do and perhaps we may feel that our experience has set us apart from our peers. Perhaps our friends' parents may go out of their way to be helpful to us, but we might not feel comfortable with this. It may seem difficult to explain to people that a parent is irreplaceable and that while we appreciate their attention, we might wish to keep our distance. But we can tell others that while we are grateful for their kindness, we have our own ways of doing things. Those who really care for us will understand and accept these feelings.

In time, we will feel proud of the distance we have covered. We may discover a new strength and self-reliance that we have acquired through the long and painful months and years. This may be a hard-won quality, but it is one that will serve us throughout our lives.

17 • Lost in a World of Couples

Anne:

You've got to come off it. You can't just be grief, grief, grief. There were a lot of people around, and that was good. The kids cried, but I would go off to be by myself if I were really going to let down. You're physically hit as if you had had a terrible disease and it's over, but you're weakened. I would go out for an hour and then I would have to come back. I would go to the office for a little and then I would have to rest. I didn't eat. Other people would probably eat too much. The dead person is still alive in your mind at that time. You're constantly saying, "But you're not here." You're constantly saying, "This is the first time it's spring without him." The first time you go to a party you say, "This shouldn't be."

That first year I was interior. It's a protective thing, like the outside of a pineapple to keep the sweetness. I had that sense, for me and my children, of "Keep it good and keep it nice. Act as if we are doing all okay. Let's not lie to ourselves." Getting through that first year was a very delicate feeling, like you have to take care of yourself, kind of what you feel like when you're pregnant. "Can't people see?" I said to myself when I was walking in an airport.

Other people say the wrong things. I'm not a mean person. I accept that. I understand. I think that probably a lot of people aren't very nice. The main thing I noticed was the feeling, "I won and you lost, Anne." They were taking a tally: "I still have my husband." It's there. It's there, in kind of a funny way, in the things they want to give you and do for you. That this happened to you means that it passed them by. That's why they avoid you in the store. You go to buy bacon and they turn away. They are ill at ease because it's such a big bad thing to have to talk about death when someone is buying bacon. They say, "How are you doing, Anne?" They want to hear the soap opera effect, they want to revel in this.

Pity is a poisoned sweetness. Pity is one guy is up on the pedestal and the other is lying on the floor and the one on the pedestal says, "Here, poor thing, have a raisin, have a grape." When you stand up and are even with everyone else it's like you have won the battle of the bulge and that scares everyone. They act weird. Many people have written me off.

I met someone I had known long ago. Death takes someone you love away from you and then society says, "Don't you dare do it, and you can't have any more or you're bad." You need someone you're at ease with. It was something for me to think about and I was very surprised at how adolescent I was about it. It kept my mind, that loving part of me busy. It didn't compensate. It's okay to use your right hand if your left hand isn't working. Of course, he's a good friend. That time everything was at high sensibilities, like playing the violin.

There's a great deal of interest in the sexual situation of a woman like me. There are men that want to take care of the fact that you need to have that because you don't have that anymore. I could have married that childhood friend. It wouldn't have been the choice that it would have been with all of my marbles intact, though he was a love. There's the "who's going to marry her and take care of her" stuff, especially towards a feminine woman. I'm not the gym-teacher type, so people do want to take care of me. I like the taking care. It's very nice. But it's nicer than the real fact of letting them take care of your physical needs. You go from being a married woman to a time-warp, to the day before you got married, adolescence. There was certainly nothing else in between. I was a neophyte. If someone asked me about my love life, I wouldn't know how to talk that way. I was brought right back to my graduation at 1962, as a girlish woman. Right now, I'm probably running about twenty-eight years old.

With the kids it was letting them see that the rest of their lives wasn't gone. No way were we going to have Bobby the man of the family. I think we've done good by letting every other fact of our lives stay the same. They think maybe Mom will be gone, the house will be gone. We did move a year and a half later but it was our joint decision; the house was too big and it made sense.

For generations women have been taught that they take care of people who are really outside the action. I've learned to come out of that. All the skills that women learn to be indirect could be put to straightforward use. They have not taken a risk. They're in a safe place. You must risk loss to gain. Widowed women are perceived as children. That weakens someone. If you help someone over every bump then that person cannot grow. It is a time that you should buy all the help you can and you take the help that's healthy that you can get. The woman/child thing is very heavy when it's given with love. I would like to please other people, but I need to take care of myself first and when I forget to do that it's wrong. Unfortunately, the most difficult road that you see ahead of yourself in the first year is the one that you should follow. It's easier to go to Grandma's and cry, but it's not quite as good for your mental health. I'm a much better person than I was.

Eric:
When the shock and numbness wears off, then the real grief and sadness comes. It's been two years and a few months and it's just getting better. It feels like a long time. The changes are almost impossible at first.

It took me a month to cry. After that, it's all I did. It would be very hard for me to believe that men don't cry. I guess people do repress their emotions. I've never been a big crier and I probably haven't cried at all since the age of twelve.

I started looking for a group right away, but most groups disband during the summer. It was just as well because groups don't want people who can't objectify their experience. You're still under shock and you're still too numb to talk about it.

I'd wake up in the morning and I'd have this weight on my chest. And I'd think I have to get up despite it, and then I would think, "Why?" If I had one meeting during the day, even for a cup of coffee at four o'clock, that was what I built my day around. I cried about three times during the day.

It was something Diane had taught me to do. We had had a chance to talk about that stuff. She sort of led me along towards her own death.

An elderly man who had been married for fifty-two years and was recently widowed exclaimed, "There's only one word I can think of to describe what it's like and it's L-O-S-T. I feel lost!" Others have described widowhood as stepping on a train, getting accustomed to the ride, and then being thrown off in a place that's unrecognizable.

The loneliness that overwhelms us after the death of a spouse is one of the biggest issues we have to face as time passes. The death of our spouse ended a relationship, yet we may still feel very strongly connected to that person. We may still reach out for them in the middle of the night or we may wake up with a keen sense of their absence. However, after a year or so, the fact of that absence is very clear to us. We know that things won't change, that we can't reverse events.

As time passes after the death of a spouse, we face our daily life without the experience of intimacy. When a spouse, or a partner in a heterosexual or homosexual relationship, or a lover dies, there is no longer anyone to share the events of our daily lives. There is no one to fix meals for or to prepare them for us, no one to comfort us and to cushion the countless irritations we encounter at work and in our other relationships. We may miss being touched and held. If we are younger when we lose our spouse, we may experience sexual frustration and desire. Our home which was once a retreat from the world is no longer a shelter but perhaps a place to escape from.

Not all marriages involve companionship. But even those which may have involved just a sharing of household routines and daily lives are a source of well-being and purpose. When I was young, the wife of an elderly neighbor died suddenly. Although the marriage was characterized by seeming distance rather than an intense sharing, the husband spent the months afterwards as if he were adrift, taking his meals at odd hours, sleeping on the living room couch and ultimately moving to another state to be closer to his daughter and her children.

In marriages where there is an intense sharing of intimate lives and a strong companionship, the adjustment period is especially difficult. Losing a spouse out of this kind of marriage is losing one's best and most trusted friend. It may seem as if we will never be able to find someone like our spouse and that we will have to spend the rest of our days in a state of longing and loneliness.

Men and women may experience this loneliness in different ways. It may be especially difficult for men who have had traditional marriages to return home after a day's work. They may go out just to avoid the long hours of solitude. Finding new companions may be a way to cope, while women may spend more time dealing with the feelings of being lonely and may take more time to look for new friends.

Older people may suffer more acutely from loneliness, and problems with health and mobility may compound their sense of isolation. For many, the stress of grief creates a vulnerability to illness. Research has shown that many people suffer from illness during the first year of widowhood. My uncle, who lost his wife when he was seventy-five suffered from a series of illnesses in that first year as he faced the prospect of the rest of his life without my aunt. For the elderly, there is no future in which to find a new companion and no stretch of time for the long process of healing.

When a homosexual person loses a partner the loneliness and isolation is heightened by the fact that the relationship wasn't legitimized and his or her grieving may be unrecognized. There are more difficulties in finding a support group and in finding understanding in the workplace, and more difficulties in reaching out for new friends. Typically, the bereaved will first check out whether it's okay to talk about their loved one when they are seeking supports and their pain may be compounded with concern about social stigmas. One's vulnerability is heightened by the possibility of rejection.

Besides intimacy, marriages also involve a division of labor within the family. As survivors we are faced with a whole set of new and unfamiliar tasks in addition to our accustomed ones. A man who must face the burden of raising children alone will have to face the immediate problems of finding adequate childcare while he is at work. Perhaps his wife had planned her schedule around the childrens' needs and now he must make special arrangements for transportation, for the time after school before he returns from work, for the times when they are on vacation or ill. He may have to travel for his work or his hours may make this adjustment especially troublesome. As single parents, we may find that the demands of family leave us little time for attention to our own pain and sadness.

A widow may find that she not only has the burden of raising children by herself but also the burden of supporting the family. Perhaps she had stayed home to take care of the children before and now has to face the job market when her self-esteem is low. Because of the gains of the womens' movement, there are now a number of organizations which specialize in helping women enter the job market and this is a good time to turn to one of them.

Taking care of younger children may be especially trying. We may feel too exhausted to get up and get them ready for school in the morning or we may be irritable and worn out from work when they come home. Our children will be grieving in their own ways. Perhaps they may act up at school and at home trying to get our attention and reassurance.

They will be greatly affected by the way we mourn. If we are open in expressing our sadness, they will be encouraged to talk and cry over their deceased father or mother. They can also be a source of great comfort. The twelve-year-old daughter of a recently widowed friend put her arms around her mother and held her while she wept as she was preparing dinner. This was the time her husband usually came home and her daughter understood her tears and wanted to be close.

Because of the demands of our lives at this time, it is not always possible for us to be the kind of parent we would like to be. We may be struggling with our dual roles as nurturer and financial support when we are least able to. It's helpful to remember that we are doing the best that we can and to recognize the ability of children to understand.

Both men and women are faced with unfamiliar tasks in the management of a household. Although today many younger couples share chores, men in more traditional marriages may be baffled by cooking and laundry or by shopping. An elderly friend of mine who was widowed developed a whole series of recipes that he could prepare once a week for the entire week, but not everyone is that inventive. Women will need to contact repair people, and take care of the finances. How to get good advice without being patronized is apt to be an issue and we may be feeling unequal to these new demands.

In the long run, we will acquire a new sense of competence and independence, but the path to these feelings is a difficult one. It's helpful to be as tolerant as possible with ourselves and not to take on too many new demands. Solving one problem at a time, living one day at a time is more than enough at this stage of our lives.

Not only do we face new tasks and roles in our immediate family, but the death of a spouse also affects our relationships within the extended family. If we are a young widow or widower, we may have to face the well-intentioned but intrusive behavior of our parents or in-laws. Perhaps our parents will try to cheer us up when we feel like being alone with our sadness, or perhaps they will try to intervene in the decisions we make.

If we are a young widow or widower our in-laws might misunderstand our desire for companionship and disapprove when we begin to date or to go out. Although we know that we can never replace our loved one, they might interpret our renewed interest in a relationship as a betrayal. It's helpful to remember that our needs are important and that a renewed interest in friendship and dating is a sign of healing. A widowed friend of mine learned how to say, "Thank you, I love you for your thoughts," and then to go quietly forward with her own plans.

As older widows or widowers we may face the disapproval of our adult children when we make new friends and begin a social life of our own. A middle-aged widower experienced friction with his adult sons when he started seeing women and going out frequently. He was able to tell them that while he did all he could while their mother was alive, he felt it was time for him to turn his attention to other things. He was convinced that someday they would understand. Some of the discomfort his sons felt with their father's new lifestyle stemmed from their own grief over the loss of a parent. If possible, it's best to keep the channels of communication open and give our children an opportunity to understand our feelings as well as to air their own views.

While it may be easier for widowers to begin a social life after the loss of a spouse, it may be harder for them to keep close contact with their adult children. In a more traditional marriage, the mother may have been the center of the family, inviting the children and their spouses to the house for special occasions and telephoning them to keep in touch with their lives. However, not all men are comfortable with this role. It may have been the wife who kept lists of birthdays and special days to remember. A widower in this situation might begin a new tradition of taking the family out for a meal or a movie from time to time. While the children may miss the old traditions, they will also learn to value these new times together.

If we are an older widow we may may find that our adult children may wish to become involved in decisions about our life. We might be confused and not know what would be best for ourselves given our changed circumstances. Perhaps what our children are saying about our housing or living arrangements sounds good to us. However, it's best not to rush into any changes until we feel that we are ready for them. Much as we may wish to please our children, in the long run, we are the only ones who can judge the timing for changing our way of life.

Perhaps we were close to our husband and we did most things together while he was alive so that we seemed to be very self-sufficient. It might be difficult for our friends and our families to realize that we have very real needs at this time. There is nothing wrong with asking for advice or help. We may not be used to turning to our children or other relatives but the worst that can happen is that they might turn us down. The best is that they might actually welcome a chance to help and were just waiting for us to open that possibility.

When we lose a spouse we not only experience changes in our status within the family but in the broader community as well. We may already be feeling a diminished sense of self-worth because of our loss and this may be heightened by the way we are now perceived by society. We face the world as a changed person and the world also looks at us differently, perhaps with fear or pity, and we may find ourselves on the margins of society.

While our spouse or partner was alive, we may never have given a second thought to our leisure activity or social life. We were used to doing things with a partner, whether the routines of shopping on the weekend or just deciding to take in a movie one evening. Now we have to make plans for social outings and we find that we need to contact people well in advance if we would like to go out. We may resent the effort it takes to have a social life.

Perhaps the people we were friendly with as a couple no longer invite us and our friends withdraw just when we feel we need them most. We may be angry at others for not inviting us over or thinking of us and we may just be angry at others for still having a partner while we are alone. Like Anne, we may feel lost in a world which seems to be made just for couples.

Even if our friends continue to invite us and want to spend time with us, we may feel uncomfortable with them, like a fifth wheel or an outsider. Perhaps we feel uneasy with longstanding friends and we can't really pinpoint the source of our unease. We are experiencing so many changes in our lives at this time that it's normal to feel discomfort in our old situations.

If we have been left with young children to care for, we may experience a keen sense of social isolation. All of our time may be taken up with our work and with childcare, leaving us little opportunity to be with other adults or to think of our own needs. Depending on our financial circumstances, this period of very real isolation may last for a number of years until the children are more self-sufficient. We may feel that we owe our children our undivided attention and that we should compensate for the fact that they now have only one parent. However, the chances are that our children will welcome a social opportunity that refreshes us and lifts our spirits even if it means we are away from them for an evening or a weekend.

As time passes in the grieving process we may experience a new growth along with our pain. We are assailed by so many conflicting emotions at this state that it may be difficult to perceive the fact of our growth. Despite the loneliness and anguish, we do acquire new perspectives and new strengths. As Anne points out in Chapter 24, it's helpful to think of this new period in our lives as filled not only with longing but with the opportunities of a blank page. This might be the time to make new friends and discover new interests.

A friend of mine who was widowed at an early age found her comfortable suburban setting to be limiting. Everyone seemed to have similar interests and lifestyles. She decided to host foreign students from a nearby college for weekends and holidays, a solution that gave her an opportunity to grow as well as an opportunity to express the giving side of her nature which had been focused on her husband. For the students, it was a welcome break from dorm life and a chance to share their culture with Americans.

While we may have experienced the hurt of being ignored by our old friends, we may also have the discovery of making new friends. As Anne points out, there is a special delight in finding that we are liked and admired in new settings. Living as part of a couple, while comfortable and secure, may not have allowed us the opportunity to test ourselves in a variety of social situations. It may be frightening to enter a new social setting with a new identity, but it's also affirming when we receive a very positive response.

Perhaps it seems as if our life is in turmoil as we change our daily routines and perhaps our work. We are not only coping with our sorrow, but experiencing the difficulty of learning new roles, new ways of being. Out of this seeming chaos may come new affirmations, perhaps a strengthening of some friendships, a loss of some relationships, but eventually a new life, one which we have built for ourselves.

All of this takes time. We may need some hours or periods of the day when we are just by ourselves, either taking a walk or simply daydreaming in our own living-room. It may seem as if we are doing nothing or that we are unproductive, but this is a good way to get in touch with ourselves, to plumb our own interests and discover our goals. For single parents, this time may be very hard to find. Perhaps a long bath at the end of the day, or listening to music while the children are in bed or watching television may be a way of finding some privacy.

We may experience pressure from our extended families or our friends to resume our activities and "get back into the swing." We may even pressure ourselves to return to a normal pace and schedule. In our achievement-oriented society, it's easy to feel guilty about "wasting" time. However, we can think of this private time as part of the healing process. So much of the work of grieving is invisible that we may be apt to ignore the toll it takes on us.

We need time to think about ourselves and where we are going. Grieving is a very self-regarding phase of our lives. As former spouses and also as parents, it may be difficult to allow ourselves this focus on self, but it is necessary not only to help us move to a new place but also to be with our feelings. It is not unusual to experience periods of depression in the year or years after the death of a spouse.

It's not only difficult to go through our daily lives without our partner but also to find a reason for living. When our spouse was alive, we may have had some very sustaining positive reinforcement from him or her. Perhaps our spouse made us feel special or important. Now, we are no longer at the center of someone's life. We may feel a low self-esteem. Perhaps our friends and our family are eager for us to "cheer up." However, these periods of depression are normal in the months after we are widowed, and there is nothing wrong with slowing down when these feelings assail us.

In losing a spouse or a partner we have not only lost the foundation for our daily life and our family, but also our dreams and our hopes for the future. Perhaps we had made plans for the children and we face experiencing the crucial events in their growth by ourselves. We may have hoped to give them special opportunities for their education or we may have looked forward to doing things together as a family. Although we can never replace our spouse, we may discover a close friend who would be pleased to attend the graduations, the Bat Mitzvah, or the confirmation of our children with us. Or we may share these moments with another person who has experienced loss.

Perhaps we made plans for the time when our children would be grown. Or perhaps our spouse was a busy executive and we were looking forward to retirement in order to be together. Our spouse's death may leave us with the sense that we have wasted time, that we could have done things together while we still had each other. Ultimately this might lead us to a reexamination of our time and values. Instead of waiting for certain things to happen, we might decide to live more spontaneously.

The husband in an older couple died a year before the retirement they had been anticipating. They had planned some renovations of their home and a long vacation. His widow did eventually carry out the renovations and this gave her a certain satisfaction, but she was left with a sense of having been cheated.

If we were younger when our spouse died, we may experience a double loss, of our mate and also of the children we planned to have. People may try to comfort us by reminding us that we are still young and will have an opportunity to remarry and start a family. However, the future we dreamed of included children with the person we loved and we may feel robbed of memories as well as of our dreams.

As widowed persons we experience profound changes in identity in the months and years after the death of a spouse. A woman changes from being a wife, to a widow, to a single woman. A man changes from being a husband, to a widower, to a single man. In this growth process we move from a self-perception of being a half without a partner to a perception of ourselves as a single person. Between these two states is an uncomfortable period in which we may feel neither married nor single. We may feel guilty about dating because we may still feel a strong attachment to our spouse. Perhaps we feel that we are betraying him or her if we decide to start a new relationship.

As younger widows and widowers we may be concerned with finding sexual satisfaction. We may experience a strong desire to be touched and to touch, to feel a physical closeness again. Or we may simply want to express that loving part of ourselves. We may experiment with new partners and encounter some disappointments along the way.

Dating may be difficult for us and we may feel awkward. As Anne points out, we go from being a married person into a time warp, to the time before we got married. We may feel like an adolescent again. We may be afraid of saying the wrong thing, experience all the insecurities of beginning a new relationship. It's difficult to go back to the early stages of a relationship if we've lived with a longstanding relationship. While some of us may find it challenging or exciting, some of us may be hesitant about beginning the long process of acceptance and compromise which precedes the attainment of mutual respect.

In the beginning we may find ourselves comparing our dates to our former spouse. If we have experienced troubling patterns in our marriage we might worry about repeating these in a new relationship. If we had a good relationship with our deceased spouse we may feel very differently from our divorced friends who may have chosen to end their marriages and who may be eager to start a new relationship. It's not unusual to idealize our spouses in the months and years after their death. An older friend of mine who was widowed in middle age told me, "It's never the same, never as good."

There are special difficulties in being widowed when one is young and attractive. Men may consider women fair game and assume that we are looking for new experiences. One of my older students was widowed when she was only thirty-five. Despite having small children, she found herself the very unwilling recipient of the attentions of the single men in her town, and found it difficult to protect herself. "People make assumptions and misunderstand my need to keep a distance," she told me.

If we were older when our spouse died, we may take more time to find a new partner. We may seek options other than marriage, such as having a relationship with a younger or older person, or dating a number of people at once, or simply living with someone else. It seems to be easier for men to find new partners because there are more women than men in most age groups.

Some of us may find living alone fulfilling after many years of catering to the needs of someone else. We may find that we have acquired a taste for making decisions about our daily lives. Also, we may have developed a strong groups of friends. There are many paths toward contentment.

In the long period after the death of a spouse, we may be

receiving a lot of advice from well-intentioned friends and family about how to conduct our life. As time passes and we traverse the difficult and lonely months without our spouse, we are making many decisions about home, work, childcare, and friendship. It may seem as if our lives are chaotic and that we are reeling from one event to another without guidance. But from these decisions and from our profound experience with sorrow, we have also experienced growth. From this growth may come the steadying and peaceful realization that the truest source for our long-term goals and our more immediate decisions must come from within ourselves.

18 • Living with the Absent Child

Phil:

The fact is that you grieve in such different ways and you don't understand what is going on in the other person's head. You might feel a little better one day and want to try to do something else and your spouse may feel quite differently. You have a really hard time expressing your feelings. Sometimes there are feelings of bitterness, sometimes of sadness. They don't just come together and sometimes you just try to deal with it privately. I think there's a real danger there. You're so caught up in your own self and dealing with your own emotions that you have a tendency not to look around you. The children miss her and they need your help and they're looking at you and your wife to see if everything's going to be all right and they need to see that it's going to be all right. Sometimes we had a hard time talking about it. Our little boy drew us out by asking about it a lot.

It had a really strong effect on my younger son who was only three at the time. He still talks about it a lot. It also had an effect on my older daughter who was only a year and a half older and was Jenny's best friend. She didn't talk about it but she manifested it. She was very fearful about things.

The first year or so you just basically try to survive, to get through the day. You experience a lot of different things. A lot of things, symbolic things, mean a lot to us, holidays, the change of seasons. The first day of spring means a warm day, a feeling that there's something happening to all of us. After that it feels exasperating. You feel worse. I can remember driving home one day in early March and having a very awful feeling about it. It's a nice day but it's really an awful day. It just heightens it, like Christmas. You're upset and you're bitter. You're out of control. The feeling of not being in control is not something that we're used to. You always face life with a certain amount of hope. No matter what happens to you and your family, there's always a way of overcoming, but this, there's no way of overcoming. The idea of hope isn't there. You can spin your wheels and try different things but they don't make any difference.

I'm more of an activist and I tend to resolve issues by going out and doing something about it but I couldn't do anything about this. It was much bigger than we were. We do think about it every day, but we do have some perspective, maybe, now. We have recognized that we are going to survive. You think about things in the beginning and you wonder if you are ever going to be able to work. You wonder if you are going to be able to interact and function in a professional way. You really have doubts about that. It's like learning to walk all over again.

You have a sensitivity to injustices, to inappropriate behavior, a lot more understanding, but not tolerance. Within a year or so afterwards I was in situations at work where I thought people's ethical behavior was inappropriate. You realize it if you put it in context with what's important in life. You have to deal with it. I felt stronger about things like that afterwards.

I presented a film I made about the grieving process to a group of women in my network one evening. During the discussion after the film, a woman stood up, and in a hushed voice told us that her eighteen-year-old daughter had drowned the previous summer. She moved like a person who had experienced a serious illness. Her suffering was evident in her face and the way she held herself. It was as if her body mirrored the pain she was feeling.

Losing a child is losing a part of ourselves. As bereaved parents, we believe that a child's death is the worst kind of loss that anyone can possibly endure. We may feel that we are beyond comfort and beyond hope. We may even wonder if we will survive the tragedy of losing a child.

We may find it difficult to communicate with others about our loss because of its very depth. The fact that the woman who lost her daughter was able to stand up and speak about it was a tremendous step in her healing process. After the discussion a number of people went up to her and put their arms around her. Because she shared her story in such a personal way, the people around her were able to draw close to her and she was able to receive comfort. But afterwards we were all going home to our lives while she was left with her terrible burden.

After the loss of a child, our friends may try to comfort us, but we know that after their visit or their phone call, they will return to a home with an intact family or with their child waiting for them while we face what seems like an endlessly bleak and lonely future. It may seem as if the only people who can really understand what it feels like to have one's very being torn apart are parents who have suffered similar tragedies.

A child is part of our own being, physically and emotionally. As our child grows up we continually see traits of ourselves and members of our family in that child. We may be surprised and amused to discover traces of our own personality in our child's reaction to events. Or perhaps our child has the same color of eyes or hair and walks with a similar gait. When we bury that child, it may seem as if we are burying part of ourselves.

A child is not only a part of our past, sharing our genetic makeup and certain family traits, but he or she may also be the center of our hopes and dreams, especially our dreams for the future. We may have spent the growing years planning for the child's education, trying to arrange our lives so that his or her unique talents could develop in the best possible way. We may have started to save for their college education.

If our child was already an adult when he or she died, we may have experienced the pride of seeing his or her potential begin to unfold. Perhaps the child was just beginning a successful career or a family. A friend of mine lost her son when he was just beginning his career as a musician. He never really had a chance to develop his considerable promise. One of my colleague's sons was killed in an automobile accident as he was driving to graduate school. We will always wonder about the potential of our deceased child, the talent and personality that will never unfold.

If our child was a young adult when he or she died, we have not only lost our child, but also the grandchildren we will never have. Perhaps we have lost a son or daughter who had a young child and the spouse of our child remarries. We may find ourselves in the difficult position of arranging for visits with someone who we believe has replaced our deceased child. The couple may want to keep their distance from us until they feel more comfortable with each other. They may wish to begin their new life together with as few complications as possible.

It is easy for misunderstandings to develop in such a situation and we might wish to seek help in communicating with each other. Certainly this is a difficult time to have to face new realities and a time when we may want to seek advice from counselors or other parents who have faced similar situations.

Whether we already have grandchildren from our deceased child, or we will never have the opportunity of grandchildren, we may feel as if we had lost our whole future and the perpetuation of our family. There is a very real sense in which children represent our immortality. Not all of us imagine our child fulfilling dreams that we ourselves were unable to realize, but most of us think of our children as our eternity.

There are parents who have lost more than one child. A middle-aged couple I met lost both of their sons in an automobile accident. Another couple I interviewed had lost an infant child through illness and then lost another son in an accident when he was nineteen. There are no words that can describe the pain and suffering of multiple losses. Although both couples have not only managed to survive but to live fully, they bear the scars of their tragedy.

This feeling of lost potential or utter waste may come up again and again as we share life's events with our family and friends. When we attend the graduation or the confirmation of a cousin or a friend's child, we may think our child would be having this experience if he or she had lived. A friend of mine who lost a young daughter thinks of her continually as graduation approaches in the college where he is an administrator. He keeps thinking that if his daughter had lived, he would be attending this ceremony with her. Knowing that we will never witness the development of our child can be a source of renewed sorrow.

There are so many painful reminders of the child we lost. If our child was still in school when he or she died, the opening of school in September or the end of the semester in early summer may awaken our grief. So much of our family schedule is involved with our children that in the months after a child's death, we feel their absence keenly every day. We may find ourselves reaching for things our child may have liked when we are shopping at the supermarket. We may find it painful to prepare a meal, to scale down the portions, face his or her favorite foods.

Our home may still be filled with mementos of our child such as photographs, toys or trophies. Deciding what to do with the deceased child's room may be very difficult especially when there are other siblings. Some neighbors of mine who lost a daughter decided to keep her room the way it was before she died. The surviving siblings felt comfortable with this.

However, it is not always easy to make this kind of decision. The brother of a child who died of an illness wanted to take his brother's room and wear some of his clothes. It was difficult for his mother to negotiate with him about those things. She was torn. On the one hand, she knew she couldn't keep his things forever unused or on display and yet seeing them on her other son was painful.

It's normal to want to keep our child's favorite things. Keeping our child's room intact is a matter of personal timing. The time to change is when we feel a need to rearrange our life and move on.

Not only life's everyday events, but holidays and the mere changing of seasons may spark a return of our bitterness and sorrow. Holidays are a time when families gather together, a time when the memories of Christmases or Passovers we spent with our child may cause us deep pain. As Phil mentions, the return of spring after a long winter may fill us with a sense of futility and despair. As he points out in his narrative, the idea of hope isn't there any more.

We are not only deeply affected by the joyous holidays, but also by illness and death among our friends and acquaintances. At these times we may feel renewed grief for our own loss. At my aunt's funeral one of her best friends mourned not only her friend's untimely death, but the son she lost in the Algerian War many years ago.

We may have strong anniversary reactions when we reach the time of year our child died and these reactions may be with us for many years. Sometimes the anticipation of this period may seem as difficult as living through the anniversary itself. A friend of mine whose adult son died of cancer a number of years ago always experiences a renewed surge of grief as April approaches.

Some parents have found that commemorating the anniversary of a child's death in a special way helps them through this difficult time of year. Those of us who practice religion in a more traditional way may wish to have a special service in memory of the child. If we don't participate in an organized religion, we might want to design our own anniversary commemoration. Even though our child has died, he or she is still part of us. Spending an evening or an afternoon remembering that child and talking about him may be a source of great comfort.

If we have other children, especially teenage children, they might not wish to participate in anniversary events. Children grieve in different ways and some children may not want to talk about their feelings. They might be more comfortable with the choice of keeping their distance from these events. They might not wish to attend a service, but be perfectly willing to go to the dinner following.

As parents, we feel responsible for the well-being of our children. We expend so much of our energy and our lives trying to fulfill their needs and expectations that when a child dies, we are consumed with guilt. We feel as if somehow we should have been able to prevent that death, that we have failed as a parent. In the months after our child's death, we may think about all the things we might have done differently, or we may remember instances when we lost our temper or quarreled with our child.

If we had experienced conflict with our child, we may be placing too heavy a burden of blame on ourselves. Perhaps our deceased child was a teenager and we find ourselves focusing exclusively on our memories of angry exchanges and misunderstandings. It's helpful to remember the mutual and unspoken love beneath these quarrels. Sometimes expressions of frustration are the only way to communicate our love and concern. Sometimes we may have to forgive ourselves to be able to move on to a clearer view of our relationship.

A woman I interviewed was very candid about her relationship with her deceased daughter. "We were very different," she said, "and we had difficulty with each other." Then she added, "If she had lived, that would not have changed." She told me this with great peace because she had resolved that relationship and was able to distinguish between the deep love she felt for that child and the differences in personality between them.

Although they have no bearing on the death of our child, we may review our own shortcomings or behavior and see a connection where there is none. As parents, we seem so powerful in our responsibility for our child's daily life that it is all too easy to believe that through some fault of our own, our child died. Perhaps we prayed intensely during our child's illness or in the hours or days after an accident and our child was not spared.

The fact that other people may avoid us and that many people find it difficult to talk to a bereaved parent may contribute to our loss of self-esteem and our own feelings of failure. We may feel as if we have been marked or that we are being punished. In our anguish, we may search for a reason for such a senseless tragedy and because we are at the center of our child's life it is all too easy to blame ourselves. Try to remember that while we are able to control certain events in our lives, we have no power over matters of life and death, nor are we responsible for tragedies that strike those we love.

We are more likely to blame ourselves for a child's death through accident than through disease. Most parents who must watch a child die through an illness such as cancer or heart disease are less apt to blame themselves because they can see that illness as something over which they have no control. When our child dies because of a long illness, we are also victims as we suffer through that child's agony.

However, if our child died through an accident, it's all too easy to feel as if our own decisions where the cause. A friend of mine whose son died in an automobile accident was tormented for a long time because his son was killed crossing the street after school while a babysitter was taking care of him. He felt that if he and his wife had not been at work, their son would never have died. A good friend or a counselor will remind us that we have no power to control such events and that these tragedies do not represent a judgment against us.

When our child dies, we not only feel a sense of having failed as parents, but we are overwhelmed by our powerlessness, our inability to control events. As parents, we can provide the best schooling for our children. We can seek out ways to fill their leisure time. We may believe that money and the hard work which procured it and which can buy the best medical care can also shield us from death.

We react to our feeling of helplessness by anger, rage and despair. In our society, where the nuclear family has replaced the extended family as protector of the children, there is great emphasis placed on parenting. When a child dies, we feel our impotence as parents. We may also feel angry at all those other parents whose children are still alive and who have no idea of the depth of our pain.

Men are apt to feel this sense of impotence very keenly because many of them are accustomed to bend events in their work and because they are more apt to see their efforts bear fruit in concrete ways. Regardless of the socio-economic level of fathers, they often see themselves as responsible for the welfare of their families. A mother may see herself responsible for a child's health and may feel frustrated at her inability to save her dying child despite her devoted efforts. Both parents suffer from the feeling of loss of control.

If the nuclear family bears the burden of parenting alone, it also is under pressure from the high expectations our society places on a marriage. It is the source of much fantasy about togetherness, about two people becoming one and sharing everything in their lives. When a tragedy such as the death of a child strikes us, people expect that as a married couple we will draw strength from each other.

However, quite the opposite may happen. Studies reveal that the majority of marriages will suffer from serious strain after the death of a child. For those marriages that are already in difficulty, such a death is often a strain that is too much to bear and the marriage may dissolve. After the death of a child, a couple is squarely in front of the fact that grieving is a solitary process. Everyone grieves in his or her own way and the grieving process itself is subject to abrupt shifts as we move from despair to periods of calm and back again.

Perhaps we had expected support from our spouse and now we find that we are moving through grief in different ways. This can be a devastating discovery. If our child has died after a long illness, we may have been able to draw strength from each other during that trying period. After the death, because each one of us is bowed under his own grief, we may not be able to comfort each other or live up to the expectations we placed on each other.

Perhaps our husband had always been a tower of strength through the trying times in our lives. It may be very difficult to understand his inability to be a support while he is grieving and he may resent this expectation. The reverse may be true if the wife had always acted as the steadying force through the shoals of their life together. Perhaps as a woman we may feel more free to express our sorrow through tears and conversation. Our husband may be trying to keep himself together in order to get through his day and may resent what appears to him as an attempt to pull him down. Our up days and down days may not coincide, causing further friction.

In our culture, men are expected to behave with stoicism and to be silent when confronted with disaster. Therefore, men may not feel comfortable talking about their sorrow or weeping openly. A wife may conclude that he feels less deeply than she does. The husband may be unsettled by a wife's insistence that they discuss the dead child and talk about their grief.

Sometimes, in our anger and despair, we may blame our husband or wife for the death of our child. Especially in the case of an accident, both of us may be tempted to point at the other for not being more careful, for letting the child cross the street, or go out on a date, or move to another city. Perhaps each of us had different parenting styles, one of us more easygoing and casual, the other very protective. In such a situation it might be easy to slip into mutual blame and create images of each other that might be difficult to live with. In our need to find an answer to that question which can never be answered, we may lash out at our spouse. This is the time to seek counseling.

It might be helpful for each of us to seek separate supports or to seek counseling as a family after the death of a child. A woman who is more expressive and who feels the need to talk about her deceased child may find comfort in talking with friends or with her own counselor. A father may find he needs time to be alone with himself. Scaling down our expectations and demands on each other at this time will help ease the burden on our marriage.

Today, many of us are in our second or third marriages and the child we lose may be the child we had with our first husband or wife. As a bereaved mother or father, we may feel that our spouse just can't understand how we feel and we may find ourselves resenting him or her. Perhaps we were the parent who did not get custody of the child and our grief may be overladen with feelings of guilt that may complicate our new marriage. It's not unusual for tension to arise between spouses at a time like this. It may be wise to seek the help of a counselor in order to prevent our marriage from deteriorating under such pressure.

Many of us may feel that while we are grieving over a dead child and trying to deal with the grief of our spouse, this is not a time for pleasure or for socializing. This is precisely the time to be especially kind to ourselves, to find a form of entertainment that both partners feel comfortable with, whether taking in a movie or spending the evening with close friends. Nor is this the time to deny ourselves the pleasures of intimacy in a way that accounts for both partners' feelings.

We may find that we have made a new set of friends after the death of our child. There may be people who know our situation and who are comfortable with us that we can turn to for a quiet dinner at home or a night out. It's helpful to plan these moments of pleasure when both of us are feeling ready to socialize. They may seem like small things, but over a period of time they may lighten the burden of our daily life and help us on the road to healing.

If our deceased child had siblings, they will need our attention and comfort just when we may be least able to provide it. We may be so overwhelmed with our own sorrow that we can neither see their needs nor respond to them. Or perhaps we may think that we are doing a great deal for them, and yet our children may have a different perception of our response.

If as spouses we grieve in our own ways, this is especially true of parents and children. If we have younger children, they may want to know that everything is going to be all right in the family. Listening to their questions and answering them even though we ourselves have no answers to matters of life and death can help them. It's best to be as honest as possible in responding to them. For instance, if we tell a child that God wanted his sister or brother, or that death is like a long sleep, they will grow up feeling angry and distrustful of God, or being fearful of falling asleep. Sometimes, as in Phil's case, our children may draw us out by their questions. If they are unusually silent, it is we who must elicit their fears and anxieties.

Older children are apt to feel a special burden of guilt over a sibling's death. They may remember the times they quarreled or were jealous of their brother or sister. They may recall feeling anger or hatred toward their sibling and somehow feel that the death of that sibling was a form of judgment upon them. We may be able to help them through these feelings if we remind them that there is nothing wrong with a normal sibling rivalry and that there is no connection between any negative feelings they may have had and the death of their brother or sister.

If our surviving children are teenagers, they may want to express their feelings in private or with their peers. It's helpful to them if we respect their sense of privacy and also accept the fact that even though they are feeling a deep sorrow over the loss of their brother or sister, they are young and may want to participate in events such as dances or ball games with their friends.

Having lost a child, it's easy for us to feel protective of his or her surviving brothers or sisters. We may want to spare our children any further problems and therefore we make special efforts to become involved in their lives. With the best of intentions, we may be placing a burden on them. Real as our fears are for our children, this is not a good time to change our parenting styles.

Above all, this is not the time to place extra burdens on ourselves. We should feel free to weep openly at home even if we are afraid it will frighten our children. At best, they will learn that grown men and women feel pain and cry. Perhaps we will be able to have moments when we share our sorrow. Some friends of mine who lost a daughter have times when they reminiscence about her with her brothers and sisters and when they just cry together. If we were unable to do this in the early months after the death when our pain was just too great, we can always begin this sharing in the years to come.

One of the difficulties we face after the loss of a child is our reentry into society. People we were once friendly with may be avoiding us and we may also be meeting new people. How to respond when people question us about family depends upon the individual. Although in time, we learn to live with the loss of a child and to let go of our role as a parent to that child, our love for that person endures. Some people feel comfortable with saying that they have three children who are alive and one who died. Others may feel that it's not necessary to share this information in a more casual social setting.

However, the friends who knew us before our child's death may be experiencing great difficulties themselves. They may not know how to communicate with us and may hesitate to discuss our child for fear of causing us further pain. Although it's not easy, taking the initiative to talk about our child will ease the difficulty. Chances are that many of our friends have children of their own and like most parents, their conversation and attention is focused on family matters. If we are comfortable talking about our deceased child with them, they will feel free to talk about their own children and also about our child. Since there are no social practices to deal with this sensitive situation, they may have been waiting for a cue from us.

One of the discoveries that we make in the long months and years after the death of a child is that although we thought we could never move beyond the emptiness, we recognize that we're going to survive. We find that our family life continues and can be a source of deep satisfaction. This might be a time to make some important decisions about our life. Perhaps we want to move to a new house or a new town. Perhaps we may decide to have another child. Perhaps our marriage isn't working and we might feel that this is the time to end the marriage. We may find that we can continue our lives in new ways and even be helpful to each other despite the end of our marriage.

We find that although we still feel sorrow over our deceased child, we regain the energy we thought we would never retrieve and may discover new avenues for it. A friend of mine who lost both sons and who made his living by farming, joined a local theater group and found new outlets in both acting and writing. Another friend changed jobs and moved to a new town. A colleague of mine who lost her only child adopted a young boy of ten years old. Although her adopted child is very different from the brilliant child who died, he has been a source of joy to her and her husband. We can never fill the place our child had in our lives, but we can find new outlets for our emotions and our abilities. The loss of a child changes us profoundly, but as time passes, we find that it is once again possible to invest in life.

19 • *The Conspiracy of Silence: Living without a Sibling*

Jim:

I thought that I had worked it out with the help of friends, that I had come to some kind of acceptance of the death, that I had made a place for her in my heart and that I would now be able to move on. When I first felt that was last fall, five months after she died. A student at my university had committed suicide, a young girl I didn't know. But when she died, it was clear that she had had an impact on a number of students in the community. So one afternoon I found myself writing a letter to her parents to say how much I shared in their grief even though I didn't know their daughter, because I too had a sister who died very young and suddenly. I knew how difficult it was to experience something like that. A lot of friends and people who cared about me had helped me to come to understand that you can't measure the value of a life in time, that no matter how much time a person is here, their spirit and the effect they had on people continues. They live on in us. I felt this sense of peace that I hadn't felt in six months. And I felt that maybe that would be it and I would move on from there.

But in the beginning of summer, I started finding myself thinking a lot about it. Every time I would walk into my office, I would sit down to try and work on a paper but instead I would end up going back and looking at letters I had written to her when I was in college, or at things that I had collected after her death; a letter from this guy that she ended up going around the country with, the coroner's report, just reading the hard clinical file. Then I started thinking a lot about this plant that I had in my office that a couple of my colleagues gave me when she died. When I got this plant it became very important to me to keep it alive and I have, much to my pleasure. It has survived even though I don't know how to take care of plants. I spent most of the month of June trying to write down my feelings about this plant. When leaves would fall off I would think about fall, and how we played as kids and how it was difficult to deal with my parents. I started writing a poem about it.

I couldn't write my research but I would work on this poem. Again I thought I had reached a kind of mini-resolution, but in fact. . . this was really initiated by a note from my mother right after Mother's Day. She sent me a picture of my sister's gravestone and on it she had written, "Mother's Day, 1984." It wiped me out. And that's what she has always done, tried to make me feel so guilty, while at the same time caring about me. I don't think she realized what she was doing. That was the stimulus that brought me back to my feelings.

As July came, again I had done a lot of short-term represssion and found myself thinking about my sister's viewing and just about the cold hard shock of seeing her in that casket for the first time, how difficult it was to accept and how angry and hurt I felt.

Maureen:

After she died, I went down to the Cape with my cousin. We had a great time. Kids that lived in the neighborhood came down. We had fun just drinking and being crazy. I got away from everything. That was the most helpful thing I had, just getting away. I didn't have any wildness in high school, but I had it there and on the weekends when I went there.

When I went back to school I felt that everyone was feeling sorry for me and looking at me even though they probably weren't. I felt like they were saying, "Hey, there's the girl whose sister died." People acted as if nothing had happened. I wondered why life had to go on. Life at school had just seemed to go on. But for my sister, life was over.

I had this boyfriend. He was three years older than I was. I tried to tell him things, but he was no help whatsoever. He didn't understand and that was the worst of it, nobody understood.

I certainly was not myself. I was insecure about a lot of things. I lost a lot of friends. At fifteen you build a lot of friendships that you are going to have for the next few years at school. I didn't build a lot of friendships. The other kids had all these common experiences that I missed out on. I was never a bad kid and I think that was because I didn't want to upset my parents. If they said to be in at ten p.m. or at midnight on Saturday night, that was fine. I wouldn't rock the boat to upset them.

My mother believed that God did it. She believed that God took my sister because he wanted to have her near him. She could justify it. I'm not sure I can. I suppose the church gives you some way of justifying a thing like that. I think that peoople just die and that everybody's got their number. When it's up, it's up. It's fate. I never think about giving it a reason. The day she died was terrible for me.

My parents and I would talk about it. We would sit down, talking and crying. It was so hard. We'd sit at the table sometimes and say, "Do you remember when? . . ." and then we'd start crying. Then Christmas came. It was happy, but it was also very sad. Joan wasn't there. We tried to talk about how we felt. But what can you say? The tears just fill your eyes.

My mother asked me if I wanted to see someone to talk about it, but I never even thought about talking about it with somebody else. I felt that everybody had to deal with it in their own way. My mother took two jobs and worked sixty hours a week. That's how she dealt with it. I felt badly that she kept her mind so busy she couldn't think about it.

My father, I don't know how he dealt with it. He cried, but he would never really say anything.

When we think of the losses that are the most devastating in our lives, we may think of the loss of a spouse or of a child or parent. We rarely see the loss of a sibling as equally traumatic and therefore, sibling loss is not as likely to elicit sympathy or understanding. However, the death of a brother or sister strikes at the very heart of our own identity and may have an important impact on our relationship to our parents.

As siblings, our identities are shaped in relation to one another within the family structure. For instance, we may have been the more outgoing child, the one most likely to take risks, or we may have been the smarter child, the one who went to college. We may have been the sibling who always assumed the responsibility of caring for the younger members of the family. Or the reverse may have been true.

Perhaps, as the surviving brother or sister, we may have lost a sibling who was perceived as more talented or better looking. We may feel guilty that we were spared. Always, we ask ourselves why our sibling died rather than us.

Not only do we develop our identities in relation to our siblings, but these relations are also colored by our perceptions of parental attitudes towards ourselves. We carry these identities with us all of our lives so that even if we may live in widely separated cities or in different countries we still perceive ourselves in the sibling role.

Often, the empathy we feel for our siblings in early life is strengthened over the years. This is after all, potentially one of the longest relationships we will have in our lives. Even if we may lose contact with each other during our adult years, we still share childhood memories and carry with us the experience of shared family life, and critical life events, whether an illness, a move to a new place, or the experiences of holidays and vacations.

Given the fact that our identities are shaped in relation to each other, we are like foils for each other. We form part of a whole. After the death of a brother or sister, we feel within us that missing self. The middle-aged woman who lost her sister when they were both children will always see herself as a sister and feel the loss not only of her sister but of the self she was towards that sister. Although no person can ever replace another, widows or widowers may eventually remarry, but we cannot seek another sibling.

Although the loss of a sibling strikes at the very heart of our identity and affects us throughout our lives, we are apt to receive very little recognition for this loss from society. One of the most common experiences of those who have lost a brother or sister is the silence of the people around us. It's as if we take our cues from that silence and bury our own sadness within it. When I began this project, a number of people came up to me of their own accord to talk about their loss. Some of them were colleagues whom I had known for years without ever being aware that they even had a sibling in their past.

Because many of us may have lost a sibling when we were teenagers or younger we may still carry our childhood understanding of that tragedy with us. We may also carry our childhood feelings of guilt and responsibility. One woman I interviewed was in her fifties and yet her perception of the death and her own reactions to it were those of a twelve-year-old. She still felt all the ambivalence of her feelings toward her mother's reaction, still felt that sense of abandonment from parents who were sunk in their grief. For many of us the loss of a brother or sister continues to be an unresolved and unexplained event.

It helps to begin thinking and talking about this loss with our parents if they are still alive or with trusted friends or even to seek counseling. As we mature, we need an adult understanding of loss and we need to express our loss in a way that is meaningful to us. One woman I interviewed who had lost her sister fifteen years ago started a support group for people who had lost a sibling. It was a great relief for her to talk after all these years and she was also able to bring her own experience to bear for those who were newly bereaved.

As siblings we spend so much of our time together and so much of our life revolves around our family. Even if we quarreled a great deal, and that is normal, we may have thought of ourselves as allies before our parents. We may have drawn strength from our differences. We may have leaned on the more outgoing sister or brother and relied on them to deal with our parents. After the death of a sibling we may feel great loneliness. We have lost a peer and an ally and either a buffer against the world or someone we protected. We may carry this loneliness for many years.

Some of us may miss our deceased sibling so much that we find ourselves taking on some of their characteristics or trying to pick up the threads of his or her life. A woman I interviewed described herself as the shy and retiring one and her deceased sister as the one who was adventuresome, who always moved in a swirl of friends and projects. After her sister's death, she assumed her sister's identity, took on her personality. Another woman who had lost a sister joined the organizations her sister belonged to and kept up her sister's friendships.

In their own ways, each of these women tried to keep the essence of their sibling's personality. "It's been almost twenty-five years now and I don't think of her that often," one of them admitted. Her efforts to assume some of her sister's traits was a way of resolving her grief.

Losing a brother or sister is apt to bring changes in family behavior as well as changes in the family structure. When a sibling dies, we may become the only child and experience the burden of our parents' exclusive attention. We may feel that we must not only make up for the loss but be the best person we can for our parents' sake. Some of us may feel that we must remain geographically close to our parents, whether going to school close to home or taking a job or a home in the same city.

Some of us will want to move away from what seems like burdensome parental attention. Sometimes this can give us an opportunity to strengthen our own sense of self so that we can ultimately forge a better relationship with our parents. In some cases, we may want to stay close to home to help keep the family intact. A young woman who lost both her father and her brother in an airplane disaster decided to commute to college rather than live on campus. That solution gave both her mother and herself an opportunity to recreate a sense of family continuity.

The death of a child may change the patterns of coping that families develop over long periods of time. Perhaps the brother or sister we lost had been a negotiator on our behalf with either our mother or father. He or she may have been the one who communicated more easily with our parents or who seemed to have more in common with them. We may not only have lost a sibling but may also experience conflict and tension with our parent or parents once our sibling is no longer there to mediate. For some of us, this conflict may be so burdensome that we will seek relief through an early marriage or by leaving home.

If the sibling who died seemed to have an easier relationship with our parents or seemed to be more gifted than ourselves we may feel a sense of distance from our parents. This might be a distance that we perceive because they may be absorbed in their sadness and have little energy or emotion left for us. We might feel that they preferred our deceased sibling or that somehow they no longer care for us as much. Many people I interviewed told me that their parents were never quite the same after the loss. It is not unusual for parents to alter their behavior over long periods of time and for the family's ways of coping with events to change. We not only carry our own sorrow over the loss of a sibling, but also the strains of a new family situation.

Strains may develop within the family simply because adults and children have very different ways of expressing and responding to grief. If we are a teenager or a young adult, we may still be looking forward to important events like dances, ball games, and vacations with our friends. We may feel a very deep sorrow over our loss while wanting to continue with our lives. It's very helpful to enjoy our peers and be able to let off steam. However, this may create strains with our parents who might interpret our behavior as one of forgetting the loss. Our parents might misunderstand, but it's important for us to have some happy times in our lives.

If our brother or sister died when we were adults, we are also faced with complex family issues. Jim's mother turned her anger and despair on him just when he seemed to be moving through his own grief. In addition to coping with his own sorrow, he had to face the burden of his parents' difficulty with grieving and his younger sister's silence. On the other hand, if our deceased sibling was the center of the family, receiving everyone for holidays and for special occasions, and acting as the emotional support for our parents, we may find ourselves trying to fill that role.

If our sibling was married when he or she died we may have to deal with changed relationships throughout the extended family. Our sister or brother's spouse may remarry, yet we still have deep ties with our nieces and nephews. While we may welcome the remarriage we may feel some resentment towards the new partner who seems to be replacing our deceased sibling. There is a whole new family structure to be learned when we have the least energy and when we are absorbed with our own sadness.

A woman who lost her married brother felt that everyone saw his widow as the primary mourner. It seemed to her as if her brother's wife expected everyone to be there for her when she herself barely had the energy to survive. "It's another way of having my own grief ignored," she exclaimed.

Whether we face the death of a brother or sister when we are children or when we are adults, our own death suddenly becomes a possibility. When we lose parents, we lose the shelter from death that an older generation provides, as we become the older generation. When we lose a sibling, we are faced with our own vulnerability.

If a sibling who died was older we may fear our own mortality as we reach their age. Even if many years pass before we reach the age our sibling died, we still may have anxieties about our own health and mortality as we approach that particular time in our lives. A woman whose brother died the day after his forty-first birthday found herself experiencing considerable anxiety when she was approaching her own forty-first birthday even though it was ten years after his death. After the date passed, her uneasiness subsided. She needed to get past that point to have assurance about her own future. These feelings are widely shared by those who have suffered loss, and they are perfectly normal.

HOW WE CAN
HELP OURSELVES

When the waters of loss rose
I built an ark of words,
took two of every part of speech
and rode the flood.

After long buffeting
by wind and waves,
I dangled tentative lines
but didn't touch bottom.

Now the waters have receded:
I feel solid ground under my feet.
My words multiply,
gambol like lambs.

Ruth Feldman

20 • *Maintaining Stability*

Phil:
It was good to move away. It also heightened our loss. All our friends, the people who were our support system, weren't there. After a while you do realize that you're really all alone. You go through a lot of things, but you're just alone. In the short term, it is more painful to lose your place of comfort, the little house on the hill, your friends and whatever else you identify with. And yet it may be good because it is really saying that you need to start again. It isn't a clean slate but at least it's a beginning, and you reconstruct yourself with some new foundations. You have to be focused all the time on making sure that the family stays together and at the same time, you want to be productive in your work. It doesn't ever come back like it was.

We have all heard of the expression "Time heals." What really happens is that we heal over time, and since we are all unique, the length of time we need to heal will vary from person to person. For many of us grief is a new experience. We have not been taught what to expect and how to cope with it. While we all have unique personalities and coping styles, we can help ourselves through the grieving process in a number of ways; by maintaining stability in our living situations, by expressing our feelings, by taking good physical care of ourselves, by the memorials and rituals we carry out for our loved ones, by reading, and also by seeking and receiving help from friends, support groups and counselors. While we grieve, we need to focus on ourselves as much as possible and to be very gentle with ourselves.

The period of grieving for the death of a loved one can be a time of upheaval and disruption. Any major change is stressful and requires a lot of energy. When we lose a loved one, we also experience far-reaching changes in our circumstances. For instance, if we are widowed, we also lose a companion, we may lose our source of income, our social status, and the friends we knew through our partner.

To cope with such a major loss and its accompanying circumstances, we may find it helpful to refrain from making any further changes in our lives at this time. Any decision involving a major change in job, home or significant relationships can add to the stress we are already experiencing. Even what we might consider as a positive change, such as a move to a better job or a more convenient house, is still a source of stress.

When our feelings are in turmoil, we may be tempted to seek relief by doing something immediately, such as getting rid of certain things in the house, or moving in with an adult child if we have lost a husband or wife. With the best of intentions, our family and our close friends may also wish to change our living situation in order to alleviate our loneliness and sadness. Making decisions about jobs, living situations or mementos in the early stages of grieving may be cause for regrets. Months later, we may long for a reminder of our loved one, or we may find that our old apartment had many advantages that we were unable to consider at the time.

Sometimes because of our circumstances it is not possible to avoid a major change in our life. There are some guidelines we can follow which can help us make the best choices for ourselves. When at all possible, wait for a least a year before making a major change. After a year or more has passed following a difficult loss, we will have gained a different perspective on our lives. By then, we will have a clearer view of the choices available and the directions we may wish to take.

If it's necessary to make a change sooner, we can approach that change in a systematic way. For instance, we can look over the course of a typical day or week and determine which elements in our lives, such as job, co-workers, home, friendships and family, would remain constant, and which elements would be different if we were to make a change. We can list these changes on a piece of paper and try to imagine what it would feel like to live with them every day.

A woman I know was unhappy with her job and had been considering a change for some time. Her unhappiness increased significantly just when her mother became seriously ill. Although she had already decided to change jobs and had even given notice, she reconsidered after her mother's death. Having familiar people around her was more important than a job change as she mourned the loss of her mother, and her job became more tolerable as the months passed.

When all considerations point to the necessity for a major change, there may be ways to lessen the stress involved. We can look at the list again and pick out the elements that would remain the same. Then we can try to imagine ways to strengthen these, such as more frequent contact with supportive people, planning a trip to visit family, or scheduling time to spend at home.

The essence of this technique is to keep as much stability in our lives as possible, allowing ourselves to grieve the loss of our loved one and to adapt to our new situation with our resources intact.

Home

It is common for a newly widowed person who is left alone to consider selling a house in favor of a smaller one or to move in with other family members. We may make this decision hastily and without considering our need for stability in our surroundings. Often, it is our adult children who may press us into such a move with the best of intentions for our welfare, but often without considering the difficulty of adjusting to such dramatic changes.

Such a move should be carefully considered over a period of time. Even if our home may seem too large or is far away from the rest of the family, it contains all the memories of the life we lived with our spouse. Moving to another city or neighborhood may entail leaving well-established friendships and routines, and getting rid of our furniture and personal possessions. Then we may have to face the difficulties of adjusting to a new family situation and unfamiliar surroundings when we are still torn by grief. Because we all face different circumstances, we should carefully consider our attachment to our home and the meaning of that attachment.

If we are an adult son or daughter wishing to take in a widowed parent, we should also carefully consider the changes involved. The addition of another family member may create stresses in our lives as we face the reworking of our daily routine, living arrangements, family relationships and workload. We might find ourselves in a role reversal as we take care of a dependent, elderly parent.

After all is considered, we may find that moving in with our son or daughter seems best. In that case all the family members involved will want to have time to talk about such a move and to prepare for the new family situation. If we talk about it over a period of time, we may come up with creative ideas of how to live together while allowing each family member to consider his or her own needs.

There are a number of other choices which can be explored. Perhaps we might prefer to remain in our own home and arrange for home services or either daily or live-in help. Perhaps we might find housing close to our children which would allow them to look in on us while leaving us both with a measure of independence. Some widowed persons have opted for shared home arrangements in their town, group living or senior citizen housing. Remaining in the same town allows us to keep in contact with old friends and former neighbors.

If we are a widowed parent, our children will be wanting reassurance about their lives. Any changes in their daily routines, their living arrangements or the school they attend may be very difficult for them. They will be comforted by being able to keep the same friends and the same playtime activities. They may already feel as if their lives are in turmoil and any additional change may cause them to be fearful or withdrawn. Stability also means trying to keep our style of parenting as consistent as we are able. It may be as disorienting to children to suddenly become the focus of a great deal of attention and protectiveness as it is to be neglected.

There are some things we can do to give ourselves and our families a sense of continuity and stability even if we have to move to another home or apartment. It can be very helpful to keep even a small thing that reminds us of our home, whether a picture, an object or a daily routine. For instance, the widowed father of a three-year-old decided to keep his wife's car in the driveway for a number of months after her death because it was a source of comfort to his daughter. Perhaps we used to have a family outing on Sunday afternoons. Continuing our family practices may give us a comforting sense that our lives together will remain as they have been in the past. What may seem like very small things can actually help us through difficult periods.

There may be other reasons to prompt a move from our home beyond financial considerations. After losing a child, we may feel that there are too many painful reminders around the home and neighborhood. If we have lost someone through murder or through vehicular homicide, we may want to change our home or even to move to another town because of the painful memories. For some of us, leaving behind old friends may be the price we choose to pay for continuing our lives. In Chapter 6, Phil's family found it so difficult to pass the street where their daughter was killed that they gave up their friends and memories of happier times to start over again in another state. However, they made this decision only after many months of deliberation.

If our loved one committed suicide in the home, we may think we could never live there comfortably again. In these situations too, time is needed to determine what the best decision may be. Living anywhere is painful when we hurt so much. Many people have had a suicide in the family and have remained in the same home, finding a way to transform the space as they healed inside. Only time will help to determine what is best in our own case.

Schools and jobs

Besides keeping our living arrangements as constant as possible, it may be helpful to keep stability in our jobs. For some of us, the loss of a loved one may suddenly bring to the fore an unsatisfactory working situation. However, because we are experiencing the stress and all the powerful emotions of grief, we should carefully consider the timing of any change we might want to make. We can try the same technique of appraisal that we used to decide about our living arrangements, listing on a piece of paper what elements would remain constant and what elements would change with a new job. We should consider the nature of our work, the surroundings, our co-workers, our boss, and decide how important each factor is and how much energy we have to make the necessary adjustment.

Allowing enough time to pass is important in making the right decision. Sometimes it's possible to take time off from our jobs to work through our grief and to consider what kind of change we would like. Eric had been unhappy in his job and therefore decided to use the life insurance money to take off a few months. He ultimately found new and fulfilling work in film-making. However, that decision came only after many months had gone by. A recently widowed woman found that she no longer identified with the values expressed in her career. She realized that she wanted a change but decided to postpone that move for another year until she had sorted out her personal life.

Many of us are satisfied with our working situations and have no thought of change. However, we all need time not only for change, but also for the work of grieving. Often we return to work a few days after the funeral with very little energy and with difficulty concentrating. Some people arrange to take time off for a few months after the death of a loved one. This is not always possible but it may be possible to negotiate a reduced work week until we feel less fatigued. In Chapter 13, Merryll describes how she took time off from her job and then returned on a part-time basis until she felt ready to take on a full-time work load. Anne describes her very gradual return to a full working day. We may be surprised by our fatigue, but we shouldn't be impatient with ourselves or try to force ourselves into a full schedule. The profound emotions associated with grieving take up a great deal of energy.

If we are a college student or about to become a college student when a loved one dies we may want to consider taking off a semester or delaying our entry for a year until we adjust to our new family situation. As an incoming freshman suffering grief, we might find it very difficult to adapt to our new surroundings and to our new living situation.

Even when we go back to a familiar college setting after the death of a loved one, just keeping up the pace of our courses and our social life may be difficult. Also, we might find very little support and understanding for the feelings of grief in the college atmosphere.

There are a number of choices we can make as students and we can discuss these with a counselor or a family member. It has become a common practice to defer going to college for a year after one has already been admitted and taking time off may help us to do the best we can when we eventually return to our studies.

If we have lost a loved one when we are adults, chances are that we have responsibility for other members of family in addition to responsibilities in the workplace. We might consider reducing our workload at home as well as at work. If we have lost a spouse we might feel that we have to take over our spouse's chores and responsibilities right away. Anne (Chapter 22) suggests calling repair people rather than trying to do everything alone. We should make as few demands on ourselves as possible and get as much help as we can in the household. We can let our family and friends know if they can help us in any way. Most people who really care for us will welcome a chance to express their concern in a concrete way.

Personal effects and possessions

When a loved one has died, sorting out his or her personal possessions may seem like an unpleasant chore and we may want to finish this task as soon as possible. Usually, we are not immediately aware of what these things may mean to us later on. Also, the things that will matter the most to us as time passes may not be immediately obvious. For instance, our loved one's favorite chair may be in poor condition and we may wish to quickly dispose of it. Yet in the months to come that chair might be a comforting memory of that person.

It's best to take plenty of time to make decisions about clothing, furniture and personal effects. Sometimes the most insignificant objects can be a source of comfort. A young woman whose father died kept his pillow to sleep on. A older woman who lost her mother kept her sewing box in her study.

If circumstances make it necessary to dispose of belongings soon after the death of our loved one, it may be helpful to use the following method. Make three piles of things. Label one pile Yes, definitely keep, label one pile No, definitely dispose of, and label one pile Maybe. We can store the Maybe pile in a suitable place and let time pass. After six months we can take out those things and re-examine them. By then we will have a clearer perspective on our attachments and needs and it will be easier to decide what to keep.

Sometimes the advice of a trusted friend or even a friend of the deceased can help. When my mother died, I was under great pressure to sort out her things because of the high rent on her apartment. Her best friend helped me with this and gave me some good advice both on where to dispose of furniture and what things to keep. It was a great comfort to donate some cherished pieces to charitable organizations because I knew that would have pleased my mother.

Unfortunately, the sorting of personal effects can create conflict within a family. Conflict over things like a piece of jewelry or a rug may actually reflect some more deep-seated disagreements among family members. However, there is a way of handling this type of conflict that is simple and effective. Each family member can take a piece of paper and make a list of things that person would like to have for themselves. The list can be rated in this way: the first level would be things the family member would really like to have, the second level would be things he or she would like but which are less important, the third level would itemize things that person would like but could do without. The list would also include an explanation of why each thing is important to that person. Then the family can meet together and discuss each member's list. Perhaps it will be possible to agree on some things but not others. The effects that cannot be agreed on could be put aside for six months or so until the family can meet again for further discussions.

Bear in mind that decisions about cherished possessions do not need to be made on a permanent basis. For instance, a prized ring could be shared among the daughters of a family for a year at a time. Other possessions could circulate among family members for months or even years.

If after drawing up lists and meeting together, we still experience conflict over the disposition of our loved one's possessions, we can call upon an outsider, a trusted family friend for instance, to moderate our discussions.

We can think of this kind of decision as a process that takes place over months. Both the time and the frequent communication over these decisions may help us to minimize the conflict and to arrive at a solution that while not ideal, at least satisfies some of our wishes.

Relationships with family and friends

When we are torn by the powerful feelings of grief we should avoid making any decisions about our relationships with family or friends. When we are in the process of grieving, we are extremely sensitive to other people's behavior towards us. For instance, people whom we considered as good friends might cause us great disappointment by staying away from us while we are grieving. Although we might be tempted to break off such a relationship, it's best to give ourselves time. As the months pass we will have a clearer view of the role that person plays in our life. Or perhaps we disagreed with a family member over the disposition of our loved one's possessions. We might be tempted to sever our relations with that person. We should bear in mind that we often regret decisions which are made on the spot and at a time when we are in great pain.

We may be overwhelmed with loneliness after the death of a loved one, and therefore we may be looking for new relationships and may even want to make them permanent. If we have been widowed or if we have lost a partner, it's normal to want to go out again and to want to express the loving, affectionate sides of our nature. If we have been left a single parent we may also miss the support of our spouse in bringing up the children. Remember that the relationship we had with our spouse or lover was the result of years of mutual adjustment and compromise, and that any relationship needs time and hard work to become fulfilling.

We can use the same guidelines that we used in making decisions about home and job when considering what to do about our personal relations. It's always a good idea to give ourselves time and to ride through the strains as well as we can. We can enjoy new people, but it's best to leave the decisions that will create permanent changes until later.

21 • Expressing Our Feelings

Jim:

I cried a lot just after. Sometimes it was by myself and sometimes it was with a close friend. I remember one of the most important things was to have people be there and willing to listen and not telling me that I shouldn't feel this way, but just listening and accepting that I felt these things. That was very helpful.

I wrote poems in the year after her death. I carry these poems around with me and at least once every two weeks I take them out and reread them. I've since written other poems, more about my family. It's opened up a way of dealing with my feelings that I didn't have available before.

It's been a year and five months. I still am moved to write. This fall a student died at my university and I wrote to her parents, as much for me as for them. I just know that having people with whom to share this thing was immensely important.

The way my parents are avoiding her death makes it much more difficult for me. On the one hand it has forced me to realize that I can no longer avoid certain things in my family. So I've begun to try and express things to them.

I have been able to communicate a little bit more with my younger sister, although she doesn't like to talk about it. I've begun to talk directly to her.

Bill:

A year later, after I had met a new lady, the two of us went up to the cemetery together. We took a potted plant to plant. We had to dig the hole with our fingers because we forgot the trowel. We planted the plant and I still didn't cry because men don't cry. We started down out of the cemetery and Mildred said, "Go ahead and cry." I did. That was probably the hardest cry I ever had.

Anne:

By the second year, I was keeping copious journals and that helped me a lot because I was in this private time. I was writing down my observations, lists of alternative actions. I was also working but this was my personal life. I was

*like Sherlock Holmes. I knew I had a big case and that I had to pay attention.
I wanted to pay attention. It wasn't meant to be for a woman to be alone and
have four kids. Once you've said that you can go on.*

Eric:

*I did start trying to write things. I kept a journal all along. Then I tried to write
short stories and then an article. That just didn't come. It felt so forced, so
removed. I really couldn't express what I felt. I was quite bitter that no one had
ever told me somewhere along the way how powerful grief was, what grief was.
If someone had asked what the major emotions are in life. I would have
answered, "Oh, well, love, hate, anger." I don't think I would have mentioned
grief. I don't think people are taught about that in this culture. I felt I have been
a little cheated.*

When we grieve, we experience profound feelings including sadness,
guilt, anger, fear, hate, frustration and despair. These feelings may be
fleeting or prolonged. We may live with them on a daily basis or they
may arise spontaneously under the most unexpected or seemingly inappropriate circumstance. Experiencing these feelings may feel like
riding a roller coaster or living at the bottom of a dark pit.

One of the most important things we can do to heal ourselves is
to express these emotions in ways that are comfortable for us. Living
with these feelings is extremely difficult. Anyone who has suffered loss
can attest to this. But when we face them head-on, we can move
through them. When we try to push them away they may surface later
on in our lives. When we express our feelings we allow them space
outside ourselves. Then, their power inside us is diminished.

We all have our own ways of expressing feelings. Some of us are
highly verbal. Others may prefer a more physical means of expression,
whether becoming absorbed in a project like carpentry or in a sport.
Some of us are more private and are less comfortable in sharing our
feelings with others. We can choose a means of expression that is
consistent with our own personal style.

Talking

Talking is the most obvious way of expressing our feelings. We can
describe them in all their fullness and detail. We can give examples,
bring up shades of meaning, color, intensity and nuance. We can even
use metaphors for the subtle feelings that are not so easily defined.

Talking about how much we miss our loved one, sharing our

memories about that person or the circumstances leading to his or her death can be a healing experience. We may need to repeat our story many times and it may seem as if we are saying some of the same things. Yet over time, what we say and how we may say it changes. The circumstances of our loved one's death don't change, but our perception of these events does change as we work through the process of grieving.

Some of us are comfortable talking with whomever is available while some of us may prefer to talk to a trusted friend. Often we find that someone who is just an acquaintance or even a stranger but who has had a similar experience can listen to us with sensitivity. If there is no one readily available, we can turn to a counselor or a support group sponsored by one of the many grief programs which are listed in "Resources" at the end of this book.

The pain of loss is like an open wound. Sometimes it may feel as if no one could possibly understand what that pain is like and therefore it may seem risky to let someone know. Choosing someone we trust to talk to is important, but most people who have really lived have experienced pain. It may not have been the same experience as our own, but those who have suffered generally have compassion and understanding of others. Talking about our grief can help us feel less isolated. By expressing our pain, we also learn what others have experienced. It's no coincidence that many of us who are grieving learn about the sadness that others around us may feel.

Some of us may feel very private about our thoughts. A widowed friend of mine rented a cottage by the ocean for occasional weekends during the first months after her husband's death. She poured out her anguish and despair into a tape recorder. When we talk into a recorder we can express our feelings as if there were someone to listen. We can play it back at another time and even have a conversation with ourselves.

Those of us who aren't able to take time away from home can always talk out loud within the privacy of our apartment or house. We can talk to the person who died, to the presence we feel near us, to the picture or to the grave at the cemetery. Our behavior may seem bizarre to us, but this is not the time to censor or judge ourselves.

Writing letters

Another way to express our feelings is to write letters. We can address our letters to the loved one who died, telling them how much we miss them, how much we loved them, or how angry we are at them for leaving us. We may not have had the opportunity to say goodbye to our loved one and even if we did, there are always things we wish we had said. This is a good way to deal with the unfinished business of a relationship.

Perhaps we lost someone with whom we had a troubled and unsatisfactory relationship. We can write a letter saying what we had hoped for and expressing our anger at the failure of this tie. Unresolved relationships may haunt us for years. It is never too late to express our sorrow and frustration about our unmet hopes.

We can also address letters expressing how we feel to a mythical or real friend, to a family member or to God. If the letter is addressed to someone who is alive, it may be wise to leave it aside for a few days after writing it, and to reread it before deciding to mail it. This type of letter really doesn't have to be mailed. Its most important purpose is to allow us to pour out our feelings.

Keeping a journal

Many people keep journals in the months and years after the death of a loved one. A journal can be a daily companion and an impartial listener. In Chapter 14, Margaret describes how she kept a journal during the first year after her son's murder. It enabled her to express her agony in an uncensored way. At the beginning of this chapter, Anne describes the use of her journal as a problem solver and as an aid in getting through the long and lonely days.

Keeping a journal allows us to record the dreams we have about our loved one, and to note all the discoveries and difficulties of living without him or her. These are all significant episodes in our healing. When we reread past entries, we gain a sense of where we have come, or how we are doing at a certain period of time. This can be very helpful since we usually have few ways to measure our progress through the long months of grieving.

It's not unusual for people who have never written before to begin writing poetry after the death of a loved one. Jim wrote a number of poems about his sister during the first year after her death. It was a way of expressing his sadness about her death and also of exploring the mystery of that death and the depth of his feelings for her. Eric wrote both poems and short stories about his wife. He wrote a story about an unusual and joyous day he had with her when she was already very ill. Marilyn ultimately wrote a book about her experience with loss.

Writing poems, stories and essays is a good way of giving free rein to our feelings and also of trying to express the significance of the relationship we had with the deceased. It's also a way of holding on to the memory of our loved one. We don't have to be professional writers to enjoy the relief and fulfillment of expressing our feelings in this manner.

Expressing anger

For many of us, anger is a difficult feeling to express appropriately. We may have been taught that it is wrong to show anger, and being angry may conflict with the image we have of ourselves. But after a loss, we often react in anger to irritations around our home or work, or to frustrations and conflicts with a partner or spouse, family members or friends.

Sometimes we may be angry at a specific target such as the doctor, the police officer who informed us of the accident, or even God. Other times we may experience a more diffuse anger and simply feel angry at the situation in which we find ourselves. Each of these different types of anger may call for different expressions.

In the early weeks and months after a death, our anger may be directed at the nurses, clergy, paramedics, anyone involved in or present at the time of death. Though we may help ourselves by expressing these feelings to someone who will listen, or by writing a letter, it may not be helpful to confront those who are the targets of our anger. If we find ourselves considering action such as writing a letter of complaint, we should allow some time to elapse before doing it. If we are considering serious action such as a lawsuit, it is very important to give ourselves enough time to heal. A lawsuit will serve to refresh all the circumstances of the death and the accompanying pain. One must feel strong enough to go through with sustained action of that kind.

We may be angry at the person who died and who we may feel abandoned us. A woman whose lover died went to his grave and screamed at him for leaving her. If God is the target of our anger, we can express that feeling by talking out loud or in letters or in a journal. No matter how much we loved the deceased, it's normal to feel angry at him or her. And no matter how religious we may be, it's also normal to feel angry at God for allowing our loved one to die.

Anger may not be expressed satisfactorily by just talking or writing. Often, our anger may require a stronger expression. Instead of talking, we can scream or yell. Many people find it helpful to scream in their cars, especially on long trips home from work or in a traffic jam.

Exercise is a good release for our anger. We can walk, run, swim, play tennis or bicycle. A friend of mine who was widowed went to an aerobics class every morning when the children had left for school just to work off her anger. We can clean the house, clean out a desk or a closet, wash the walls, or rake the leaves. With these kinds of activities we may find that our actions become more energetic as we do them.

Sometimes it takes very vigorous activity to get at our anger. It may be helpful to pound a pillow or even use a bat or a tennis racket to hit a mattress. We can do so and yell at the same time. Often, after doing this, the tension of pent-up anger is released and we feel relaxed. We may find the sadness that was held back by our anger.

When we feel angry towards someone close to us, a family member or a friend, we may want to carefully consider how we deal with this feeling. Often this anger is aroused by some circumstance around the death, or disagreements around the funeral arrangements, wills or estate. We may be angry that a person did not fulfill our expectations for help or empathy. We may be so distressed that we are inclined to do something that will sever the relationship. This situation deserves extra consideration.

Though we may feel hurt and angry at our family or friends, we cannot be aware how important a relationship will be to us when we have reached the other side of grief. Our perspective will be quite different then. Meanwhile, we can relieve our pain by talking with a trusted person. Perhaps we may decide that we need some distance in a particular relationship for a time. However, severing a relationship may cut us off from a nurturing resource for the future.

Expressing sadness

The most obvious way to express our sadness is through our tears. Tears well up when we remember our loved one, or hear a song, or see something our loved one might have liked, or for no apparent reason. The tears come at what seems like the most inappropriate time.

We may have been taught that adults don't cry or that men don't cry. But we should allow plenty of space for our tears. As men, we are just as entitled to shed tears as women and we suffer the loss of a spouse, child or sibling as keenly. Tears can be cleansing. Some of us may prefer to go to the cemetery and cry, or to read old letters, or to cry in the privacy of our rooms or during our daily commute.

Some of us prefer to cry with a close and trusted friend. Although Bill had some strong ideas about male behavior, the fact that he was able to cry at his wife's grave and in the presence of his new friend was a turning point for him. He was then able to go on to new interests and a new life. Both Eric and Jim found crying a great relief, whether with friends or by themselves.

We may consider weeping as a sign of weakness or as shameful. As men, we are urged to "be strong." Yet tears are not a sign of weakness. On the contrary, they are the source of our strength and they are also the wellspring of our joy. If we are able to cry, then we are also capable of laughter.

We may think that weeping is appropriate only in the early months after our loved one's death. However, many of us will be caught by surprise and find that the tears well up months or even years down the line when an event or a familiar landscape suddenly remind us of our loved one. Perhaps someone else's tragedy may remind us of our own.

A widowed friend of mine was attending a skating party for fathers and daughters at the local rink. When she saw the fathers glide out onto the ice holding their daughter's hands, she had to leave the bleachers so she could go out and cry. Afterwards, she felt relieved. Trying to push away our sadness doesn't mean that we get rid of it. Our unexpressed sadness may haunt us and surface when we least expect it.

Expressing guilt

Guilt is a very difficult emotion to deal with. Our guilt may be especially strong if we are parents who have lost a child, if we have lost a young sibling, or if we have lost a loved one through suicide. We feel guilty for having done things or for not having done things, for having been there or not having been there, for actions done or not done years ago.

We may have spent months by the bedside of a very sick child, parent, or friend, and have been out of the room just when that person died. We may feel guilty that we were not present at the time of death even though we gave ourselves wholeheartedly to that person. We may feel guilty if a parent or child died when he or she was in another city. We may feel guilty if our relationship with our loved one was a troubled one.

If we express our guilt to friends and acquaintances they may very well reply, "Oh, don't feel guilty." But that doesn't take the feeling away. A woman whose husband committed suicide reflected a year and a half after the death that the best resource she had were those few close friends who listened to her say, "If only . . ." over and over without judging her. When she did finish, her friends would then remind her of all the ways in which she did care for her husband and how she could not have been responsible for what he did. Her friends heard her out before they responded, and they let her repeat her guilt feelings without admonishing her.

If we do not have friends who are able to respond in such a supportive manner, we can turn to a counselor or find a support group where it's all right to express feelings of guilt. If these are not available we can write about our guilt. We can list all the things we feel guilty about, all the things we didn't do and wished we had done. Then we should be sure to make a list of all the things that we did do that were caring or helpful or loving towards the person who died. Referring to these lists from time to time may help give us a sense of perspective.

It's not very useful to think of guilt as being justified or unjustified. Guilt is a feeling. It keeps us attached to the person we lost and we need to feel it for a period of time. Once we have expressed it for as long as we need to, we can let it go. We can live for a long time with a sense of responsibility for an action, but that does not necessarily mean feeling guilty about it. There will come a time when we will be able to gain a more objective view of our loved one's death.

Expressing despair

Some of us may find our religious beliefs strengthened by the death of a loved one, but others may view the death as a challenge to our faith. We may feel abandoned because our prayers were not answered. We may question the existence of a benevolent God and our whole structure of meaning may be called into question. Even the most devout followers of religious faiths may experience a sense of hopelessness after the death of a loved one. Those of us who have lost someone through murder are especially apt to feel that things will never be all right again. It's helpful to remember that this is a normal feeling and that we can move through it.

These emotions may be very difficult to hear and our friends may not be able to listen to us. We can talk to a counselor, or turn to a support group where we may find others who have had similar experiences and who will not feel threatened by our feelings.

One way we can help ourselves during the weeks and months of anguish is to create positive visual images for ourselves through a relaxation technique. To do this, we will need a place where we can have solitude and quiet. This can be our own car if we live with a number of people, or the privacy of our bedroom. We can begin our relaxation by sitting quietly with our eyes closed, and paying careful attention to our breathing. As we breathe, we can tense and relax each muscle in our body from our toes to our neck. Once we begin to feel our tension ease, we might start by counting as we hold our breath. For instance, we might count to five for each time we inhale and exhale.

As we become more and more relaxed, we can think of positive images. Some of us might call up the image of ourselves swimming past an obstacle, or swimming across a pond. Others might see themselves skiing or walking or even sailing past that obstacle. We can even imagine ourselves climbing up a fireman's pole, reaching above our difficulty. Each one of us will be comforted by a certain type of image. As we relax, images may appear in our mind spontaneously and we may feel as if we are being lifted out of ourselves. Both the breathing exercises and the conjuring up of images will relax us. It's best to do these exercises for at least ten minutes and as often as possible, once a day if we are able to. Throughout the day, we can call up those images whenever we feel despondent. Gradually, we may gain a sense that we can move through the tunnel of our pain.

Many people have found it helpful to record feelings of despair in letters or in a journal. In Chapter 14, Margaret recounts how she recorded the painful weeks and months after her son's death, and her deep sense of hopelessness. Three years after his death she was able to reread those journals and chart the distance she had covered. From feeling utterly without hope she had regained the energy and confidence to begin a new project of victim rights advocacy.

The loss of hope may be frightening for those of us who have lived with the view of an orderly universe. However, many of us who face this feeling and allow ourselves to experience it have come through it with a new sense of life's meaning.

22 • *Coping with Daily Living*

Anne:

Have everything taken care of. Take that time of your life and realize only once is this big thing going to happen to you. Take every cent you have and have things done for you. Have someone clean your house and do your garden. Don't take the offers of your friends to fix your pipes and do that stuff because it involves you in a whole thing that holds you down. I called the plumber and paid retail and made sure that the driveway was shoveled. Spend the money. I don't care if you only have ten thousand dollars left, take care of everything so it's smooth. What you have to deal with is this big thing. That's big enough. I don't say don't take from other people because it's bad, but because you won't know if you're gaining in strength. You won't know if you can handle your house. You won't know until you try and it's working and your kids see that it's not done by everyone else's fathers. When they say they want to do something, make a list and tell them what it is. The ones that would really help, will. Pay the lawyers, pay everyone and then you'll be taken care of. You're not being taken care of any more and you'd better well take care of yourself because you might not find out that you can.

Do everything for yourself that you can. Buy yourself presents, personal, lovely things. I think going on a trip is good.

Don't look at the whole picture. Look at the next thing you're going to do. Don't say, "My husband is dead. I have four kids and how am I going to pay for college?" You can't do ten things at once. Do one thing. That's all you can do. It's brought me into a whole new place.

Widows should know this, look forward to certain things. Value in a special way people you meet for the first time after your husband dies. Don't have this view of you as being part of a past. You're you because you're you. Seek something new, not "Widows of the world unite", but take sailing lessons. Mrs. Widow, you won't believe how special you feel when you strike up a friendship at the office. You don't have that much self-confidence at first because such a big bad thing has happened to you that you might think of yourself as diminished. It isn't true. It's nice to look forward to meeting someone new. Even if you don't try to, you do as time goes by. It's a blank notebook like the beginning of school in September. Don't say, "Oh, I shouldn't think that, oh I wonder if a man will like me, I shouldn't think of going to Paris." There are some changes from death that are not negative. Now you can do damn well what you please. Ask yourself: What can I do new, who can I meet new?

Eric:

I went to the Boston Film and Video Foundation after Diane died. I took a workshop there. I took the summer off because I had Diane's insurance money. I was fortunate not to have to work. I thought, "What I am really interested in is grief and that's what I know something about." I also thought, "People are going to think this is morbid, but I'm going to propose it to the Newton Television Foundation anyway." I did a year later when I saw a notice for a competition. I called them and they said, "It sounds good, when do you want to start?"

The documentary felt good. I thought, "Here's something that I can learn that is new." It is a kind of compensation. It's the only thing that I have done that's valid since Linda died. Her death took a great toll on my self-esteem. It takes a lot to crawl back. The documentary made me realize that there is something I can do.

It was broadcast May 1, 1985, two years after Diane died. You become a believer after these kinds of things.

After a loss, it may seem very difficult to manage the routines of our daily lives and to muster up the energy for all the things we are used to doing. It's helpful to remember that we don't have to keep up the same pace or to shoulder the same burdens after the death of a loved one.

We can let go of some of our responsibilities while we are grieving and we can do that in such a way as to avoid a loss of self-esteem. Many of us see ourselves in relation to our jobs or our roles within the home. We may feel as if we are less worthy if we are unable to be as active as usual. But we cannot be the person we would like to be if we are fatigued and overwrought. It's all right to focus on ourselves while we are grieving.

The following are some suggestions that many people have found helpful. However, each one of us is unique and it's important to find ways of coping that are comfortable for us.

Eating and sleeping

Many of us change our eating habits when we are under great stress. Either we eat less than usual or we may eat more or turn to different kinds of food. Minor changes may not have much effect on our health or need special attention. However, if we have been unable to eat as much as we need over a period of time there are a number of things we can do to assure ourselves the proper nutrition. We can try eating small amounts more frequently, perhaps six times a day. We can ask our pharmacist for a good nutritional supplement, usually a powder to mix with milk or other liquid, and we can get a good stress-formula vitamin as a supplement. If we find that we are still unable to nourish ourselves properly, we should see a physician.

If we change the kind and variety of food we eat, and begin consuming more junk foods, we can also benefit by using the kinds of nutritional supplements mentioned above.

If we find ourselves over-eating to a great extent, we may try to vary our activities so that eating doesn't become a major focus of our day. However, if we gain weight, we should avoid berating ourselves for the gain. That won't help our self-esteem. We can live with it for now.

Our sleeping patterns are frequently disrupted when we are grieving. Some of us may not be able to sleep during the night, sleep very little or awaken several hours earlier than usual. Lack of sleep or diminished sleep can lead to fatigue, stress, and a low tolerance for the irritations of work and home.

When our sleep is disturbed for a period of time, there are a few techniques which may bring us relief. We can take naps whenever possible during the day or in the early evening when we feel fatigued. We can also take extra periods of rest from our activities and re-sponsibilities. Even if we are unable to sleep, leisurely rest can be restorative or even help us relax enough to be able to sleep. Sometimes a walk in nature, or simply curling up and listening to music, may have the same effect as sleep.

Sometimes we may have difficulty falling asleep at night, or we wake up during the night and are unable to go back to sleep. If this disruption is caused by anxiety or tension we can use some simple techniques to relax. We can progressively tense and relax each muscle in our body from our toes to our neck until we feel totally relaxed. Or we can try some simple breathing exercises such as focusing on our breathing and counting to a certain number each time we exhale and inhale. We can also play a cassette tape of music that comforts and relaxes us. If the sleep just won't come, it's best not to fight it. Perhaps we can pick up a favorite book and plan for a rest period during the day.

It's not unusual to dream about our loved one, especially in the early weeks and months after the death. If our loved one had a painful death through illness or accident, we might replay these events in our dreams. In the solitude and darkness of the night, our fears may be heightened. One way to cope with a dream is to have a notebook handy. We can describe the dream and also the feelings that the dream aroused. By writing it down, we can place it outside ourselves and may be able to relax.

If we dream frequently throughout our grieving, we may discover that our dreams change over time. In the early months we may have more troubling dreams about our loved one's illness or well-being. As time passes, our dreams change and tend to become more comforting.

Care of our health

Because grieving is so stressful, it's important to take good care of our health. If we develop any symptoms which concern us we should see a physician without delay. Even if we are feeling all right, it may be helpful to have a check-up just to give ourselves peace of mind about our health.

It's not unusual to experience symptoms which are similar to the disease that our loved one had. We may worry that we have or will develop the same disease. When my mother died of a heart attack, I was certain that I would develop heart disease even though I had no rational basis for my feelings. Our physician happened to be an older and very understanding person. He looked at me and said, "Just because your mother died of a heart attack doesn't mean that you are going to have a heart condition."

There are many physical symptoms that are associated with grieving. Some of these are chest pains, shortness of breath, tightness in the throat or chest, dizziness and disorientation. These may be the effects of stress. In any case, we should do our best to take good care of ourselves and see a physician if we are at all concerned.

Exercise is an important way to assure our physical well-being, especially when we are under great strain. However, there may be times when we just don't feel like exerting ourselves. If that is the case, it might be helpful to try some mild form of exercise every day like walking, or to join a more structured program which many health clubs offer. A structured program needn't be a strenuous one and it does provide us with motivation and places us in an environment with other people.

While we are grieving we need to be especially cautious about the use of alcohol or drugs. Our doctor may prescribe anti-depressants or tranquilizers and these might help our symptoms for a time. But they will not be helpful when we are ready to face the feelings of grief and cope with them. These kinds of drugs should not be prescribed only for grief. If our doctor does prescribe them, we can always ask the reasons for the prescription or seek a second opinion.

If we use drugs to help ourselves fall asleep or to feel calmer, we should limit their use to a certain period. We can monitor their use and regularly question our need to continue them.

Turning to alcohol as a way of numbing our pain can also develop into a habit that might become difficult to break. As with anti-depressants or tranquilizers, the use of alcohol will not allow us to face the feelings of grief and to deal with them. Like drugs, alcohol covers up feelings. The resolution of grief can only happen when we allow ourselves to experience difficult feelings as fully as possible.

Caring for ourselves

Besides paying careful attention to patterns of eating and sleeping, and to our health, there are many other ways we can care for ourselves. Grieving takes up a good deal of our energy and is very fatiguing. This is the time to be especially gentle with ourselves. Losing a loved one diminishes our self-esteem. We need to be good friends with ourselves.

When we grieve, we experience both good and bad days. When we are having a relatively good day, we can do a simple exercise that will help shore us up over the weeks and months. We can take a piece of paper and make a list of twenty things we like to do or twenty things we can do to be good to ourselves. These can be hobbies we like to pursue, special interests, or projects we have wanted to do but postponed because of other obligations. They can be simple treats like buying some flowers or going to a ball game. There should be several items that are simple and require little planning and energy. For instance, many of us find that being in a natural setting is a restful, healing experience, whether walking by the ocean or in the woods, or simply lying on the grass.

Each day, we can choose at least one item from our list. We can select whatever feels right for that day. It's important not to judge or censor ourselves for what we decide to do with our time. Reading a favorite book for an hour or listening to music is a good way of taking care of ourselves.

This is also a time to think of doing the things we have always wanted to do but postponed because of our responsibilities. Perhaps we have always wanted to take a trip to another state or even another country. We might not be able to fly across the country or to Paris, but we might arrange a weekend with a friend or by ourselves. We might have dreamed of learning a new language or acquiring a new skill. As Anne suggests, this might be the time to take sailing lessons or look for a new pastime.

This might be a good time to meet someone new. Often when we lose a loved one, we receive sympathy and support from people we knew only slightly, in our office or in our neighborhood. In Chapter 13, Merryll describes a new friend who reached out to her at the office and who was a very important support to her. Anne suggests meeting someone new. Some of us may find it difficult to meet new people casually and might prefer more structured opportunities through organizations or church socials. Everyone has their own timing for moving through grief. We alone know when it's time to resume social activities. As Anne points out, these things not only help us through our grief. They also help us look forward to the future.

Maintaining a schedule

We may find it helpful to maintain a regular daily schedule or routine after we have lost a loved one. This won't be an issue if we continue working or if we have the same responsibilities at home. However, if our lives are greatly changed after the death, we may feel more secure with a regular schedule of duties or activities.

If our lives at home or at work are largely unstructured, we may want to take time either by ourselves or with someone's help and write out a schedule for ourselves. Even one major activity during the day can help us focus our energies. Meeting someone for coffee in the afternoon or taking a walk to the library may help get us through the day, as Eric describes in Chapter 17.

Making a list of activities for the day can give us a reference and a place to check off accomplishments. It's best to avoid crowding our schedule. The emotions of grief are extremely fatiguing and we may find that we can do much less than we are accustomed to, and that even a simple outing tires us.

Balancing solitude and activity

Some generations ago, it was customary for the bereaved to withdraw from society for a period of time. It was felt that people who had suffered loss needed time to heal before reentering society. When a loved one dies today, we are relatively free to arrange our periods of privacy and sociability. We might find that there are periods when we feel like spending time alone and there are times when we wish to do things with friends or family. We can examine our daily or weekly routines and see if our schedule allows a balance that is comfortable for us.

If we have a great deal of responsibility at home or at the office, or both, we may need to structure both the space and the time to be alone. We can look for ways to incorporate that private time in our daily or weekly schedule. It can be as simple as extending our commute on the way home from work so we can be alone in the car to cry or to think. A widowed friend of mine scheduled a weekend away for herself without the children once a month.

After the death of a loved one we may not feel at ease at social gatherings. There are a number of ways of dealing with our new sensitivity to social situations. A widow who felt uncomfortable going to parties by herself began her reentry into social life by attending some events with her best friend's husband. A widower who disliked attending weddings and large social gatherings alone found a friend in his bereavement support group who was willing to accompany him.

Some of us would rather not attend social functions. When it is a matter of obligation such as a wedding or graduation, it's always possible to make a brief appearance and then to leave quietly. Often we might feel uncomfortable with large family gatherings during the holidays or at special events. Some people have found it easier to go away during the holidays in order to have a quieter celebration. These occasions may make the pain of our loss more difficult and therefore we should feel free to make a decision that feels appropriate for us.

Just the opposite may be true for some of us. We may find that we have too much time alone. There are a number of ways to be among people. We can go to a park, or we can read in the main reading room of the library or attend a lecture or concert. We can seek out a more structured experience such as joining a club, or a support group, or taking a course.

Manageable pieces

When we are grieving, we sometimes tend to want to take on difficult problems. We might ask ourselves "How will I ever manage the house alone?" or "How will I ever love someone again?" or "How can I bring up three children alone?" These kinds of questions can loom very large and cause us to become discouraged.

As Anne suggests, it's better to do one thing at a time and to concentrate on manageable problems, such as arranging transportation for the children. Big questions do not and probably cannot have ready answers today. It may be more helpful to focus on the present, on this very moment, and to let go of six months from now, or a year or five years from today. It's enough to face each situation as it comes and to do the best we can to take care of ourselves. When we do focus on ourselves, and let go of our worry, we usually find that those big problems fall into place.

23 • Supports

Eric:

It takes a while before you can be part of a social process. I did find a group and some of us still see each other. I had been with myself during the summer. When I found the group it was a great relief.

Marilyn:

Some limited reading was helpful. Books that helped me were those that talked more philosophically about how we deal with tragedy and loss, that gave me some clues as to how other people met their tragedy, lived through it and fended off the assaults of people who were not understanding and sympathetic.

One of the things I found helpful was reading about other people's reactions to those around them so that I knew that some of the anger I felt towards people who were not understanding was a normal thing to feel. I have gained some ways of dealing with people that say such things as "It's all for the best. You don't know that now but you will someday." I think I would say now, "I just don't feel that way."

Two kinds of reading helped me immediately after my first loss when I was sick and actually bedridden for a while. One was just imaginative literature that took me out of myself. I thought at first that I wouldn't be able to turn my mind to anything. The other was books that talked about loss in general. I didn't want to read things that talked about specifics of other people's losses because at that point, I wanted to have hope that I would succeed eventually. Reading about other people who had all different kinds of pregnancy problems made me feel more overwhelmed and made me think, "Well, maybe I'll run into that wall next time."

I did go through counseling immediately after the loss and we are continuing now so that the counselor is ready to deal with our adoption issue. That was tremendously helpful. The counselor was also very helpful in teaching us to accept our responses and to communicate them to people so we could fend off unhelpful comments.

Phil:

One of the things that helped was a psychologist who met with us hours before Jenny died and told us what was going to happen. He invited us to come and see him and we did and continued to see him for months. Even after we moved we did. We went as a family a couple of times and as a couple most of the time. That was important because you never grieve at the same time. You bump up against each other and one of the things he was trying to do was to make sure that we came out of this together.

It wasn't just professional help. This man really had sensitivity and experience. I occasionally still call him. I value him as a person.

We need not be isolated with our grief. In fact, it is often true that the more support we have, the better we are able to express our grief and to heal ourselves. Support allows us to be ourselves without being judged or admonished. It allows us to express who we are and what we feel, no matter how difficult those feelings may be. It lets us know that we are not alone and that others feel pain.

Supports can come in many different forms. We can receive support from people close to us like a spouse or partner, a family member, or a friend. We can also receive support from our co-workers, neighbors, and acquaintances, and from our hobbies and interests. Most importantly, we can support ourselves in the ways we care for ourselves and make room for our needs.

Supportive people

Some of us may have a supportive spouse or family member who is able to listen to us and understand our grief. However, it is likely that our family members will also be grieving the same loss. Since we all grieve in different ways and since we may expect support from each other, we can experience great strains in our relationships.

In these circumstances, outside supports can be of great help. Also, if we only have one supportive person or someone we see only infrequently, other supports might be very welcome. Surprisingly, it is often the casual acquaintance or even a stranger who has been through a similar experience who can be most helpful. When my mother died, some of my closest colleagues withdrew, yet someone I knew only in passing wrote the most helpful letters and called me from time to time. She had suffered a great deal in her life and knew how to respond to someone else's pain.

We may find ourselves looking for just that, someone who can affirm our experience and serve as a model for us. One of the best places to find such people is in a support group.

Support groups

There are many bereavement support groups around the country. Some are independent groups formed by concerned people, others are part of national or international networks. Some are focused on a specific group of the bereaved such as widowed persons, bereaved parents, or those who have lost loved ones through suicide. Some groups serve all bereaved people. The Resources section lists some major bereavement support groups and gives a brief explanation of how to contact them.

While there may be variations from one support group to another, they all have common elements. These groups are self-help groups. They provide a place for people to come together, to talk about their issues, feelings and concerns, and to receive support from one another. It is comforting simply to know that there are others who are going through the same experiences as ourselves.

Some of us are used to groups and find it easy to turn to a support group when we are grieving. Others have never been to a support group and may wonder what to expect. Usually, support groups meet weekly or twice monthly. They may meet for a series of sessions, perhaps eight or ten weekly meetings. A meeting may last from one and a half to two hours.

Meetings may be run by a facilitator or a leader. A meeting may open with a statement which speaks of the atmosphere of the meeting. It acknowledges the pain and sorrow that people bring, emphasizes that talking, silence, and crying are allowed, and requests that participants give each other space to explore feelings and refrain from giving each other advice. Finally, the facilitator will ask each person to offer support, to keep all in confidence, and to leave with the belief that each person can pick up his or her life enriched by the gift of the members of the group.

For some people, the group is a safe place, maybe the only place to express feelings of grief and to talk with others about ways of coping. Participants talk, weep, tell each other about their dreams, and discuss difficulties with loved ones and with marking anniversaries. The participants listen to each other without making any judgments.

Sometimes a parent whose child has committed suicide may search for clues to that child's motives. A participant whose parent committed suicide may respond and they speak to each other almost as if they would be speaking with their loved one. Each one of them gains a little more understanding through this exchange.

Perhaps a participant speaks of his struggles and expresses his anxiety and fear. Another participant who has had similar feelings shares her past experience and urges him to be easy on himself. The first speaker may feel his anxiety diminish, and the group as a whole may experience a sense of comfort.

Sometimes a person may be totally silent during the whole meeting, yet may speak animatedly with just one person right after the meeting has ended. Each member of the group determines his or her own level of participation.

After the weeks and months pass, there are many changes in the participants' feelings. Some of the members have become calmer and experience less anxiety and tension. Others may speak less of sadness and more of learning to cope with being alone. Another person may still feel guilty, but is able to tell herself that she is not responsible for her son's death. Yet another finds some good memories beyond those of illness and can even laugh at them. Someone who may have expressed a lot of pain for the first time may tell a newcomer just how valuable these meetings are and urge him to continue attending.

Members of support groups learn to trust the process, to trust that at each meeting people will be there for each other, and that they are helping themselves in ways they may not even be aware of. Each may be there for the other, in a unique way. Such groups have demonstrated the resources we all have to heal ourselves and that we all have the resilience, the strength, and the ability to reach out to each other and to give something of value.

We may find more than one group in an area. It's all right to explore and try out different groups. It's also best to attend more than one meeting to see if we feel comfortable in that setting.

A support group is not a permanent solution to our grief. It is a help along the way. As we move through our grief, we will come to a time when it feels natural to move away from the group. Some people may continue to attend a support group meeting at difficult times such as the anniversary of the death. This kind of occasional attendance may help us through a time of slump even though we are getting on with our lives.

Reading

Some of us may feel less comfortable with a group or may want to have intervals of private time for our grief. Reading about other people's experience can be a great comfort, as Marilyn attests. There are many types of reading that we can turn to: books dealing with loss, personal accounts of loss, novels. The Additional Reading section suggests some further reading on the topic of grief.

Novels often deal with the most difficult human problems, with issues that many people generally shy away from. In a good novel we may be lifted out of ourselves, as Marilyn describes in her narrative, and we may also identify with someone's experience or discover that someone's expression of feeling matches our own. We can come away feeling less isolated, knowing that ours is a common human experience.

Poetry can offer us comfort while we are grieving. Poetry deals with our deepest feelings and contains images and metaphors that may express the emotions we cannot describe. We can carry copies of poems with us and take them out when we feel in need of comfort. In Chapter 28, Anne tells us how she memorized poems and repeated them to herself when she felt in need of solace.

Professional help and therapy

The stresses created by grief may be greater for some of us than for others or we may be faced with especially difficult circumstances. In such cases, we might want to seek the help of a professional therapist.

Our relationship with a spouse or partner after the death of a child might be riddled with tension. We may judge each other's behavior surrounding the death or have expectations that neither can fulfill. Relationships within our family might be strained if we have lost a key member like a parent. It is not unusual for children to become estranged after the death of a parent. Often in tragic deaths resulting from suicide or an accident, we blame each other. With the help of a therapist, we can learn that each one of us is experiencing his or her own pain and we may begin to interact with each other in more caring ways.

Some of us may be isolated either because we have just moved to a new town or because we are estranged from our families or live at a great distance from family and friends. Some of us may have very few close friends, or perhaps our friends and acquaintances are unable to meet our needs as we are grieving. When we find ourselves without regular supports, it may be helpful to find a therapist who can be an ongoing presence for us.

A local woman found herself very isolated after her twenty-year-old son committed suicide. She had been divorced for many years and her two other sons had chosen to live with their father leaving her with her twenty-year-old. Linda found herself with no one to talk to about this painful death. Her former husband and her sons lived one hundred miles away. Her parents were unable to talk about her son and wanted all the pictures of him cleared away. Her best friend found it too difficult to listen to her.

When Linda first attended a support group, it was clear that she needed a great deal of help, more than the group could give. Linda was very verbal, very expressive and needed many outlets for her feelings. She experienced a great deal of anxiety simply because she was so alone. Very wisely, she knew that she needed a number of supports.

Linda began to attend two different support groups, one for

bereaved parents and one for those who have lost a loved one through suicide. She requested a volunteer counselor for one-to-one support and she sought out a therapist. She continued to use all of these supports on a regular basis throughout the first year after her son's death. Because of this effort, she had people around her who cared about her and she learned new ways to cope with being alone. From her therapist, she learned more about the feelings she was experiencing and became able to express them in a safe environment.

For some of us, the death of a loved one brings up the pain and anxiety of past events, perhaps the death of someone many years ago. These old wounds can be as fresh and painful as when they first occurred. Yet our friends may not be sympathetic because the event took place so long ago. The death of a friend can spark the pain we felt at the death of a parent or a younger sibling years ago. In these cases, a therapist can help us to face the pain and deal with it now.

Sometimes the death of a loved one propels us towards a new identity. When our parents die, we are no longer a child. When our spouse dies, as Anne so aptly points out in Chapter 17, we are no longer part of a couple and begin to see ourselves as a single person. These changes in identity are profound. They may create burdensome new responsibilities for us and cause great inner turmoil. In any of these situations, we may seek a therapist to help us move through our struggles towards a new identity and new roles.

Some of us may tend to view a therapist as a professional only for people who are "crazy" or mentally ill. Most people are becoming aware that professional help is intended for all of us who experience difficulties with our lives. A therapist is a listener, someone who cares, someone who adds a perspective that we may not have, and someone we can lean on. However, even with the help of a therapist, we are still the ones who do the work of grieving and of coping with our lives. We simply turn to the therapist for help along the way.

When seeking a therapist, it is important to select someone who is appropriate and comfortable for us. This is very much a matter of individual taste. A therapist may be a psychiatrist, a psychologist or a social worker. A psychiatrist is a medical doctor and is only necessary if we require medication. In other cases, a psychologist, social worker or other counselor may meet our needs.

When we are looking for help while we are grieving, it is important to engage a therapist who is both sensitive to the issues of grieving and who has had experience in dealing with the process of grief. We can ask for a referral from a physician or trusted friends. We can call a local bereavement counseling center or support group and ask for the names of therapists. In all cases, it is important to interview a therapist either over the phone or in person to determine whether we feel comfortable with this person.

In a therapist-client relationship, we should feel completely at ease and we should feel that we can be totally honest. We should also feel that the therapist genuinely cares for us and is interested in furthering our well-being and growth. Even if some painful issues come up in therapy, we should be able to feel that the therapist is supportive and caring. If we have any doubts or concerns about a therapist and about what is occurring during our sessions, we should feel free to say what we think about the situation. If we are not satisfied, it is best to seek someone else.

Building support structures

One of the many lessons of grief is to make us aware of the need for regular and varied supports in our lives. Many people who have suffered loss experience a change in their scale of values and come to appreciate just how important personal relationships are. We may have considered our careers, or material well-being, of primary importance, but after the death of a loved one we may consider the task of creating supportive relationships for ourselves as more important.

We might begin by trying out some new activities. Eric turned his creative talents in journalism and writing to film-making. He started out by taking courses at the Boston Film and Video Foundation. We can learn new things by taking courses at a local school, an adult education center or at any of a number of university extension programs. We might also be interested in joining a club, a church group or a group focused on a particular project, perhaps providing a service or entertainment

One of the most common discoveries of the grieving process is our need for more or closer friends. Yet friends do not just appear, nor do friendships grow in a short time. Often the longing we feel for friends cannot be fulfilled when we are most in need. But we can gradually meet new people as we take part in activities, in courses, groups or local events. When we take care of ourselves and develop new interests, we will find that people will be attracted to us and we will discover new friends. Many of us who have lost a loved one have found close friends in a support group.

Building supports is not an easy task, especially after a loss. We may have to experience some trial and error and some disappointments along the way. Yet when we find an activity or a group of people that we can relate to, it usually leads to others. The possibility of networking is endless.

24 • Reminders, Memorials and Rituals

Eric:

I wrote Diane's obituary and it ran in the Herald *and the* Globe. *Apparently because of the B.B.C. film Diane had participated in, the wire services picked it up. It ran in San Francisco which is really bizarre because it's Diane's favorite city and it's where her siblings live.*

Anne:

There are certain things I still do. I have to keep pictures of him above my eye level. I still keep them in the house and I will look when I want to. I know another widow that had a huge portrait of her husband made. Do not conduct your life as if your husband was alive. You'd never have to think again if you're one of those widows. Don't set up a shrine.

The first Christmas afterward I took the kids to Disneyland because everywhere we went our family and friends would go into states, crying and everything. I knew we had to get out of there. Get out the next Christmas if you've got this problem.

Sue:

There are quite a few of her clothes I still have. There's an old friend of mine who said to me when I had on this sweater that my mother had made, "It's just like having her arms around you." It was true. I have her china which means a lot to me and I have her wedding ring. If my father had died there wouldn't have been that same connection with the clothes. Sometimes I'll see myself in the mirror or I'll say something that makes me think of my mother.

Reminders

A young woman whose father died keeps his sweater to wrap around her shoulders when she has a hard day. A widower keeps a picture of his wife in his living room. He feels her presence whenever he looks at it. A husband and wife visit their son's grave every Sunday after church. There are so many reminders of our loved ones: pictures, clothing, personal possessions, places. Sometimes a gesture may suddenly bring up the memory of our loved one.

We can use these reminders to bring up our memories and these can comfort us. They can help us to feel less alone and to remember what the deceased meant to us and all the good times we had together.

Pictures can be especially comforting reminders of our loved one's features and expressions, their gifts and their energy. By looking through albums or even at one picture, we can review our love and understanding for that person. If our loved one died after a long illness we can use pictures to bring up memories of the happier times.

A woman, whose husband committed suicide, periodically takes out an album with pictures of her husband and the family. She gathers her children together to look at the album and to talk about their father. Because she is concerned about the young childrens' reaction to their father's suicide, she uses the pictures as a way of stimulating conversation about him.

We may also have various objects to remind us of our loved one. Perhaps a gift we once received from that person may have special significance. After her mother died, a woman rescued an almost dead purple passion plant from her house and took it home. Within a few days, it showed new life. Although she moved several times and kept neglecting the plant, twelve years after her mother's death, the plant is still alive. For her, it symbolizes a continuing source of life and a sense of connection with her mother. Jim kept a plant that someone gave him when his sister died. He kept the plant in his study as a reminder of his sister and as a comforting presence. The plant even inspired him to write a poem about his sister.

Many of us may keep a piece of clothing or an article belonging to a loved one. It may be a watch, a robe, or a Christmas tree ornament. My grandmother's cane leans against my study wall. Whenever I look at it, I see her setting off on one of her long walks. It's both a reminder and an inspiration. She never stopped walking, even when her health and her vision failed. We may keep letters or tapes of our loved one's voice. We can take them out whenever we feel the need to be with our loved one's memory.

A room or a place we associated with our loved one may be special for us. Our loved one's bedroom, or a corner of the living room with his or her favorite chair may be a place of comfort. We may keep our loved one's room unchanged for a while as we sense their presence. As time passes, we may rearrange that space as we make changes in our own lives.

We may want to visit places we shared with our loved one: a favorite vacation spot or a place close to home where we walked or picnicked together. Going to these places may help us feel connected to our loved one.

Some places may cause us discomfort and awaken painful memories. We may find ourselves avoiding places that remind us of the circumstances of our loved one's death or of how much we miss that person. There is no need to confront that pain. We can take plenty of time to choose the reminders and the places that help us to feel connected and that give us comfort.

Rituals and memorials

There are many rituals in our lives that express meaning, celebrate events, and give external expression to a particular reality. Rituals are not only religious. They can be as simple and ordinary as a birthday party, a Thanksgiving dinner, or lighting a candle with a special intention or memory.

There are rituals that are common to our whole society and rituals that are shared by a particular culture or ethnic group. These rituals are there for us. All we need to do is to participate and to give that ritual our own particular expression.

Some of us may want to visit the grave of our loved one at regular intervals. We may plant flowers around it. Tending a grave site is a family ritual in most Latin countries. It gives family members a sense of continuity as a unit as well as a sense of connection with the deceased. Some of us may like to spend quiet moments alone by the grave of our loved one. We can talk to that person, read a poem or say a prayer. We may prefer to keep an urn or container for the ashes and put it in a special place. Tending that place with flowers or other decorations can be a comforting ritual.

We may want to plant a tree in memory of our loved one. We can do this as part of a ceremony with a gathering of family or friends and perhaps with a reading. Some of us may want to plant a garden or create a special spot around our homes. When Maureen's sister died, her parents planted a tree and a flower garden behind their house as a memorial. When the flowers appear each spring, that spot is a source of great comfort to them.

Special days or events can be an appropriate occasion for a ritual. A birthday, a wedding anniversary, or the anniversary of our loved one's death can be spent in a special way. Because there are no prescribed rituals for these events, we may wonder how to mark that day. Some of us will feel anxious as one of these days approaches.

It may be helpful to focus on planning how to spend that day. If we want to spend the day with others, we can decide who to share it with. We can go to a special place, read an appropriate poem or passage, or share memories. We may simply decide to go out to lunch or dinner with friends.

Some of us may choose to spend such a day alone. In Chapter 13, Merryl describes spending the first anniversary of her husband's death reflecting at the beach. Being alone with the memories of our loved one in a beautiful setting can be healing . We may want to have a number of rituals over a few days, spending some of our time alone with our letters and pictures, and some time with trusted friends. We can choose the format that meets our particular needs.

Linda wanted to commemorate the anniversary of her son's suicide. She planned to have her ex-husband and her two sons come to her home for dinner and afterwards to join her at the cemetery and share a piece she had written in memory of her son. Her family did not feel comfortable going to the cemetery, but they did come for the dinner. Linda then decided to share what she had written with the members of her support group.

A woman whose husband died wanted to mark the anniversary of his death in a way that would involve the youngest child. She and her sister and brothers and all their children wrote messages or drew pictures expressing their love. They placed each one inside a balloon and blew up all the balloons. Then they all walked to the top of a nearby hill and released the balloons into the air.

A ritual needn't be elaborate or require a lot of planning. Some of us may simply want to light a candle, read a poem, or listen to a favorite piece of music.

A local bereavement counseling center holds a yearly memorial service for all those who have been members of its support groups. The service is held just before the holidays, in early or mid-November. Participants contribute by sharing poems, or passages that have special significance for them. The readings are followed by prayers

and songs that are read and sung by everyone. The service is not
directed by clergy. Rather, the readers are introduced by group facili-
tators and staff. At the end of the service, the participants light a taper
candle from a light passed on from a central candle. As each person
lights the candle, he or she says the name of their loved one. The
church is filled with light as they say a final prayer and sing. After the
service, all share in a light meal prepared by the participants. Such
services are a comforting way to express the importance of the relationship we had with our loved one and of our memories.

Holidays

The holidays can be a difficult time and we may be filled with anxiety
when we must decide how to celebrate them, especially in the first year
after a death. For instance, Thanksgiving may mean a family gathering, but this time that gathering may heighten the absence of a key
member of our family. Christmas and Hanukah may be joyful times
yet we may not feel like being joyful or buying gifts.

We can decide how to participate in these events and choose a
way that feels most comfortable for us. For instance, we can talk with
our family about where and how to celebrate Thanksgiving. Some
members may want to keep as much of the family tradition as possible.
Others may not want to participate at all. This is a time to respect
everyone's feelings and to make it as easy as possible for one another.
Perhaps we can lessen the strain on ourselves by buying prepared food
instead of spending long hours in the kitchen or we may want to go
out for that dinner.

Often, conversation around the table may be strained. Each one
of us may want to protect the other by not mentioning the deceased.
We may wonder who will sit in Dad's chair at the end of the table and
who will carve the turkey. We can ease these awkward moments by
taking the risk of mentioning the deceased and what he or she used
to do. We can talk about who will sit where and who will serve the food,
or say the blessing. It's difficult to talk about the changes taking place
in the family, but once the ice is broken, the conversation will flow with
greater ease.

It's important to take plenty of time to plan how we can best be
at ease during Christmas or Hanukah celebrations, knowing that total
comfort is not possible. Some of us may want to refrain from decorat-
ing a tree or giving gifts. Some of us may want to keep these traditions
for the children, but not for ourselves. Others may find it helpful to

keep everything the same. It's best to talk among ourselves before the holidays, and listen to one another's needs. Then we can set those plans aside for a while and discuss them again as the holiday approaches.

Some of us may prefer to take a trip during the holidays either to be alone with our feelings or because we don't feel up to a family celebration. Anne planned a trip to Disneyland with her children over Christmas. Another young widow planned a ski trip with her children. Holidays can heighten our sadness. It's important to be easy on ourselves and one another.

It's best not to project the first year's holidays onto future years. If we are disappointed by an overly simple celebration, we can remind ourselves that each year will be different as time passes. We will have new choices and new perspectives to help us make those choices.

HOW FRIENDS AND CO-WORKERS CAN HELP

When you need them most, to ask
where to go from here, your hair
growing sparse as February grass,
they've gone, singly or united
under stone in the safest place
where the stranger who cares for them,
pulling a mower behind his International Harvester
to trim the grass they vivify,
setting poison out for mice and squirrels
that mate nearby, for weeds,
knows them better than you, seasons
laboring by like old city buses against the wind
but too far away to disturb
a parent's rest, their reward for teaching you
that being their child's the same
as being no one else, that mourning them's
the final thing you have to learn.

David Citino, "The Funeral"

25 • Helping a Friend

Understanding the grieving person

Bill:

It's helpful to have someone that understands. My new lady knows all about my wife. We talk about it now and then. I don't overdo it. She's been good to me.

Eric:

My friends were as helpful as they could be, but if you haven't been through the experience it's difficult. People were scared to talk, to ask anything. I remember being at the beach with a friend and I started to cry and that really frightened her. People do their best and I think actually all my friends learned a lot. I did too because I didn't know how to help people in those situations. You give some sign that you care and that you're really willing to listen to them talk.

Phil:

Men do have a hard time with this. Some people in general were trying to be helpful and did say the wrong things: "Oh I know how you felt, my daughter was sick." Before long you realize you're role-reversing with them. They don't need to say that, just to say they're sorry and just be there sometimes. There were a couple of people like that. There was a friend of mine who was highly sensitive. He always knew. We were friends since undergraduate days. There was another friend who has experienced certain kinds of setbacks and who really tried to draw me out, to get me into sports, going to events with him. I knew it was just a strategy, but I knew I needed it. I knew I needed him to be able to carry the ball for me, whereas maybe I was carrying it for him before. You have some help from family, some professional help and your friends.

Marilyn:

One of the big things we learned was that when it's a pregnancy loss, people neglect to think about the loss to the husband. One of Tim's big difficulties after our first loss particularly, was that people would say things to him about their regrets on my loss. It wouldn't occur to them that he had had a loss too. This hurt him tremendously. We even had good friends who would send me cards. He was crying and grieving too.

I think it's been one of my and my husband's greatest difficulties, that so many people do not understand this kind of a loss. Many people who have been through this type of a loss have gone on to have children, and a much smaller number have had repeated losses like we have and finally given up. You find yourself picking out people you want to be near because it's so painful to be with people who don't understand. Sometimes it's all right to be around people who don't know what you've been through but who are generally sensitive people and you know if the subject came up they would be okay. But some people who know everything about what happened are so insensitive to what it really means to you that it just hurts to be around them.

Sue:

For a while my grandmother's sister started writing to me quite a bit, incorporating me in her family, becoming a surrogate figure. Her presence was very important. She and then my mother's sister became very close to me although I hadn't been in touch with her for a long time. Only the female members of the family gave me that sense of family feeling.

I never heard my mother's father speak about my mother's death. He's eighty-seven years old and never talks about her. It's very strange to go and visit him and not have it be a topic of conversation.

Often we are uncertain about how to act when a friend suffers the death of a loved one. We may be torn by conflicting feelings ourselves, by deep sympathy for our friend's loss and also by the fear of our own vulnerability to loss. In the face of the death of a friend or relative's loved one, it's normal to feel that it might happen to us and to want to withdraw. If we have not experienced loss ourselves, with the best of intentions we may wish to see our friend bounce back to his or her former state. We may feel this way because we truly wish our friend to be happy, and also because all of us tend to be uncomfortable with someone who is in deep pain. Finally, we may be so baffled by how to treat the bereaved that we may avoid mentioning the death or simply keep our distance, believing our friend needs the privacy to work out his or her feelings.

Perhaps we may believe that any mention of the deceased would only cause him or her pain. We may simply be afraid of making things worse or we may be uncertain just how to respond to such a tragedy. An important thing to remember is that we cannot cause our friend or relative to feel pain by mentioning the deceased. The pain is already there and it is a heavy burden to carry. By visiting our friends and talking to them about their loss we can actually help relieve that burden.

It is not as difficult as we might imagine to help a grieving friend. We can give solace to our friends and family in a number of simple ways. The first, and one of the most important ways we can help is to understand and to accept what our friends or relatives are feeling. This may mean accepting the fact that a friend or relative who was formerly a source of great support for us can no longer play this role at the same time as mourning a loss. It may mean understanding that a grieving person is often torn by the very strong emotions of anger, guilt and sadness. It may involve taking the time to see just what a particular loss may mean to our friend.

Someone who is in great pain may not behave in their usual manner. If our friend or relative is a man we may be surprised at his tears and his expression of emotion. Men have a right to grieve too, even though society expects them to put on a stiff upper lip. Perhaps a friend or family member might be unusually silent or irritable and withdrawn. We may feel that this behavior might be directed at ourselves, but it's only a reflection of their inner turmoil. Our quiet and unjudging regard for the grieving person will actually help that person to move through their suffering.

Accepting the strong emotions a bereaved person feels means also accepting the time it takes to work through these emotions. A person who has suffered loss cannot return to his or her previous behavior in a matter of days or weeks. With the best of intentions, we may wish to help our friend return to his or her usual disposition. We all want to see our friends and relatives happy. However, there are times when we can help them more by understanding that they need to feel their sadness or their guilt for weeks and even for many months. They need to feel accepted as grieving persons.

We may grieve for a friend or for a lover as deeply as we may grieve for a parent or other member of our family. It's best not to make judgments about whether our friends are justified in grieving for someone who we may feel was not close enough. A young adult who has lost a close friend will experience all of the pain and turmoil of grief and will need the same acceptance and consideration as someone who has lost a relative. Perhaps someone we know has lost a child through miscarriage. Because that child was invisible to us, we may not think such a loss is truly a tragedy, but a mishap. But such a loss is as searing and painful as other types of losses and the parents feel as great an emptiness and despair. Although as a society we tend to overlook the importance of a pregnancy loss or the loss of a friend, co-worker or lover, we can be helpful if we understand that these kinds of losses are deeply affecting.

The narratives tell us that one of the most important supports a grieving person needs is to have his or her pain acknowledged and accepted. This means very simply not trying to coax our friends out of their pain and not ignoring that pain.. There are a number of ways in which we can do this. One important point to remember is to be ourselves and to act naturally towards the person who is mourning.

What we can do for the grieving person

We can express our acceptance and understanding of a grieving person in a number of simple ways. We can pay very careful attention to how we communicate with a grieving person and we can also do a number of practical things.

One of the most important things we can do for someone after a loss is to stay in touch and let that person know that we care. This can be as simple as a phone call to let that person know that we are thinking of them.

People who have lost a loved one appreciate it when friends stop by for a visit in the weeks and months after the funeral. Perhaps we may feel uncomfortable about making such a visit, but we don't have to say anything terribly wise during our stay. Usually, a few words expressing our sympathy will suffice. Just pressing someone's hand or giving them a hug will convey our concern.

After all the activities associated with a funeral, the survivors begin to feel the full impact of their loss. That is the time a visit or a phone call will be the most welcome. When the services are over, we all go home to our normal lives, but the bereaved returns to an empty apartment or to a house with an empty room.

We may also want to say just a few words about the deceased. For instance, we might say, "Your mother was a wonderful person. It's so hard to lose a person like that." Even though our friend or family member may have buried a loved one, that person is still very much alive in their thoughts. They will be pleased to know that others are thinking of the deceased and that others also cared about their loved one. Generally, if we just speak very briefly about the deceased, that will give our friend the permission to talk and that conversation may be a great relief.

Or perhaps our friend is not verbal and would rather be silent about his or her memories and feelings. We can sit in silence with that person. We don't always need words to comfort. Just our presence alone is a sign that we care. We may have expectations about what our friend or relative may want us to do or say when we visit. It's best to be open and to take our cues from our friend.

Sometimes, just holding someone is a great comfort. A close friend of mine who lost her mother broke down and wept while we were sitting in the living-room after dinner. She held out her hand so I could hold it while she was crying. She needed to feel that someone was with her while those tears were flowing.

However, not all of us may feel comfortable with someone else's tears. It's best to know our own limits, and if we have a low tolerance for weeping, we might do something practical and more active to show our friend that we care. Our friend will respond more to our attitude and our concern than to any specific gesture we might make.

We can also help the bereaved in a number of practical ways. We can lighten the burden of everyday chores by driving the children to school, picking up the laundry, or preparing a simple meal. When my mother died, my relatives came from Europe for the funeral and suddenly I had a full house. A close friend of mine made up the beds for me and left some casseroles in the kitchen. Another friend arranged for a light meal after the funeral. These were simple gestures, but they meant so much to me then both because of their thoughtfulness, and because in my grief, such small tasks seemed too much to handle.

The recently widowed will appreciate practical help in the months and weeks after the death of a spouse. We can help a widow with legal matters or with organizing child care. We can help an older widow to re-register the car, get social security, or put in insurance claims. If our friend or relative is a widower, we can help with managing the household and with finding childcare. Our friend may have to juggle a demanding job and get his children to school or arrange for their care after school before he returns from work. Sometimes we can just be there to discuss issues around children or household. A widowed person not only misses the companionship of a spouse but the opportunity to discuss all the small problems of work and home.

There are a number of less obvious things we can do for someone who has suffered loss. If our friend or relative is a mature adult who has lost a cherished parent, just talking about that parent and the place that parent had in our friend's life can be helpful. And although we can never replace a person, we can do some of the nice things a parent would do for our friend, whether inviting them out to lunch or to a movie.

We can also help our friend to clear out his or her parent's clothing and personal effects. This is not only a very painful task for our friend, but a difficult one too, because he or she might not be able to think clearly about keeping mementos that might be a source of comfort later on.

If we happen to have a photograph of the deceased, we might have it enlarged and give it to our friend as a gift. When my neighbor's daughter died of cancer, one of her friends had some pictures of the daughter from a wedding party. She had them enlarged and mailed them to my neighbor. Or perhaps we might have a memento of the deceased that we know will please our friend or relative.

A young adult who has lost a parent might appreciate our interest in their studies or in their job. After the loss of a parent, a young person may feel invisible or of less importance. A phone call inquiring about life at school or courses may be very welcome.

Then there are some simple but thoughtful things we can do for bereaved friends: bringing a few flowers or a plant, or bringing over something we baked. After a loss, people experience dips in self-esteem and this kind of attention will help them feel better about themselves.

Staying in touch may mean calling or visiting on a regular basis. A person who has suffered a loss may feel terribly isolated in his or her new situation. Since most of us have very busy lives it may not be possible to give as much time as we would like. Yet we can encourage other friends to get in touch. If we are too busy even to make a phone call we can always send a card or a brief note. Any expression of concern is always deeply appreciated by someone who is grieving.

People who have lost someone close will have strong reactions to that loss during holidays and also on the anniversary of the death or on the birthday of the deceased. Sending a note or card on Mother's or Father's Day to a parent who has lost a child is a way of letting that person know that you share the memory of that child and their sense of loss. We can send a note to mark the anniversary of a death, or the birthday of the deceased. We can continue to acknowledge our friend's loss as the years pass. While our friend or relative may not wish this loss to be in the forefront of their lives as time passes and they heal, there are times when they would like to know that the deceased and their own pain have not been forgotten.

Holidays especially are times when survivors not only feel a fresh surge of pain but also feel most keenly the contrast between the good fortune of intact families and partnerships and their own situation. It may be a period when we are absorbed in preparations for our own families and partners, but a few minutes of our time can bring great solace to friends.

As the weeks pass after the death, we can very gently draw the bereaved person towards outside activity. A bereaved person may not have the energy, the initiative or the self-esteem to take part in social events. We can invite them out for coffee or a simple meal or a movie, some activity our friend would feel comfortable with. For instance, a recently widowed person will not feel at ease at a large party attended mainly by couples. We need to be sensitive to the changed circumstances of our friend and to the fact that the customary social settings may now emphasize their sense of loss. Phil's friend helped him renew his interest in sports events at a time when he was unable to seek out diversion. He knew the kinds of things that gave Phil pleasure and used them to draw him out.

When our bereaved friend begins to take part in social activities, we should avoid treating him or her with pity or dwelling on their loss. Pity diminishes a person's self-esteem. It's better simply to acknowledge the loss and the change in that person's life and leave it at that. A good guideline both for ourselves and for our behavior towards the grieving is to be ourselves and to treat our friend as a normal person.

We can be sensitive to the grieving person's need for a balance of solitude and social times. This balance varies from person to person. Sometimes our grieving friend may long for someone to talk to, but there are times when he or she would prefer just to be alone. Being in tune with our friends' different needs may mean just letting them know that we understand their need for some private time, but that we are available when they want to be with us. Friends' or relatives' need to be alone with their pain does not mean that they are rejecting us. Sometimes we all need to be alone with our tears and with our memories.

Not only does a bereaved person experience great emotional upheavals, they also experience change in their lives beyond the change of circumstances that a death leaves. After the death of a loved one, a person begins a long process of self-discovery that may lead them to changes in activities and even in life style. As our friend goes through these changes we can be helpful by being supportive and understanding. For instance, we may be surprised that our widowed friend has begun to see other people in the months after the death. It's useful to understand that this socializing is not a betrayal of our friend's deceased spouse or partner, and that because everyone is unique, no one can be replaced. Sometimes, bereaved friends may go through a period of experimentation in both relationships and lifestyles. It's best not to make judgments about our friend or relative's social efforts. It's part of the grieving person's journey to a new sense of self.

Being supportive means allowing our friend or relative to change and encouraging new activities and new identities when that person is ready. Any change is not only stressful but can cause the person making changes to feel lonely. If we are supportive we may help that person reach a new and fulfilling way of life. Being supportive may mean very simply that we are available to our friends, and that we accept them for who they are at any phase of their lives.

In Chapter 28, Anne will describe her decision to sell her house in the suburbs and move to an apartment in the city. This new living arrangement reflected the person she had become, a business woman with children who were almost grown up. She was terribly disappointed when her mother questioned the move and treated it as an act of betrayal. A widower decided to move in with a woman he had begun seeing a year after his wife's death. His sons were so upset that they stayed away from their father. It may be very painful for us to see our friends and family change. No one really likes to experience change, but if we understand that a friend or a relative is the best judge of their happiness, and that the old ways may be a source of discomfort, it will be easier for us to face that change.

How to talk to the grieving person

Faced with the enormity and finality of death, we are often at a loss for words. We don't know what to say to a grieving friend or relative. Often we feel that we must say something that will "make things all right." It's helpful to realize that one of the best ways of communicating with someone who has suffered loss is simply to listen and to be a sympathetic and responsive presence.

To communicate effectively with a person who is suffering grief we need to know our own feelings. We need to know whether we feel uncomfortable with sadness and tears, whether we feel uneasy if someone expresses anger or bitterness. This can help us avoid projecting our feelings on others, such as telling a grieving person that we don't want them to feel sad or angry. We need to know ourselves, so we can be helpful without exceeding our own limits. We needn't change our personalities in order to be helpful to a friend. There is always a choice in how we handle both our communication and our actions towards the grieving.

But what do we say to someone immediately after the funeral, or the first time we meet a friend after a death in that friend's family? The simplest comments are always the best. We can say what we feel: "I'm so sorry." The way we speak means as much as what we say. If we talk with feeling and with sincerity, if we act naturally, we will communicate effectively.

In the first days and weeks after a death, it's best to say little when we visit our friends. They may not feel like talking much, but will welcome our presence. A simple hug may be just what they need for comfort. This may mean that we sit with our friend's silence. In our culture, we often place negative interpretations on silence. However, after a death, when feelings are in turmoil, it is often not possible to be articulate. We needn't feel that we have to force conversation. Nor should we press for details about the death. The best practice is to let the grieving person take the lead.

When talking to the mourner, we should avoid clichés and pat statements such as "It's all for the best," or "She had a good life," or "He's out of pain now," or "Aren't you lucky that . . . " In our discomfort with death, we may be tempted to make these kinds of remarks when someone has died after a long illness or at an advanced age. It may be helpful to remember that when a person has had a long life, his or her friends and family have had that much more time to love him and to build the relationship, and therefore it's very difficult to lose such a person. We should also remember that even if someone died after a long illness, the friends and relatives of that person will have always hoped that their loved one would survive. They may not feel that "it was all for the best." These kinds of comments are a way of cutting off communication about the deceased, and denying the powerful feelings of grief.

It's especially important to avoid minimizing the loss of a child through miscarriage with such comments as "It's all right, you can try again," or "It wasn't really a baby." The man and woman who have lost a child in this way were parents, and they need to have their loss and their pain acknowledged.

We should also avoid encouraging denial about the death. Our friend or relative may feel a strong need to know about the details of the loved one's death. It's helpful to know that this is part of the grieving process and is not at all morbid. Jim was very anxious about the real causes of his sister's death beyond her fall and felt restless until he had the results of the autopsy. Our friend might need to go over and over the story of his or her loved one's death. We can listen quietly without comment, and without saying, "It doesn't matter now that she's gone." Our friend is trying to understand the death, and also trying to hold on to the memory of his or her loved one. It's perfectly normal to dwell on the death, and he or she will move on to other topics of conversation as time passes.

Comments about God, such as "It was God's will," may anger the grieving person if she or he does not share the same religious beliefs. This type of comment also tends to minimize loss and to break off conversation. A grieving person often feels that the world is unjust and may direct his or her anger at God.

As time passes, one of the best ways of communicating with a grieving friend or relative is to listen without contradicting. We should not tell the mourner, "I know how you feel." We can ask how a friend is feeling, but it is presuming too much to tell someone how they are feeling. It's best to inquire gently and then to listen without either rebuking or comparing. Everyone's experience with grief is unique. To try to compare is to belittle or deny that person's experience. Telling our friend, "Don't feel guilty," or "Don't feel sad," is both a way of projecting our own feelings on others and of denying our friend's feelings.

Friends and family must be allowed to express such difficult feelings as guilt, anger and even suicidal feelings. Many survivors of a death express the wish to die themselves after such a tragic event. This may be the case when a parent loses a child and his or her life suddenly seems meaningless. It may be very hard for us to listen to comments like this but they are valid feelings. When our friends express these feelings, they are putting them outside themselves literally. Saying them out loud is a way of getting rid of them, while holding them in may cause these feelings to grow.

Guilt is always a very strong element in the grieving process, and it's best to allow our friends to express their feelings of guilt without contradicting them. In the case of a suicide, guilt is an especially powerful emotion. Survivors of a suicide need to go over and over their behavior in their search for understanding the suicide and also ultimately to be able to let go of guilt. Sudden deaths as a result of illness or without any previous warning also cause survivors to feel guilt. They may think of all the things they wished they had said or done. We can be helpful by not denying these feelings, by not saying, "Don't feel bad," or "Don't worry." As time passes, we can gently remind them of all the good things they did for their loved one, but in the early weeks and months after a death, mourners need to feel guilt.

Because grieving is a self-regarding process, we may be surprised to find people who were always so interested in others talking exclusively about themselves. It's helpful to understand that this is necessary and that it is temporary. The grieving person is exploring his or her new situation and talking may be a way of thinking out loud, of examining those new circumstances.

We should also avoid talking about our own troubles and pain in front of a grieving person. Their own feelings are so raw that they may be very susceptible to other people's distress. What may seem like a complaint about a trivial matter at work may feel like an intolerable burden to our friend.

We can help our friends and relatives by listening actively, not only nodding our heads, and by the things we say. We can tell someone that their feelings are valid, or we can draw them out by gently asking them questions about what they may be feeling. As time passes we can tell them that the directions they are moving in and their other decisions are sound. The chances are that our friend is uncertain and that such support will give him or her the courage to make that decision.

Listening can have its unexpected rewards. Over a period of many months, I had a number of long lunches and dinners with a close friend who had been widowed. As I listened to her, I responded not only to her feelings but also to her search for new goals and a new lifestyle. Over the months, my friend moved from feelings of anger, bitterness and chaos toward the discovery of a new set of goals and a brand-new sense of herself. I felt as if I had participated in her unfolding, and as if I had shared her triumphs as she journeyed through the dark period of the early months after the death to a new excitement about her life.

Sometimes our friends may feel that they need permission to talk about the loved one who died, and if we mention that person it is a great relief. The unspoken can loom very large when we are with someone who is grieving. A young woman in my neighborhood lost her mother shortly after she had given birth to her first child. When I met her as she was walking her baby in the stroller, I said, " Your mother would have loved being a grandmother." "There's not a day I don't think about it," she replied. And then we moved on to speak of her child and her new home. Acknowledging loss is very helpful to a grieving person. They may feel that their pain is invisible if those around them fail to mention it.

After those first weeks and months, we can take our cues from the person who has had the loss. If we have made them feel comfortable and they are secure about our concern they will take the lead in conversation. As our friend begins to talk about his or her loss we should avoid pressing them about the future. A grieving person is in such emotional turmoil that they have enough difficulty just handling the present. The months after a death are much too soon to think about the demands of the future.

Some days our friend may want to talk about the one who died. Some days he or she may want to talk of other things. Grief is unpredictable. A person may experience a string of good days and then plunge back into a renewed sense of sadness. We mustn't feel as if this means a sliding back or a lack of progress. Frequent ups and downs are a normal part of bereavement.

Because loss may be a new experience for us, we may feel uncertain about just how to act. Helping a friend or relative who has suffered loss can be very simple. What is required is not a superhuman effort, but a quality of sensitivity and caring, listening with concern, and allowing our friend to express whatever he or she may be feeling. It's also a matter of admitting that in this society of ours, where every illness seems to have a cure and every problem seems to have a solution, there are limits. There is no cure for sadness. However, if we allow friends and relatives to express that sadness, to shed those tears, we are actually helping them move through them. We will not only have helped our friend, but will have learned something about ourselves and how to cope when we may be faced with a similar situation.

26 • How to Write a Letter of Sympathy

Perhaps one of the most difficult things for us to do after a death is to write a letter of condolence. We may not be able to think of things to say in the face of such an event. Some sample letters are given here. There are a few things we can keep in mind when writing such a letter. Keep it simple. Let your friend or co-worker know that you care about them and their loss. Make a reference to that loss, and express your own sorrow about the death.

Writing a letter is a way of acknowledging our friend or relative's pain. People often keep such letters for years after the death and reread them from time to time. After a loss we are extremely sensitive to other people's reaction towards us because we are in such pain. A letter may bring more solace than we might ordinarily imagine from such a simple act.

When a mature adult loses a parent

Dear Andrea,

I just learned from Doug that your mother died. What a terrible blow for you. I remember feeling that the bottom had dropped out of my world when my mother died. No one ever loves us or knows us like a mother. You spoke of your mother so often and with such love that although I never met her I gained the impression of a wonderful and understanding woman.

I want you to know that your friends are with you during this difficult time. I know just how busy you are, but I hope you will be able to have some time to be with your feelings. I will be thinking of you in the weeks and months to come.

Please accept my sympathy and my deepest concern.

Fondly,
Marianne

When parents lose a child

Dear Joan and Ray,

We were shocked and saddened to hear of the death of your Elizabeth. It seems against nature to lose a child, especially such a young and gifted little person. We know what a close and loving family you are and how tenderly you cared for Elizabeth while she was ill. What a terrible loss for you and for all of us who loved her.

We want you to know that we feel very close to you during this very difficult time and that you will be in our hearts and

thoughts during the months to come.
Please accept our concern and our deepest sympathy.

Sincerely,
Julia and Richard

When a younger person loses a spouse

Dear Barry,
I was so sorry to hear of Evelyn's death. The two of you had such a good marriage and so much to look forward to. It seems terribly unfair to lose a spouse when one is so young. All of us who loved Evelyn will think of her and remember her courage and her talent.
I want you to know that we are thinking of you and of your tragic loss. You will be very much in our hearts in the long months to come.
Please accept my deepest sympathy and concern.

Yours,
Andy

When an older person loses a spouse

Dearest Emma,
I was shocked and saddened to hear about Alfred's heart attack and death. I know you had been looking forward to his retirement and to some travel together after all those years of hard work. Even though the two of you were very different, you complemented each other so well. We always thought of you as one. What a terrible loss for you.
I want you to know how much Peter and I are thinking of you and that we will be there for you in the long and difficult weeks and months ahead.
Please accept our deepest sympathy.

With my love,
Susan

When someone loses a sibling

Dear Craig,

I was so sad to hear about Annie's death. I know that she had been having some difficult times and just how worried you were about her. I know too that the two of you had had a lot of disagreement lately, but that you were always a loving and concerned brother. You did so much for her.

Losing a sister is a terrible blow. No matter how old we are or that we have our own families, a sister is always part of ourselves.

I want you to know how sorry I am and that you will be very much in my thoughts in the weeks and months to come.

Yours,
Matt

When someone loses a child through miscarriage

Dear Karen and Allen,

I was so sorry to receive your letter telling me that you had lost your baby. I wish I had been there to hug Karen and to talk to you both. It's hard for me to be so far away when you are in such pain.

Perhaps the baby wasn't visible to many people, but you were three and the two of you were a mother and a father. You made so many preparations for this baby, but it wasn't just the room and the furniture you chose, she was part of your life, your hopes and your dreams.

Please be good to yourselves during the difficult months ahead. Take the time you need for your sadness and pain. I will stop by as soon as I return from California and I will be with you in the time to come.

Fondly,
Martha

27 • *Helping a Fellow-Worker*

Understanding the grief of a fellow-worker

As co-workers, supervisors and employers, we may feel unsure how to relate to a bereaved worker. We may have difficulty balancing our expectations of productivity with sensitivity towards the grieving person. In too many cases, the work environment leaves little room for the strong feelings resulting from personal tragedy. Yet a little understanding and creativity can help to create a more comfortable environment for everyone.

Someone who has lost a loved one experiences many strong emotions, and these may occur at any time during the day or night, even in the middle of work. The sadness, anger, guilt, depression and fear a grieving person feels cannot be controlled at will. And while a person may find it difficult to brush these emotions aside, he or she may also feel guilty or embarrassed when revealing them.

In the weeks and months after a death, the bereaved person may experience a great deal of disruption in his or her personal life. Because of this disruption, he or she may not seem like the same person and may even seem less capable than before. For example, a grieving person may experience a diminished ability to concentrate, and may forget small things and even more important things like showing up for appointments. Because grief affects our self-esteem, someone who has suffered a loss may be reluctant to generate ideas or to try new things. He or she may become irritated at small annoyances, speak harshly to co-workers or even become angry over what may seem like a small matter. A grieving person will also be depressed and therefore display a lower level of energy and productivity. He or she may be absent more frequently and have more illnesses.

It's important to recognize that these behavior patterns are not due to laziness or unwillingness to work, but are a reflection of the disruption occurring in the bereaved worker's life. It is likely that the person is aware that she or he is not acting normally and would welcome a chance to talk about how they feel and what could be helpful to their work.

The grief a person experiences is an important source of stress and will not disappear in a matter of days or weeks. A bereaved person will have some good days and some bad days. He or she may even welcome work as a way of setting the grief aside for a while. Yet he or she may still manifest the symptoms of stress in a number of ways. Grief takes many months and in some cases many years to work through.

How employers and co-workers can help

Funerals, wakes and viewings are important rituals of leave-taking and are significant events for the bereaved. It's best for the worker to be able to participate fully in these events and without pressure from the office or plant. In some types of workplaces this might be difficult to achieve, yet if possible, everything should be done to assure the grieving worker adequate time off.

Many companies offer a bereavement leave as part of their personnel policies and practices. For example, a worker may receive a three-day leave for the death of a family member. Often, the length of leave varies with the closeness of the relationship. Many workers use other allowed days off for extending their leave from work. For example, one woman took one of her four allowed days off to attend the funeral of a close friend, telling only her supervisor the exact reason for her absence. Some employees may have their leave extended at the supervisor's discretion.

As co-workers or supervisors, attending the funeral or viewing and expressing our condolences in person may be a great comfort to the bereaved. During these occasions, it's best not to discuss work except to assure the grieving person that they need not worry about the office. For those of us who are unable to attend the funeral, sending flowers or letters expressing our support is an effective way of letting our co-worker know that we care about them and their loss. The bereaved often keep letters and cards for many months and refer to them as a source of comfort. What may seem like a small gesture to us may be a source of lasting support to someone who has suffered loss.

Within the workplace, we can notify the appropriate people, our co-workers and those in personnel or managerial positions who would want to know that our colleague has lost a loved one. Sometimes a department circular or newsletter is the place to mention personal events. Often, these notices inspire people to speak to the newly bereaved person or to send a note. Because there are no common practices for announcing a death beyond a notice in the obituary columns of the newspaper, we may be uncertain whether we should share such news or even how we should do so. It's helpful to remember that a grieving person may feel isolated and even invisible in their grief and may welcome any kind of acknowledgement of their loss.

Sometimes the return of the newly bereaved person to his or her workplace can be a difficult time for all concerned. The bereaved person may not know what to say, and we as co-workers and supervisors may be at a loss for words. The situation may be awkward yet we can do some simple things to ease the way.

First of all, as a supervisor or manager, we can be in touch with the person to talk about his or her return. We can carefully discuss the day and time, whether the first day or week will be full or part time. We can also discuss how the person would like to return. For instance, the person might want to return to a normal workload and regular schedule right away, or perhaps might want to ease back in, meeting with the supervisor first and taking on a lighter workload or fewer responsibilities. In Chapter 13, Merryl described how she worked only a few days a week when she returned to work and also how she was able to discuss her sadness and low energy with her secretary. In some circumstances, it might be appropriate to arrange for a different set of responsibilities or even a different job description for a newly bereaved worker.

On the other hand, it may be just as difficult to return to work after a funeral and to have everyone come up to one's desk and express condolences as it is to have everyone act as if nothing had happened. While silence may isolate the grieving person, being overwhelmed with condolences may make one feel pitied. As co-workers or managers we must be sensitive both to the person's need to feel useful in the work environment and that person's need to have a major loss acknowledged. In these circumstances, a touch, a look of understanding or a simple note can be comforting. When it comes to tasks, we may want to avoid the extremes of being overly protective or too demanding.

As the weeks and months pass, we may feel that things have returned to normal at work and we may easily forget the bereaved person's grief. Perhaps it is not evident. Yet often this is when the grieving person will be feeling the disruption in his or her life most acutely. He or she may display irritability, spurts of crying, or the inability to concentrate or remember more frequently than before.

When a worker displays these kinds of behavior, he or she might find relief in someone to talk to on a regular basis, perhaps once a week. Some places have an Employee Assistance program with trained counselors. Sometimes the personnel or human resource departments have counselors who are able to spend time with employees. Taking even one hour a week to talk and express their feelings will often make a grieving person much more productive.

If the bereaved worker is having difficulty with schedules, tasks, memory or concentration, as supervisors we can help by assisting with the preparation of a schedule. Also we can be clear and direct about our expectations. Perhaps a particular job requires time after hours, and yet the bereaved person may not be willing to work overtime. It's helpful to understand that this lack of interest in overtime work may be due to decreased energy or to the need to spend time alone or with family. We can be sensitive to these needs and refrain from requiring long hours at such a period in a worker's life.

Some bereaved persons will need additional time off either because of symptoms of stress, or because of family needs. If we are sensitive to such needs and allow sufficient time off, a person will be able to return to work with renewed energy. The accumulation of stress symptoms can cause illness and result in long periods of absence from work. Allowing time off for the demands of grief can be an investment in that worker's future productivity.

There are many community resources for the grieving: support groups, counseling centers, support/education programs. Today, many companies keep files on such resources for their employees. As a supervisor or manager, we can assist the bereaved by directing them to the appropriate resources.

Some of these suggestions, for time away from work to attend a funeral, for a gradual return to a full schedule, or for time to see a counselor or participate in a support group, may seem like time lost. Yet the opposite is true. A valued employee will be far more productive in the long run if we allow sufficient time for the disruptions of grieving. If a worker is allowed periods to deal with the stresses of grief, the time at work will be more concentrated and energetic. In addition, employees tend to be more productive when they are happier at work. When we address the disruptions caused by grieving and try to meet the needs of the bereaved, we are creating the conditions for greater productivity and greater satisfaction in the workplace.

This is not to say that there won't be difficulties: questions from co-workers about "excess" time off; jealousies; pettiness. However if we are caring and tactful, we can handle such situations, and employees can learn that each one is taken care of as the need arises.

Often such situations inspire the development of new policies for employees that are more humane, reflecting individual needs.

REACHING THE
OTHER SIDE OF GRIEF:
THE FINAL PHASE

Grief opened the sluice-gate:
words flooded forth
faster than I could set them down.

Something sweet
washed up on this salt shore.

Ruth Feldman, "Flood"

28 • *The Path to a New Life*

Sue:

I don't feel like I walk around with the heaviness of it every day. I have incorporated that. As I've grown up I've come to terms with myself in many ways. Even though I was in my early twenties and on my own, it would have been great to have had more of a family than I had at that time. Now I feel like I have a lot of long-term friendships in the community. It's very very different from when I was just a year out of college and not having many connections to places or people. Sometimes I wonder if her death and my grieving didn't prevent me from relating to other people. I had so many things to work out, I couldn't give as much energy to someone outside. It affected my relationships with men and women. And then I was trying to figure out how I was going to make a living, doing all kinds of odd jobs and trying to write.

Jeremy:

I am just sad that he had to die. He was only fifty-one years old. I think if he had lived longer we would have had a really nice relationship. I see a lot of people with a lot of worse things than I have had. I see a lot of kids at work that have never had a father. I'm just happy that I had twenty-two years of my father and a good last year with him.

There's grief in life and life isn't easy. But if you can't live with grief, it's much harder to live your life. I can't see myself stopping to live because of what happened. I can't see myself stopping everything so I can wallow in my grief. I don't think I want to do that. I don't think my father would want me to do that.

Anne:

I decided to buy a condominium in the city. It was just right for me. It was surprising, my decision to sell the house and move into the city. It was a question of timing. There were the children before, and I had to prove to the world and the kids that we could keep the house, that we'd have two cats, a mom and four kids. The apartment in the city is more for who I am these days. I'm not the mother with little children drooling all over me. I'm dressed up more. I think I will like this elegant new situation.

There are still some difficulties. When the children are in a play or at graduation, I find myself wishing there were someone with me that I could be proud with. But when I find myself feeling that way, I use mental exercises. I memorize things as I did when I was a kid in school. You can make yourself learn from that.

Bill:

Every time I see my daughter's new baby, I think, "Wouldn't Ginny have loved to have this baby to play with?" That always reminds me of her. There are a lot of things that remind me and I have a moment of grief. But there are a lot of other things in my life and I don't dwell on it. I could never forget someone I'd been living with for over thirty years any more than I could believe she was dead in the first few days after she died.

I have always liked to talk about this. I'm not so sure the kids want to talk about it. They don't want to be reminded. The most I say is, "Oh, your mother really would have liked that," or "She wouldn't have liked that."

Eric:

It's been two years. It is still hard, although I feel much better. If I feel better it's because of that film project. I also met a woman and even though that relationship fell apart, it did because of its own problems, not because of Diane, and that actually felt good.

The sadness is still there, but now I can control it. I know where it is. I can live with it. I feel better about being in this apartment. Diane and I were happy here.

The last two winters were very hard. I never could figure out if it was because that was the time when Diane was dying or the bad weather. I used to dread winter. Now I feel this winter is not going to be bad. I think a lot of it is just the passage of time. I knew it would happen, but I thought it would happen sooner.

It doesn't ever go away. There will be other relationships and I will probably get married, but I will be thinking every day of Diane. It means that there's always that sad place inside you. You wish it weren't like that. Even though things are getting better, I wish I could let go of that. You always wonder what it would have been like if she had lived.

Marilyn:

You invest the child whom you actually never knew with the ideas of what you would like the child to be, the things that all people invest their child with during a pregnancy. When a pregnancy is suddenly brought up short, those ideas never take form and you never see the real person. Yet you still carry those ideas with you. The problem is that there actually was a physical being there, and because you never got to know that person, you've lost not only the idea but the specific individual which you can't possibly ever know. You often look at other children and wonder what yours would have been, blond or dark, cute or ugly. You just wonder. I think that's one reason you actually find yourself not wanting to be around children.

Writing has always been an outlet for me. I found myself automatically writing some poems that dealt with the experience. I also found myself writing down a lot of the details that I was going through because it was the deepest experience of my life, and it seemed important that I remember. I think part of that was for the child that I couldn't get to know. This is really the only existence she had. Gradually I began to see that I really wanted to write a book that narrates my experience and explores some of the ideas that I invested this child with. When I started writing this I was very hopeful that I would have a child, and I envisioned a book that would end with my succeeding in bearing a child. I know now that it will end with my coming to terms with the fact that I am not going to have a child through birth. Questions of adoption are really separate from all this. I see it now as a book about coming to terms with this kind of loss, finally saying no to pregnancy. The doctors may be saying you still can succeed, but you see yourself as being so battered in the process that you have to say no. It's an act of will. It's very difficult to do.

Another aspect of coming to terms with this type of a loss is dealing with the question of whether to adopt a child. We have had a moratorium on talking about that for several months. Now we are just beginning to deal with looking ahead to that type of answer.

Phil:

We had a fund started in her name, and we sometimes put on a little children's program anonymously. Sometimes we take our kids to it. My wife has had a real good feeling about being able to do that as an outlet for herself. It's a small thing, to give annually to help children in that area educationally. I think you have to do those things. That keeps her alive.

Our son is now two and a half. He's full of life. It brings us some dimension of hope and expectation. I go through life in a different way, a lot different. My memories are different.

I have four children and one of them is not with me. It depends on who asks me that question, whether it's someone that you are going to get to know or it's more formal. Most of the people where I live don't know that and they don't need to. It's not something you stop and dwell on. It's somewhat private. I feel like I have four children.

It's been three and a half years. I still feel very sad, and I feel unfortunately at times that there are little pieces that ebb away. I try to keep memories fresh in my mind. But you just know that human faculties are such that you're going to lose little pieces now and then. Other things and experiences are coming in and they're fresher. Our life is so different now after three and a half years. Our life seemed so different then. We were living in a small town and our children were small and life seemed so tightly knit. You can feel the void that has transpired since then. You try to hang on. I try to hang on to what she represented. When I have difficult decisions to make or issues that are highly moral, I try to think about my daughter because I think that helps. She's a part of maintaining what religion is to me. If I didn't have that connection, even though the way she died is hard, or if I didn't adhere to Christian beliefs, it would be hard.

I don't try to set many long-term goals. But I try to make sure that what I'm doing is as fulfilling as possible, particularly the depth of my relationships with my students. Some of the students I get to know well. I could see what it would have been like for Jenny if she were nineteen or twenty. I'd want someone to help her in her education. The students give me a lot. I can see how some of the students are growing here. I feel good in being a participant observer and seeing them prosper. And then I see them leave and I can cherish that. They represent a lot.

I'm an achievement-oriented person and I've got a lot of drive, but I'm not so sure that's important any more. When you get knocked down, you get to look at the world from a whole different angle. You're looking up instead of looking down. That humbling experience gives you another perspective.

I was out running around the track, and I got to talking to this elderly man that I had always seen there. He was probably in his late seventies. I walked around the track with him when I wasn't running and discovered that we both went to the same college, and that he lost his son when his son was in his early twenties. He was his pride. That was really interesting and I asked him how he dealt with that. He said that it was really hard but you have to be really tough. It increases your sensitivity. You can't let it all overwhelm you. You can get help and have friends reach out, but you have to have inner toughness. It is a word that is important to me. I understand now what he meant when he said that. He gave me a lot of hope because I saw him going about his life and putting things in place. I said I could do it too.

Maureen:

A few years later, my friend called me when her grandfather, whom she was really close to, was dying. The first thing she did was call me and say, "I really want to talk to you about death, and how you dealt with it and where we go from here." It made me feel so good that she turned around and said, "I need your help now. I know you've been through it and you can tell me how it's going to feel." You can have all the compassion in the world, but until you've been through it, you don't know what someone is feeling after a death. I knew what she was feeling. I didn't know if what I was saying was going to help her, but I said what I would have liked to have heard. She asked me, "Did you feel lost, this emptiness that you couldn't fill?" I said, "Yeah, that's how I felt, and no one can tell you that you'll feel better or how to feel." I felt so needed. I felt that the death gave me something that I could give to somebody else.

I still feel my sister's so close to me. For Mother's Day, my mother and I went up to the cemetery. I've introduced my husband to her and my best friend has been up there with me. I know she won't slip away from me.

There are plenty of older people that have died in my life, a lot of great-aunts. When they died, I don't think I ever really cried a lot. They were old people. I loved them. They had a good life and they're gone. But I think of my sister, how much life she missed, how I miss her, how much life we could have shared. All I have now are memories.

When I got married, it was Maureen getting married rather than Joan. I could see a lot of things that my mother and father were going through. I had my best friend as my maid of honor, but I missed having my sister there. It was Mary Beth and me, but it just wasn't the same as being close with Joan, sharing the looks I know we would share, jokes that we would have shared. I had her favorite flowers on the altar. I had a bouquet of daisies right next to me because that's where she would have stood.

When I see someone that's handicapped or anyone that is suffering, I just feel for them. Little things don't bother me anymore. When my husband leaves the house every morning, I have to tell him that I love him because God knows what can happen to him. I say, "I love you," every time I hang up the phone with my mother, my grandmother, my father. I never knew when I was 15 that my sister was going to die.

There's this man at work. He never goes to funerals or says goodbye to anyone. If you can't say goodbye, you can't feel right about that relationship later. After living through what I have, I'd never want to give that cop-out to somebody. I find that the best things I can do for people now is to send them cards, or call them out of the blue, or just be aware of their thoughts and their feelings. Someone I hadn't seen for years just had a baby and I sent her a card. She called me up and was so pleased. That made me feel great. And now I don't say I won't do things, or think I won't go out of my way for someone. I do go out of my way.

When I hear something about someone else, I get upset and it brings back all the feelings I have for Joan and that is good. Sometimes I need those to bring me back, because sometimes I put her out of my head for a while. Sometimes, she'll pop into my thoughts for no reason and those are the best times.

Jim:

It is always there. I expect that I will again get back into periods where I will be able to think of nothing else. I still feel very angry at my parents and I feel angry at myself, partly for not seeing the light sooner. It will be there for a long time. I'm struck by how powerful the emotional part of our life is, and at the same time how mysterious.

Two weeks ago, my university wanted me to talk to a newspaper reporter about how to prevent alcoholism and drug abuse in teenagers. So I did the interview. I emphasized things like communication in the family. I did all of this interview without ever once thinking about my sister or myself. It was the strangest and most amazing thing that I could do that without thinking about her. Yet the things that I said apply to her situation and my own.

I feel that I will continue to struggle with it, but it has made me pay more attention to what the important things are. There used to be a time when I thought my job was so important. Since this happened, well, it's not so important. What's important now is my own family, my wife and son, but also accepting the things in my family that aren't helpful, and not being afraid to tell my parents that we're not healthy. I've only begun. It's so much easier to just not rock the boat and just not say anything; easier in the short run, that is.

Living again

One morning we wake up and suddenly notice that the trees are in bloom or that the leaves are beginning to turn color. A student of mine told me how months after her father's death she walked out her front door one morning and noticed the apple trees bursting into flower. We find ourselves looking at the sky again or noticing the people around us. There does come a time when we accept our loved one as lost and begin to take pleasure in new things. We feel that we are going to live again.

This means different things for each of us. For some of us it means that we are beginning to experience more good days than bad days. For some of us it means that a day has gone by without our thinking of our loss, or perhaps when we think of that loss, the pain is not as sharp or overwhelming. It is no longer the center of our lives. We find ourselves investing our emotion and energy in new things rather than in our grief. We begin to think about spending time and emotion on new projects.

If we are a young adult who has lost a parent or a sibling, we may begin to see ourselves as young again, and we will want to start going out with our friends or putting our energy in our studies or job. We may be out at a movie with our friends one evening and realize that we are enjoying ourselves and that it's possible to have fun. Sue describes the long-term friendships that she began to build after a long period in which she was unable to give herself to relationships.

If we have lost a husband or a wife, we may begin to see ourselves as a whole person again. One day we may look in the mirror and be pleased with ourselves. We may begin seeing other people again and invest in new relationships for their own sake rather than as an antidote to our loneliness. A widower friend of mine spent a great deal of time playing tennis after his wife died. It was a release from tension, a way of lessening his pain. Months later he met someone he could care about, and he found himself going out for enjoyment. He had started believing in life again and began to experience moments of ease and contentment.

These changes occur almost imperceptibly. They are extremely subtle and gradual. They seem to take place almost like a change in weather. This does not mean that we no longer think of our loved one, or that we no longer experience the pain of our loss. It simply means that our pain has become manageable, that the energy we spend on living again is increasing and the emotion we spend on our loss diminishes. In his narrative, Eric spoke of his new film project and new friends. He also spoke of the place his wife will always have inside him. In Chapter 13, Merryl told us that although she has a new relationship and plans to marry, she still thinks of her husband at times during the day. We learn that we can carry our loss around with us and still invest in our lives, or as Eric so aptly put it, the sadness is there, but he knows how to live with it.

When we reach the other side of grief, we find that we have experienced tremendous growth. We have learned to incorporate loss and sadness in our lives without being overwhelmed by them, and also that we can go on living in new ways. It isn't necessarily what we might have expected before the grieving began. We may have thought that our lives would be the same and that we would forget. It's not a question of forgetting or getting over our loss, but finding that indeed our life is significantly different now, and that we are not the same person we were before our loss.

We create a new relationship with the loved one who died. This may be one of our most surprising discoveries. As time passes we continue to see our loved one in different ways and to understand his or her personality with greater depth and perspective. If we have lost a parent, we may begin to develop an appreciation of our parent as a person rather than just as our parent. We may come to understand what they experienced in their lives, and to learn from that experience. Thinking about my mother, I gain understanding of the aging process and of what she might have experienced. I feel that I shall continue to learn from her throughout my life.

If we have lost a child, we may develop a greater understanding of the place that our child had in our lives. In his narrative, Phil spoke of how memories of his daughter serve as a reference for his decisions. He also described the depth of his relationship with his students. It's as if he were reaching out to his own daughter and helping her through her college years. The relationship we have with our loved one continues to be dynamic. It reflects our own age and our accumulating experience, as well as our changing perspectives of the deceased.

Those of us who have experienced traumatic losses through suicide or homicide will have gained a greater understanding of ourselves and our ties with the deceased. If our loved one took his or her own life, we may have learned a lot about personal responsibility in relationships. We may have learned what we have control over in our lives and what escapes our control, that we cannot be responsible for someone else's life. Letting go of that belief in our ability to control our loved one's destiny helps us to move beyond grief.

For those of us who have suffered the death of a loved one through homicide, living again may simply mean making the best of a very painful situation. We may have to live for years with the fact that the murderer of our loved one is out on the street, that our sense of justice has been violated by the judicial process, and that the world continues to be a frightening place. We may find that living again means simply that we have more good days than bad days, and that we can continue our lives at work and at home.

It is not unusual for families to experience estrangement and divorce after a death. We may have experienced a whole series of losses in addition to the loss of our loved one. In these cases, reaching the other side of grief means that we gain perspective on our relationships, that we cease to blame ourselves for a failed marriage or the inability to keep the family together after the death of a parent. We may learn to develop a more positive view of ourselves despite our losses, and this self-regard will help us to continue our lives in the best way possible under the circumstances.

Given our unique situations, moving beyond grief means very different things for each one of us. However, all of us who experience the suffering of loss undergo great changes. In different ways, many of us are healed by these changes and we eventually reconstruct our lives. The resolution of sorrow means being able to express it and then put it in a place inside us, weaving it in our lives as a thread in a complex and rich experience.

Building a new life for ourselves

As we move beyond grief, we begin to focus on ourselves again and we find that our view of ourselves has changed. Because of what we have been through, we see ourselves as more capable. While our loss may have dealt a heavy blow to our self-esteem, we have drawn on our inner resources and coped with that loss perhaps without being aware of our growth. The disruption of our lives may have actually opened up new vistas for us and we begin to ask ourselves what we want to explore. We begin to dream again and to see ourselves as persons with possibilities. Musing on the passage of time, Anne Morrow Lindbergh commented that the development of new energy and new interests and the discovery of new truths happen not just in our youth, but over and over again as we progress through our lives.

Although we may have believed that the building phase of our lives had come and gone, we find ourselves in the process of creating a life once again. If we have lost a parent we may have been pushed towards independence and we now begin to express it the way that Sue did, by making new friends and finding ways to support herself. As a widow or widower, we may also begin to express our independence in more positive ways, whether deciding to remain single or to marry or to live with someone again. But this time we are the ones who are doing the planning, selecting the alternatives that will best suit the person we have become.

After such a searing experience as the death of a loved one, many of us may have developed not only a sense of the fragility of life, but also a desire to make the most out of the life we have. We are more demanding in a sense. After we have traversed the grieving process, many of us look for more satisfying jobs or a more fulfilling way of life. Many of us have discovered new talents along the way.

Eric discovered a new interest and new talents as he turned his efforts to filmmaking and away from journalism. A woman I know, whose husband committed suicide, decided to go back to college and get a degree in fine arts. Some years after, she developed a career as a painter. An older man whose son died in an automobile accident became involved in local theater and tried his hand at writing, although he had been a probation officer for most of his working life.

Our changes in careers may reflect not only the discovery of new talents but also a shift in values. After his daughter died, Phil left his job as superintendent of schools to become a college professor. He wanted to make sure that his work was as personally fulfilling as possible. Working with young women was also a way of remembering his daughter and imagining the young adult she would have become. He had developed a new image of himself, beyond that of good provider and successful administrator. Anne also developed a new image of herself as a successful and competent business woman at ease in an urban setting.

Those of us who don't work outside the home may have found new sources of fulfillment in traveling or in meeting new kinds of people. We may maintain the living situations we had before the death of our loved one, but with changes in outlook. A widow I know decided to stay in the same town and in the same house after the death of her husband. But she began to travel and to make new friends. We may strike up a friendship with a person outside of our usual social circle. We may take a course in an area we are completely unfamiliar with. These are not negligible steps. What may seem like small, isolated decisions represent a steady incremental movement towards a more satisfying life.

Each one of us who has suffered a major loss can experience significant growth, spiritually, psychologically and emotionally. As we grieve we also learn a great deal about ourselves and our relationships to others. We learn how to express our feelings in new ways and how to take support and help from others. Perhaps we have learned how to shed tears and still maintain self-esteem. Some of us may have learned how to face life on our own. Some of us experience a strengthening of our faith. All of us, however, have learned that we were able to cope and have used our new strengths in different ways to enhance our lives.

Spinning gold out of flax

In the well-known fairy tale, a young woman is locked in a room with a pile of flax and ordered to spin it into gold. Ultimately, a dwarf appears and gives her the magic formula that will help her to spin the gold and thus to save her life. There is also a sense in which we can turn the experiences of our suffering and the circumstances of our loss into gold when we discover a new capacity for giving and for using our experience with loss to help others.

Not only have we developed the emotional strength and the practical skills which have enabled us to cope with loss, we may now undertake service projects or establish funds that will help others who experience tragedies. For example, most bereavement support groups have been started by people who have experienced loss, such as Compassionate Friends or Parents of Murdered Children.

The people who volunteer for one-on-one support and for peer counseling in hospice programs and bereavement centers are people who have suffered loss themselves, and who are able to use their own experience to help the newly bereaved. Most of these volunteers feel that they receive much more than they give, because this kind of work also gives them an opportunity to learn more about their own grief. Many of us find it a privilege and a source of richness to enter other people's lives at a time when they are vulnerable and in great need.

In Chapter 14, Margaret described how her anger and sorrow are being channeled to help others through her work in Victim Rights. A woman I know, whose elderly mother died, began volunteering in a nursing home. She discovered that she was able to use her experience in caring for an ailing parent in new ways. Some of us who have lost loved ones through diseases such as cancer or heart conditions may start volunteering for fund-raising drives to help research in eliminating these illnesses.

Some of us who are financially able find that starting funds to help others who suffer similar tragedies is a way of turning our loss into positive support for others. Phil describes the fund he started in his daughter's name and the solace it provides for his family. A young couple who lost an infant started a fund to help bereaved parents and to upgrade a local hospital's child-care equipment.

We needn't be wealthy to make such helpful gestures. A young woman whose daughter died donated a small amount to an organization that provides for needy children throughout the world.

Some of us write books or articles about our experience and these serve as guides and supports for others who are struggling with loss. Jim was able to provide a newspaper with some useful advice on the prevention of drug abuse, as a result of the understanding he gained from his sister's death. Anne frequently addresses local groups to share her experiences as a young widow. In our journey through grief, we may have discovered, not only that we are not isolated in our grief, but that our own suffering can be of use.

Learning compassion and sensitivity

When Maureen discussed the changes in her outlook since her sister's death, she spoke of the insight she gained into other people's pain. One of the most important things we learn when we have grieved for the loss of a loved one is compassion. While the pain of our grief may have seemed very isolating, ultimately it brings us to a deeper understanding of others. We come to see how many people labor under the burden of pain, not only through the loss of a loved one, but through difficulties in their jobs, their family circumstances or their health.

We discover a new ease in relating to different kinds of people. We also come to recognize that for all the seeming differences between people, the distinctions tend to fall away as we draw close to others. From this recognition flows an ability to communicate. Now we know what to say and what not to say when we go to a wake or a funeral. We know how to talk to the newly bereaved, or to those who have suffered loss at any time in their lives. These insights can be useful in addressing other kinds of loss.

We know what to do as well as what to say when tragedy strikes others. For example, if we are employed as a supervisor, we may find ourselves willing to bend those regulations when someone is in need, and more willing to put people's needs as a priority. We will know what to do for co-workers and friends when they suffer a loss. Maureen speaks of the wonderful discovery that she was able to help her friend who was in need of support. We become both role models and sources of solid practical help for others.

As Maureen discovered, the compassion we have gained attracts people. Someone at work may stop at our desk and tell us about an illness or death in their family. A friend will call us if he or she needs help with a difficulty. Often even strangers will be drawn to us and tell us their stories. We have learned a very important skill that will serve us in many situations: how to listen.

As we reach the other side of grief, we also learn to develop compassion for ourselves and our own difficulties. We have learned not to demand so much of ourselves and to be more tolerant of ourselves as we struggle with the problems in our lives. Because we have lived with our own need and vulnerability throughout the grieving process, we have learned to accept and even value that side of ourself.

Developing new outlooks

Most of us who have suffered loss discover that our experience with grief has changed our outlook on life and affected our scale of values. What used to seem so important to us, such as our work or perhaps our material comfort, may now take second place. We come out of the grieving process with a keen sense of both the fragility and the preciousness of life. In this future-oriented society of ours, we have gained a new sense of respect for the present.

Maureen speaks of enjoying the here-and-now and making the best of things because "the people you love won't always be there." A student of mine, whose boyfriend had a very difficult relationship with his mother, advised him to tell her that he loved her. She wanted him to realize that what he had was precious and would not always be there. She also told him that for her, having a home before they could marry was not important. After having lost both parents as a young adult, she understood that the real strength in life lies within ourselves and not in material things.

Many of us look back on our lives and perhaps wish we would have done things a bit differently. Surviving the loss of a loved one may seem almost like a reprieve, a chance to do things in a new way. We have learned what really matters, and that because time is fleeting, we need to make the most of it.

A man who lost a child commented, "For a long time, work was important to me. But work has taken second or third level. There's more things that are important in life than making a buck." After his sister died, Jim found that achieving success in his work was no longer as important to him. Perhaps because of our loss, we no longer take the people we love for granted, and have come to regard our personal relationships in a new light. We may now care more about finding meaning in our lives than about the more fleeting satisfaction of success.

For some of us, this might mean taking time to do things with our loved ones. Perhaps we might look for a job that will give us more time with our family. Or we decide to take that vacation now, rather than postponing it until we reach a certain job level or a certain salary. My mother always worried about having enough money to retire on, and therefore she went without a vacation for years in a row, and postponed the travels she often dreamed of. After she died, I developed a strong sense of the importance of taking time for living and for paying attention to one's dreams. After we have struggled with loss, we develop a sense of both the limits and possibilities of life.

The experience of grief has also tested many of our friendships. In Chapter 23, Marilyn described how she had to choose her friends very carefully after her losses. Some of her friends were insensitive to her tragedy, and she needed to distance herself from them. But she also discovered new friendships that evolved into close relationships. After our long struggle through grief, we find that we are attracted to different kinds of people, that we are both more and less tolerant. We might find real pleasure in friendships with people who are different in age or interests, but who have experienced some kind of loss. We might find ourselves less tolerant of those who are like us in superficial aspects, but are concerned with values we have now rejected or placed in low priority.

For many of us, a change in outlook means a new appreciation of the simple things in life, such as taking the time to enjoy a beautiful day or to take a walk in nature. We might find that having a quiet conversation with a friend is just as renewing as a more elaborate social event. We have come to see what is around us with new insight and to learn to take pleasure in our immediate surroundings.

Becoming our own best friend

During the long and lonely months and years of our grieving we will have often felt as if we were caught in a tunnel with no exit. We have not only suffered the loss of a loved one, but have also experienced a whole train of other losses as our former lives and relationships were transformed. Many of us will have had to change our homes and our livelihood. We may have been disappointed by the reaction of our friends and we may have developed new friendships. Even those of us who remained in place with the same friends and the same lifestyle will have experienced profound and lasting changes in our lives. We have all made an extraordinary journey, not only in our external lives but also deep within ourselves. Even when we may have felt most helpless and vulnerable, we were coping with our sorrow and learning that we have inner resources to draw upon.

While it may not have seemed as if we were making progress during the bleak time of our sorrow, when we undergo personal crisis we move forward. We have not only explored new interests and new relationships, but most importantly we have discovered new sides of ourselves, drawing on inner resources that we never dreamed we had.

While we were working so hard to build new support structures and make new friends, we may have found that we were developing the best friend of all, ourselves. Though we still look for, and are nourished by, outside support, we now have a new and strengthened resource to draw on all our lives. We have become our own best friend.

In learning that we can be comfortable with ourselves we have discovered the difference between loneliness, which we rarely choose, and solitude, which we may now cherish as an alternative. We find that we prefer spending the evening by ourselves, listening to music or curled up with a favorite book. We find ourselves proud of the way we are able to take care of ourselves instead of resenting the fact that we are now in charge of our own well-being. Most of all, we not only accept who we are, but we appreciate that person.

A widowed friend of mine, whose children had grown, described her Thanksgiving to me. She set candles on the table and after dinner, spent the evening in front of a wood fire with her dog and a good book. Rather than resenting the fact that she was alone during a family holiday, she relished the experience as an opportunity to unwind from her schedule at work and as a chance to be with herself. A well-known poet, Derek Walcott, wrote that the time will come when you will greet yourself "at your own door, in your own mirror"—when you "will love again the stranger who was yourself."

This is a time to take stock of all that we have accomplished, and to be proud of the way in which we have survived. We have gone through one of the most profound changes we will experience in our lives, and even if things didn't turn out as we had hoped, we have endured. Regardless of whether our marriage or our family relationships have remained intact, we have survived as a person. As Margaret so aptly phrased it in Chapter 14, "the human spirit is amazing." Because this may have been the most trying experience of our lives, we can face other and lesser difficulties with greater perspective. Many of us may find that reaching the other side of grief is a new beginning. Painful as the journey has been, it has prepared us for a lifetime of growth and change.

Afterword

by Phyllis R. Silverman,
Harvard Medical School

When Marguerite Bouvard and Evelyn Gladu asked me to write the afterword for their book I wondered what I could say that would add to this (already very full) volume. I finally decided that the reader might find it interesting to share some of my recent thinking. There always seems to be something new to learn about how losses of people and relationships affect us, for we are all survivors of such experiences. Yet we have lost some of our ability to know what to do when we are faced with dramatic changes in our lives. We live in interesting times, however, that provide us with ever-expanding opportunities to understand our own behavior and the behavior of others at such times.

Two major forces are for the first time receiving attention as legitimate subjects for research. In the latter half of the twentieth century, as a result of the women's movement, an entire new area of research is opening up: women and their experience have become important subjects of study. At the same time, death, dying and bereavement have come under close attention. I see these research efforts joining together and opening new windows on the human experience. Until this century the measure for human behavior has always been the experience of men. Behavior that was associated with maturity was goal-directed and reflected a position of autonomy and independence. Relationships, in this model, are seen as necessary steps on the road to independence. Sometimes I wondered if, in this

Phyllis R. Silverman, Ph.D., is co-principal investigator of the Child Bereavement Study at the Harvard Medical School Department of Psychiatry. She began the Widow-to-Widow program at Harvard Medical School and directed it from 1966 to 1974.

She is the author of four books: *Mutual Help Groups: Organization and Development; Helping Women Cope with Grief; Widow-to-Widow;* and (with Scott Campbell) *Widower: When Men Are Left Alone.*

way of looking at the world, friendships and connections with others had little value in their own right. When people—that is women—did not conform to this standard, the problem was never that the standard was wrong, but rather that the person measured was defective. Women were criticized for being overly involved with others, for being too enmeshed in caring.

What do we know from these studies of women, and how does this relate to how we cope with grief? We are learning from looking at women's experience to appreciate the importance of relationships, connections and caring in how we live. Relationships are affirming forces that frame and focus our lives. In large part, if truth be told, both men and women know themselves only as they relate to others. Rather than focusing on how important it is to be independent and able to stand on our own two feet, we are beginning to appreciate that we, both men and women, always need people. Life itself can be characterized in terms of how we connect and reconnect to people from beginning to end. We may be cheating ourselves, but in particular we cheat men when we emphasize autonomy instead of caring. This may, in part, account for the difficulties so many men have in acknowledging and expressing their feelings.

As we look at the language we use to talk about coping with grief, we see that the emphasis has been on letting go of the past. We sometimes talk of it as an illness from which we will recover. With the proper treatment we can remove this foreign substance, grief, from our bodies. But if caring and connection are the cornerstones of our lives, the death of an important person, by its very nature, will be associated with appropriate pain and with serious disruption in how we live. In fact we cannot cope by simply putting it behind us. Ruth Feldman, whose poems are quoted in this book, called her collection of poems *The Ambition of Ghosts Is to Be Seen and Heard.* Her struggle in part was that she was seeking ways to remember.

Not too long ago I was at an international meeting, the focus of which was on understanding the bereavement process. People were talking about tie-breaking rituals that freed the bereaved from their attachments to the deceased so that they could get on with their lives. This goal troubled me. I have yet to meet a bereaved person who can let go of the past in this way, and I protested that this was not a model that matched my many years of experience of studying and working with bereaved people. One of the psychologists present, a man from England, said that letting go was like having a baby. This seemed to me to be a rather unusual analogy, but I was perfectly willing to consider a model taken from the start of life for coping with the end of life. He noted that when a baby is born, we cut the cord, give him or her a slap, and the infant is on the road to autonomy and independence. At that moment I understood why we were not communicating. He was seeing the world in a male (for lack of a better word) metaphor, with the focus on separation and getting on with things. I, on the other hand, was talking from what I realized was a female view, which emphasized the need to maintain our connections to others throughout life and maybe even after death as well.

Another way of looking at birth came to mind. I had just witnessed the birth of my grandson in my home. As he was gently brought into the world he was quietly placed on his jubilant but exhausted mother's abdomen. He was welcomed by his grandparents, an aunt and uncle, and an adoring father, who carefully cut the umbilical cord without disturbing his son's new attachment and his relaxed position. All of this enabled this baby not to separate, but to change the way he was connected, especially to his mother and to all of us who cared. What is the message for the bereaved?

Robert Anderson, the playwright, says that death ends a life but not a relationship. The dilemma for the bereaved is how to go on with life, while acknowledging the past and the part it played in who they are today. They need to remember, even while changing how they live. They learn to remain connected, but change the nature of that connection. We are talking about a complex process that may require a good deal of effort.

The focus on connection is not only a problem for the bereaved but for others around them as well. People need each other at times of loss: they need comfort, they need guidance, they need to be touched and cared about. In a society that prizes separateness and autonomy, people are often encouraged to pull down the window shades and withdraw into their grief. As I have noted elsewhere, they feel stigmatized, as if something is wrong with them. They feel spoiled, broken. They turn the rejection on themselves, assuming the problem is in them, and that is why they are unacceptable and unattractive to others at a time when they need others most. They are welcomed back to society once they make no demands on others and manage their lives by themselves. We need not only to pull up the shades but to open the windows as well, to make it easy to reach out and accept the need we have to care and be cared for. This does not come easily for most of us. We have been socialized to respect people's privacy, to avoid intrusion. We have relegated caring to women, making light of it as women's work. Caring is probably the most important job any of us can have. All of us, men and women, need to be experts; to see the caring and connected sides of ourselves made legitimate and enhanced.

How will we learn? In part, from letting ourselves experience all aspects of living. We will also learn from listening to others and letting them teach us from their experience. Marguerite Bouvard and Evelyn Gladu have provided an excellent guide, integrating their own experiences with those of others. This guide is not only for those who are bereaved but for those around them who want to help. As long as we acknowledge our connections to others, we cannot avoid the risk of loss. It is a universal in the human condition. We all need such wisdom; we should all read this book.

Resources

When we are grieving, it may be difficult to find appropriate information and support, simply because we have not needed them in the past. The following pages include a list of resources, divided into several categories. Some categories overlap, so it is important to read through all of them in order to find the right resources for ourselves. This list is not exhaustive, but it provides enough leads to find the nearest resource and information center. Addresses without telephone numbers indicate contact by mail only.

Education and information centers

Center for Death Education and Research
114 Social Science Building
University of Minnesota
Minneapolis, MN 55455

Books, pamphlets and articles on many topics about death for both mental health professionals and the lay person.

Concern for Dying
250 West 57th Street
New York, NY 10017
(212) 246-6962

Information on many issues of health care and dying. Promotes the Living Will and has sample documents available.

The Elizabeth Kübler-Ross Center
South Route 616
Head Waters, VA 24442
(703) 396-3441

Besides being a retreat for terminally ill patients, the center holds workshops and seminars, and publishes a newsletter which includes a reading list.

The Foundation of Thanatology
630 West 168th Street
New York, NY 10032

Primarily educational; co-sponsors conferences on grief and death. Most material and seminars are for mental health professionals.

Grief Education Institute
2422 South Downing Street
Denver, CO 80210
(303) 777-9234

A regional bereavement counseling center; information and literature available on request.

National Center for Death Education
656 Beacon Street
Boston, MA 02215
(617) 536-0194

The Center has an extensive library of books and films; also sponsors seminars and workshops for professionals.

How to find a support group

Since most support groups are self-help, it may require a few telephone calls to find one in your area. Besides the resources listed, there are several other routes to locate a support group. The following is a list of places to contact. Many local newspapers list events that might include meetings of support groups for the bereaved.

>*—United Way Information and Referral Service*
>*—the social service department of your local hospital*
>*—the local mental health agency*
>*—the local Council on Aging (for widowed groups)*
>*—a local hospice program*
>*—a local church*
>*—a state self-help clearinghouse (see national listing below)*

National organizations serving the bereaved

The Compassionate Friends, Inc.
P.O. Box 3696
Oak Brook, IL 60522
(312) 323-5010

An international organization for bereaved parents with over 500 chapters in the United States. Local support groups are run by volunteer bereaved parents; literature is available, and often a library as well.

Concerns of Police Survivors, Inc.
16921 Croom Road
Brandywine, MD 20613
(301) 888-2264

Nationwide outreach programs to the newly widowed; group discussions, educational programs and seminars.

National Association of Military Widows
4023 25th Road North
Arlington, VA 22207
(703) 527-4565

A referral service for the newly widowed; sponsors support groups.

National Self-Help Clearinghouse
Graduate School and University Center/CUNY
33 West 42nd Street
New York, NY 10036

Support and information to self-help groups throughout the nation; local chapters in most states.

National Sudden Infant Death Foundation (SIDS)
Two Metro Plaza, Suite 205
Landover, MD 20785
(301) 459-3388

Over 70 local chapters providing information and services.

Parents of Murdered Children
1739 Bella Vista
Cincinnati, OH 45237

Many local chapters across the country offering support groups; publishes a newsletter.

They Help Each Other Spiritually (THEOS)
410 Penn Hills Mall
Pittsburgh, PA 15235
(412) 471-7779

Servicing the widowed, this group has 135 chapters across the country; also publishes THEOS, a magazine about bereavement.

Widowed Persons Service
American Association of Retired Persons
1909 K Street N.W.
Washington, D.C. 20049
(202) 872-4700

WPS has over 470 chapters nationwide of widowed support groups; sponsors a yearly conference for those leading support groups.

Regional and local support & counseling
groups for the bereaved

The Commission on Pastoral Bereavement Counseling
10 East 73rd Street
New York, NY 10021
(212) 879-8415

Spiritual and emotional counseling for the newly bereaved in the New York metropolitan area.

Enrichment Groups Child and Family Services
1680 Albany Avenue
Hartford, CT 06105
(203) 236-4511

Self-help and mutual support groups for families dealing with the loss of a member through murder or suicide.

The Good Grief Program
Judge Baker Guidance Center
295 Longwood Avenue
Boston, MA 02115
(617) 232-8390

Education, consultation and services for groups of children who have experienced a death. Also helps parents and teachers to deal with children after a death.

Hope for the Bereaved
1342 Lancaster Avenue
Syracuse, NY 13210
(315) 472-HOPE

Support groups for the bereaved, including specialized groups such as widowed, survivors of suicide, bereaved parents, etc. Publishes a handbook and a newsletter which has a wide circulation.

Kara Emotional Support Service for the Bereaved
457 Kingsley Avenue
Palo Alto, CA 94301
(415) 321-KARA

Individual counseling for the bereaved; serves several counties just south of San Francisco.

Marin Suicide Prevention Center
P.O. Box 792
San Anselmo, CA 94960
(415) 454-4544

Help for families of homicide victims

Naim

U.S. Catholic Conference
Family Life Division
721 North LaSalle Drive
Chicago, IL 60610
(312) 944-1286

Support for the widowed; has chapters in Illinois and other states. (The organization is named after a biblical widow.)

Omega Emotional Support Services for the Ill and Bereaved

270 Washington Street
Somerville, MA 02143
(617) 776-6369

Several support groups for the ill and bereaved, including suicide death. Also provides individual counseling and conducts workshops for professionals and volunteers. Serves the Greater Boston area.

Ray of Hope, Inc.

P.O. Box 2323
Iowa City, IA 52244
(319) 337-9890

Telephone counseling and support groups for survivors of suicide; presentations, printed material and videotapes.

Safe Place

call: The Samaritans
(check local telephone directories for numbers)

Support groups for those bereaved through suicide. The Samaritans is an international organization offering counseling to the suicidal and depressed.

Seasons: Suicide Bereavement

Bonnie Jo Gessel
1182 No. 575 West
Centerville, UT 84014
(801) 292-2858

Support for those bereaved by suicide; chapters in various parts of the country.

Suicide Survivors Grief Groups

5124 Grove Street
Minneapolis, MN 55436
(612) 929-6448

Presentations and publications for relatives and friends of suicide victims.

Survivors of Suicide

P.O. Box 1393
Dayton, OH 45406
(513) 223-9096

Group discussions, telephone and referral services, presentations and educational programs. Chapters in various parts of the country.

To Live Again
P.O. Box 73
Wynnewook, PA 19096
(215) 664-6565

For the widowed in the Pennsylvania and Eastern New Jersey area.

Victim Services Agency
2 Lafayette Street
New York, NY 10007
(212) 577-7700

Crisis support, counseling programs and support groups for families of homicide victims.

Young Widows and Widowers, Ltd.
4 Whiffletree Circle
Andover, MA 01810
(508) 475-2857

A support group for the widowed under forty-five years old; branch chapters in several towns in Massachusetts.

Information and services about illnesses

The following organizations can provide information or services about a particular illness.

Alzheimer's Disease and Related Disorders Association, Inc.
360 North Michigan Avenue
Chicago, IL 60601
(312) 853-3060

American Cancer Society
19 West 56th Street
New York, NY 10019
(212) 586-8700

Your local chapter of the ACS may be found in your telephone book.

American Heart Association, Inc.
205 East 42nd Street
New York, NY 10036
(212) 661-5335
See telephone book for local listings.

American Lung Association
1740 Broadway
New York, NY 10019
(212) 315-8700
See telephone book for local listings.

Cancer Information Service
1-800-4-CANCER

This telephone number will put you in touch with your local or regional Cancer Information Service. This service provides information on the causes, detection, prevention, treatment, rehabilitation, and continuing care of cancer. Also, they give referral to medical facilities, home health care and support groups.

Multiple Sclerosis National Society
205 East 42nd Street
New York, NY 10017
(212) 986-3240

National AIDS Network
1012 14th Street N.W.
Suite 601
Washington, D.C. 20005
(202) 347-0390

See telephone book for local AIDS organizations.

National Hospice Organization
1901 North Fort Myers Drive, Suite 902
Arlington, VA 22209
(703) 243-5900

Hospice programs provide care and support for people living with a terminal illness; care includes nursing and medical care at home. You can obtain the names of your local hospice programs from the national organization.

National Kidney Foundation
2 Park Avenue
New York, NY 10016
(212) 889-2210

Stroke Foundation, Inc.
898 Park Avenue
New York, NY 10021
(212) 734-3461

Other resources

American Association of Retired Persons
1909 K Street N.W.
Washington, D.C. 20049
(202) 872-4700

Families and Friends of Missing Persons and Violent Crime Victims
8421 32nd Street S.W.
Seattle, WA 98126

Mothers Against Drunk Driving
669 Airport Freeway
Suite 310
Hurst, TX 76035
(817) 268-6233

National Organization for Victim Assistance
1757 Park Road N.W.
Washington, D.C. 20010
(202) 232-8560

NOVA can help you locate resources for victim assistance in your local area.

Parents Without Partners, Inc.
7910 Woodmont Avenue
Bethesda, MD 20814
(301) 654-8850

Violence Project of the National Gay Task Force
80 Fifth Avenue #601
New York, NY 10011

Additional Reading

The following list is not meant to be exhaustive. It includes a selection of books about loss and grief for those who wish to do further reading in this area. The list includes three categories: a general list for those experiencing grief and those who wish to help a grieving friend or acquaintance, a selection of works in fiction and poetry which focus on grief, and a list of more technical works for health care providers or those who wish to do research on grief.

General

Albertson, Sandra, *Endings and Beginnings,* New York, Random House, 1980.
> *Written by a widow, this book presents one family's experience with grief and loss.*

Angel, Marc, *The Orphaned Adult: Confronting the Death of a Parent,* New York, Human Sciences Press, 1987.
> *Acknowledges the grief of adults when they lose a parent.*

Bernstein, Joanne E., *Loss and How to Cope with It,* New York, Clarion Books, 1977.
> *An easy-to-read book about loss for young people.*

Bolton, Iris, *My Son, My Son,* Atlanta, Georgia, Bolton Press, 1983.
> *The author's account of living through her son's suicide.*

Caine, Lynn, *Widow,* Bantam Books, 1974.
> *A widow's own story of living with a dying spouse and with grief.*

Campbell, Scott with Phyllis Silverman, *Widower: When Men Are Left Alone,* New York, Prentice-Hall, 1987.
> *A collection of personal experiences of a number of widowers.*

Colgrove, Melba, *How to Survive the Loss of a Love,* New York, Bantam Books, 1977.

Small practical book containing suggestions for surviving grief.

Grollman, Earl, *Living When a Loved One Has Died,* Boston, Beacon Press, 1977.

A reassuring book about coping with loss.

Grollman, Earl, *What Helped Me When My Loved One Died,* Boston, Beacon Press, 1981.

A collection of personal stories about grief and loss.

Herrman-Donnelly, Nina, *I Never Know What to Say,* New York, Ballantine, 1987

A helpful guide on what to say and what not to say to the bereaved.

Hewett, John, *After Suicide,* Philadelphia, Westminster Press, 1980.

A guide for dealing with the aftermath of suicide, part of a Christian book series.

Klagsbrun, Francine, *Too Young to Die: Youth and Suicide,* New York, Pocket Books, Inc., 1984.

A helpful book on teenage suicide.

Krementz, Jill, *How It Feels When a Parent Dies,* New York, Alfred A. Knopf, 1981.

Eighteen children ages seven to sixteen tell their stories of the loss of a parent.

Kübler-Ross, Elizabeth, *Death: The Final Stage of Growth,* New York, MacMillan, 1981.

A book of essays about the dying.

Kübler-Ross, Elizabeth, *Living with Death and Dying,* New York, MacMillan, 1981.

Explores issues of death and dying.

Kushner, Harold J., *When Bad Things Happen to Good People,* New York, Schocken Books, 1981.

A rabbi's approach to the question of human suffering.

LeShan, Eda, *Learning to Say Goodbye: When a Parent Dies,* New York, Avon Books, 1978.

A readable book for ages ten and up.

Lewis, C.S., *A Grief Observed,* New York, Bantam Books, 1980.

A diary of a widower's grief.

Loewinsohn, Ruth, *Survival Handbook for Widows,* Chicago, Follett Publishing Co., 1979.

A sensitive practical book for the widowed.

Lukas, Christopher and Seiden, Henry, *Silent Grief: Living in the Wake of Suicide*, New York, Charles Scribner's Sons, 1987.
Emotional and practical help for survivors of suicide.

Magee, Doug, *What Murder Leaves Behind*, New York, Dodd, Mead, 1983.
Stories of several people in the aftermath of a homicide.

Manning, Doug, *Don't Take My Grief Away*, New York, Harper & Row, 1984.
A minister's approach to dealing with grief.

Myers, Edward, *When Parents Die: A Guide for Adults*, New York, Viking-Penguin, 1986.
A sensitive and informative book about the loss of a parent.

Pinkus, Lily, *Death and the Family*, New York, Vintage Books, 1974.
A book about family dynamics and bereavement.

Rollin, Betty, *Last Wish*, New York, Linden Press/Simon & Schuster, 1985.
The author's story of assisting her mother's suicide.

Rosenfeld, Linda and Prupas, Marilynne, *Left Alive: After Suicide Death in the Family*, Springfield, Illinois, Charles C. Thomas, 1984.
Stories of issues surrounding a suicide death.

Shiff, Harriet Sarnoff, *The Bereaved Parent*, New York, Penguin Books, 1978.
A helpful book for those who have lost a child.

Shiff, Harriet Sarnoff, *Living through Mourning*, New York, Viking, 1986.
A guide through grief with emphasis on how to set up support groups.

Stein, Sarah B., *About Dying: An Open Book for Parents and Children Together*, New York, Walker & Co., 1974.
Simple text for young children with accompanying text for parents.

Tatelbaum, Judy, *The Courage to Grieve*, New York, Harper & Row, 1980.
A clearly written book about the resolution of grief.

Temes, Roberta, *Living With An Empty Chair*, 2nd edition, New York, Irvington, 1984.
A simple eloquent book about grief.

Wasserman, Marion Lee, *Searching for the Stork: One Couple's Struggle to Start a Family*, New York, New American Library, 1988.
A stirring personal account of a couple's struggle with still-birth, miscarriages, and genetic problems.

Fiction and poetry

Chase, Joan, *During the Reign of the Queen of Persia,* New York, Harper and Row, 1983.
  About the loss of a parent and its effects on family dynamics.

Kenney, Susan, *In Another Country,* New York, Viking, 1984.
  Living with a spouse who has a life-threatening illness.

McEwan, Ian, *The Child in Time,* Boston, Houghton Mifflin, 1987.
  Grieving the loss of a child through kidnapping.

Moffat, Mary Jane, *In the Midst of Winter: Selections from the Literature of Mourning,* New York, Random House, 1982.
  A collection of poetry and prose which the author gathered after her husband's death.

Mojtabai, A.G., *Autumn,* Boston, Houghton Mifflin, 1981.
  About the loss of a spouse.

Paton, Alan, *For You Departed: A Memoir,* New York, Charles Scribner's Sons, 1969.
  Loss of a spouse.

Watson, Elizabeth, *Guests of My Life,* Burnsville, North Carolina, Celo Press.
  A spiritual journey through the works of Emily Dickinson, Rainer Maria Rilke, Alan Paton, Walt Whitman and others after the tragic death of the author's daughter.

Woiwode, Larry, *Beyond the Bedroom Wall,* New York, Avon Books, 1979.
  The long-term effects on family members after the death of a parent.

Advanced reading

Bowlby, John, *Loss,* volume III of *Attachment and Loss,* New York, Basic Books, 1980.
  A study of loss and bereavement.

Garfield, Charles C. Ed., *Psychosocial Care Of the Dying Patient,* San Francisco, McGraw-Hill Book Co., 1978.
  Essays on the psychological issues of terminally ill patients.

Gorer, Geoffrey, *Death, Grief and Mourning,* Garden City, New Jersey, Doubleday & Co., 1965.
  An anthropological view of death, grief and loss.

Lifton, Robert Jay, *The Life of The Self,* New York, Basic Books, 1983.
  Theoretical essays on death and life.

Osterweis, Marion, et al., eds. *Bereavment, Reactions, Consequences and Care,* Washington D.C., National Academy Press, 1984.

A collection of scholarly articles about grief and loss.

Parkes, Colin Murray, *Bereavment: Studies of Grief in Adult Life,* Bloomington, Indiana, Indiana University Press, 1973.

A classic study of grief.

Parkes, Colin M., and Weiss, Robert S., *Recovery from Bereavment,* New York, Basic Books, 1983.

A study of adult reactions in various circumstances of loss.

Rando, Therese A., *Grief, Dying and Death,* Champaign, Illinois, Research Press Co., 1984.

For persons working with the grieving and dying.

Raphael, Beverly, *The Anatomy of Bereavement,* New York, Basic Books, 1983.

A clinical study of bereavement.

Silverman, Phyllis, *Widow to Widow,* New York, Springer Publishing Co., 1986.

Explains the theory behind and the growth of mutual help groups for widows.

Worden, William, *Grief Counseling and Grief Therapy: A Handbook for the Mental Health Professional,* New York, Springer Publishing Co., 1982.

A unique approach to the grieving process which includes interventions for health professionals.

About the authors

Marguerite Bouvard has been an interdisciplinary professor at Regis College for twenty-three years. As a teacher she frequently acts as counselor to students who have suffered the loss of family or friends. She holds a doctorate from Harvard University and has written a number of books in the fields of sociology, political science, and poetry.

Evelyn Gladu holds advanced degrees in counseling and education. For the past fifteen years she has counseled persons in stressful situations. She has been the director of Omega Emotional Support Services for the Ill and Bereaved in Somerville, Massachusetts.